THE RF

MW01070814

At Table

The Recipe Reader

Narratives, Contexts, Traditions

Edited by

JANET FLOYD and LAUREL FORSTER

University of Nebraska Press

Lincoln and London

This paperback reprint of *The Recipe Reader* is published by arrangement with Ashgate
Publishing Limited.

Library of Congress Cataloging-in-Publication Data
Floyd, Janet.
The recipe reader: narratives, contexts, traditions / edited by Janet Floyd and Laurel Forster.
p. cm.—(At table series)
Reprint. Originally published: Aldershot, Hants, England; Burlington, VT, USA: Ashgate,
c2003.
Includes bibliographical references and index.
ISBN 978-0-8032-3361-4 (pbk.: alk. paper)
1. Cookery. I. Forster, Laurel, 1962– II. Title.
TX643.F56 2010
641.5—dc22
2009041708

Contents

INDIVIDUAL INTERVENTIONS

CONTEMPORARY CONTEXTS

Notes on Contributors

Maggie Andrews is a freelance researcher and educationalist. Her research and publications explore the relationship between popular culture and feminism and include *The Acceptable Face of Feminism* (Lawrence and Wishart, 1997) and (co-edited with Mary Talbot) *All the World and Her Husband* (Cassell, 2000).

Margaret Beetham is a Reader in the Department of English at Manchester Metropolitan University, and author of *A Magazine of Her Own? Domesticity and Desire in the Woman's Magazine 1800-1914* (Routledge, 1996). She is co-editor with Kay Boardman of *Victorian Women's Magazines: An Anthology* (Manchester University Press, 2002) and of various articles on popular reading and feminist criticism.

Janet Floyd is a Lecturer in American Studies at King's College, London. Her research interests are in the writing and representation of the domestic, and in the writing of the American West. She is the co-editor, with Inga Bryden, of *Domestic Space: Reading the Interior in Nineteenth-Century Britain and America* (Manchester University Press, 1999), and the author of a book on the writing of the domestic in nineteenth-century North America, *Writing the Pioneer Woman* (University of Missouri Press, 2002). At present she is working on the mining fiction of Mary Hallock Foote.

Laurel Forster is a Lecturer in Cultural Studies at the Arts Institute at Bournemouth. Her research interests are in the narrative processes and creative impulses behind various forms of twentieth-century women's writing within the cultural and social context. She has a particular interest in, and has published on, May Sinclair, and is currently working on a full-length study of cultural and creative contexts within the twentieth century.

Marina de Camargo Heck is a Senior Lecturer in Cultural Studies and sociology at the Fundação Getulio Vargas, São Paulo, Brazil. Her particular interest is in food, migration and cultural memory. She has co-written a book, with R. Belluzzo, on the subject of memories and recipe adaptations of immigrants in São Paulo, *A Cozinha dos Imigrantes* (DBA/ Melhoramentos, 1998), and recently they have launched a book about sugar and the evolution of Portuguese sweet recipes in Brazilian cuisine, *Doces Sabores* (Studio Nobel Ed.S.P., 2002). Her current research explores the development of cooking and eating practices from basic routines necessary for nourishment, to leisure activities.

Celia M. Kingsbury is an Assistant Professor of English at Central Missouri State University. She has published articles in *Modern Fiction Studies* and *Conradiana*. Her book, entitled *The Peculiar Sanity of War: Hysteria in the Literature of World War I*, has just been published by Texas Tech University Press.

Andrea K. Newlyn is an Assistant Professor of English at Ohio State University at Lima. Her book manuscript entitled, 'Captivating Blackness: Transracial Crossing in American Literature and Culture' is currently under consideration. Her work which focuses on American literature, critical race theory and narrative theory, popular culture, gender and sexuality studies and 19th-century material culture has appeared in *Narrative*, *Modern Fiction Studies*, *The Journal of American Culture*, and *The Journal of Popular Music and Society*.

Sarah Sceats is a Senior Lecturer at Kingston University, London. Her specialism is in twentieth-century fiction, especially women's writing. She has a particular interest in the literary uses of food and has published widely on food and eating in fiction by Angela Carter, Doris Lessing, Margaret Atwood and Michèle Roberts among others. Her book *Food, Consumption and the Body in Contemporary Women's Fiction* was published in 2002 by Cambridge University Press. She is currently working on a number of projects, including the aging body, the idea of belonging and the fiction of Betty Miller.

Talia Schaffer is an Associate Professor of English at Queens College, CUNY. She is the author of *The Forgotten Female Aesthetes: Literary Culture in Late-Victorian England* (University Press of Virginia, 2000) and has co-edited, with Kathy A. Psomiades, *Women and British Aestheticism* (University Press of Virginia, 1999). Her recent books include an edition of Lucas Malet's 1901 novel, *The History of Sir Richard Calmady* (Birmingham, 2003) and a forthcoming reader, *Literature and Culture at the* Fin de Siècle (Longman, 2004). She is currently working on a project that explores Victorian domestic handicrafts as a paradigm for the realist novel.

Andrew Warnes is a Lecturer in American Literature at the University of Leeds. His first book, *Overcoming Hunger: Cooking and Resistance in*

African-American Literature (University of Georgia Press, forthcoming), is a study of the representation of food in the novels of Richard Wright, Zora Neale Hurston and Toni Morrison. He is currently working on a cultural history of barbecue.

Susan Zlotnick is an Associate Professor of English at Vassar College. She is the author of *Women, Writing and the Industrial Revolution* (1998) in addition to a number of articles on Victorian literature and culture. She is currently at work on a study of women, poverty and representation in nineteenth-century Britain.

Acknowledgements

First of all we would like to thank Reynold Silva, who originally suggested the idea of a book about the recipe. Our thanks must also go to our contributors as their scholarly and lively work has done much to stimulate our own thinking about recipes, cookery and writing. Miranda Nield-Dumper at King Alfred's College Library has been of great assistance to us. Our editors at Ashgate have guided us through the various stages of production, for which we thank them. And the support of Nick Forster and Richard Thompson has been, as ever, invaluable.

Furthermore, we would like to thank the *Journal of American Culture* for their permission to print a newly revised version of Andrea Newlyn's essay as Chapter 3 in the present volume. This appeared in its earlier form as 'Challenging Contemporary Narrative Theory: The Alternative Textual Strategies of 19th-Century Manuscript Cookbooks' in vol. 22:3, Fall 1999, pp. 35-49. We would also like to thank the journal *Frontiers*, published by the University of Nebraska Press, for their kind permission to reprint Susan Zlotnick's article 'Domesticating Imperialism: Curry and Cookbooks in Victorian England'.

Chapter 1

The Recipe in its Cultural Contexts

Janet Floyd and Laurel Forster

Recipes surround us: in cookery books and magazines, in newspapers and television programmes, in films and novels, we seem continually to read about, observe and be encouraged to absorb ourselves in the preparation and serving of food. Recipes, instructional or indicative, are not, of course, exclusively concerned with the more or less complicated production of routine meals or the orchestration of feasts, though, in doing just that, they evoke the elaborate scene of home, and the contentious arena of domestic politics and family values. In their different appearances, they are also persistently drawn into cultural debates around health and purity, about lifestyle and individualism, and into definitions of the national past, present and future. This volume aims to bring together some of these disparate contexts and debates, in order to demonstrate the multiple ways in which the recipe illuminates the cultural worlds in which it appears, and constitutes a textual form worthy of study in its own right. Food and cookery are crucial elements in all cultures. To say that we are what we eat has become a truism, albeit one that has generated a burgeoning field of academic enquiry into food and meals. The work of cooking and the texts that represent that work to us, situated as they are between the purchase of food and its consumption, can scarcely be less important to our sense of identity and shared values than food itself.

Cookery texts do not only define and engage with our spheres of daily experience. Cultures supposedly foreign to us are continually called up for our consumption in recipes, as are regions distant from the urban centre. Cookery writing and travel writing have much in common. The popular discussion of travel includes as a key element the pursuit of 'authentic' food familiar from cookbooks and visual cookery texts. Furthermore, as fears about the impact of fast food (food that is not prepared domestically or in ways we like to acknowledge) act as a catalyst for fears about global capitalism, so the appearance of recipes imitating the cuisine of 'simple tribal folks' may provide some reassurance. If there is no escape from tentacles of multi-national business, at least 'good' food offers some trace of a lifestyle uncorrupted by commercialism (Hall, 1991, 39).

Whatever cultural needs, desires and aspirations have inspired our appetite for cookery texts, a mass market for such material certainly exists. It is not only that thousands of such texts containing recipes in various contexts are available to us. Each of those texts is stuffed with recipes. Graham Tomlinson (1986), taking a modest sample of twelve cookbooks as part of a study of instructional texts, found himself studying three thousand recipes. And indeed, besides cookery books, recipes appear in all manner of places: newspapers and magazines, diaries and calendars, as free leaflets with food purchases, on tea towels, aprons and even tableware.

Anthropologists have seen food as a code, finding linguistic or cultural meaning through a precise grammatical or lexical system (Lévi-Strauss 1966; Douglas, 1975). Psychologists and philosophers have looked for revelations about deeper aspects of human behaviour through studies of our food habits and customs (Curtin and Heldke, 1992). Others have seen the recipe as an 'embedded discourse' with a variety of relationships within the social context: amongst friends, neighbours, relatives or even wider communities (Leonardi, 1989). The recipe, in its intertextuality, is also itself a narrative which can engage the reader or cook in a 'conversation' about culture and history in which the recipe and its context provide part of the text and the reader imagines (or even eats) the rest. It is open to subjective intervention and interpretation, putting the reader in contact with the writer, making personal connections with a cultural moment or a community, and allowing the reader to interpolate herself into the text, making the narrative her own. Through this system of exchange the reader learns more about herself and the world. Thus the recipe, besides being a narrative in itself, offers us other stories too: of family sagas and community records, of historical and cultural moments or changes, and also personal histories and narratives of self.

In putting this volume together, we have looked to address the range and multiplicity of this form and to collate work that uses a range of strategies for reading the recipe as it appears in different forms, at different times and within different contexts. Our predecessors in the scholarly field have set out generic practices or looked at particular strands of recipe writing and theorised the work that it performs within particular spheres. Our aim has been to address the variousness of the recipe's appearances within and across genres – television programmes, oral histories, magazines, novels, government documents and of course cookbooks published and unpublished – and to place the recipe within a range of disciplinary and interdisciplinary approaches. Cookery texts, long attached to discussions of the continuities of community and the conventions of the writing of domesticity, are seen here in terms of a range of shifting practices and as imbricated in difficult debates about national, colonial, postcolonial, class, race and gender politics.

Such concerns have produced texts that are the object of many responses, and indeed of misrepresentation. Mrs Beeton's writings appear in contemporary culture as signifiers of conspicuous Victorian consumption. Elizabeth David is a national saviour. But, aside from assumptions about specific texts, the role of the recipe itself is a contentious matter. As we write, there is evidently something of a backlash against the ubiquitous presence of the recipe and an attempt by the high priests of cookery writing to recast its role. The British cookery writer and journalist Nigel Slater (2000) argues that he has 'always felt that there is more to cooking than obediently following a recipe. Working to someone else's set of rules, word for word, gram for gram, not only kills the possibilities of adapting a recipe to suit our taste, but also stifles the enjoyment of preparing a meal' (9). Here the recipe, for this is what Slater goes on to provide, is defined as an aid to the creative individual, while cooking is an activity on the cusp of art. Meanwhile, cookery books that eschew the merely instructional are much praised and gathered into the high cultural sphere. John Thorne's *Outlaw Cook* (1992), according to one admiring reviewer, is 'more a novel than a cookbook': 'reading him on bread is like reading Proust on love'(Bateman, 1999). Thorne's own argument is that the continual reproduction of recipes has produced a diminished cuisine: 'cookbook writers [are] passing the same recipes around and around' and 'each time one passes through their hands, they manage to make it faster and faster, leaner and leaner, until everything fuses together in a little black box (the microwave)'. Like Slater, Thorne is keen to make a claim for the creativity of the individual cook as well as of cookery writing: 'It's easy to be seduced by other people's notions of a perfect pie and never to realise your own'(12).

As the creativity of cooking and recipe writing has become a given, at least in circles most involved with the gastronomic end of cookery, so originality has become a point at issue. Nigella Lawson, the British food writer and broadcaster, has been sharply criticised for not inventing her own recipes or generating variants on others', but instead paying others to find good recipes (*Observer Food Magazine*, 2002, 7). Yet the claims that creativity and originality are crucial to good recipe writing sit uneasily beside the other *sine qua non* of much contemporary cookery writing:

authenticity. A recent edition of the BBC's *Food Programme* (2002) that focused on the impact of the current explosion of recipe writing made much of the skill of a particular chef, David Thompson, who has learned to cook Thai dishes not through recipes but through tasting and imitating the dishes themselves. This brings us back to the creativity of the chef as artist; a recipe for the education of lesser cooks was made available on the BBC website. But, at the same time, the discussion is also characteristic of a longstanding view of the recipe writer's purpose as one of recreating an authentic 'original'. To deviate from the authentic dish is, for some, a desecration. John and Karen Hess (1972), for example, claim that only the chosen few have the talent to produce a 'delicious variation' on a dish; only in circumstances where different tools and ingredients are available may a 'different dimension' be allowed. Indeed the Hesses' argument is that most recipe writers are involved in plagiarism from 'original' writers, and 'snitchers are invariably butchers ... slovenly thinkers and poor craftsmen who do not understand the construction of a dish ... [T]hey will destroy its balance and harmony because they are intent on disguising the fact that it is stolen property' (138–139). Thus creativity and authenticity jostle with one another as terms shaping the recipe's meaning and purpose.

For as many of the cookery texts that express the cook's creativity or prompt our own, or that strive to recreate the art of the original, as many others are concerned to guide their readers and viewers conscientiously through the minutiae of the simplest of recipes. In fact the two categories are not exclusive. M. F. K. Fisher (1983), the doyenne of US cookery writing in its high cultural guise, has ruefully written of contemporary domestic cooks' dependence on instruction: 'as a spoilt idiot-child of the twentieth century, I want to be told' (17). But the association between cookery and a mode of training that embraces the inculcation of rules of social behaviour reaches rather further back. Insofar as cooking famously deals with the definition of what is raw, uncivilised and unpalatable, and its transformation into what can be shared and understood, ingested and enjoyed, it is plainly of crucial significance to the experience of social relations. Indeed for many decades food advertising has played on this so that Western culture now demands such transformations as part of the civilising process of society (Williamson, 1978).

Recipe books, as they structure meals, have participated in the formalisation of social rules. Different writers have placed this in different lights. For example, Val Mars (1993) writes of the ways in which middle- and upper-class Victorian children were permitted only blandly flavoured foodstuffs, for fear of stimulating their appetites. Their parents meanwhile feasted on meals in which varying cuisines were promiscuously mixed, and where meat, symbol of wildness and passion, dominated not only the table, but the decoration of the room (Ames, 1992). Laura Shapiro (1986) has described the cookery classes of the late nineteenth-century domestic science movement in America in which styles of cooking perceived as American were enforced, and the cuisine the domestic scientists chose to understand as foreign was suppressed. More generally, recipes may be linked with the impulse to rule, hierarchise and differentiate. Jack Goody (1977), emphasising the relationship between the recipe and the list, begins his discussion of the recipe form with the image of the high table at St John's Cambridge, where the list of diners, the seating list and the menu listing dishes recall the shopping list and the recipe that have enabled the scene of ranking and exclusion to take place (143). Recipes are lists, at least in part. Cookery books dictate the structures of meals, the size of servings. Cooking, writes Graham Tomlinson (1986), 'may represent the most instructed activity for the general populace in our society' (203).

The relationship between cooking and community does not have to be read wholly in terms of regulation, however, and some of the most important and elaborated discussions of recipe writing have seen this form of writing as working to draw together, memorialise and imagine supportive communities. The recovery of a feminist history of recipe writing is perhaps the most prominent expression of this. An important starting-point for the study of recipe writing was Susan Leonardi's 1989 article, 'Recipes for Reading', which argued that recipes do the work of constructing communities amongst women. Through the discovery, reading and even putting into practice of other women's recipes an imagined community is built. Real communities too are expressed and documented through recipes, and modes of cookery, or cookbooks, collectively assembled as a community enterprise (Bower, 1997).

Meanwhile, in the wake of Leonardi's article, literary scholars have revisited cookery books and have recast them as a form available for women's creative expression. Food, cookery and recipes, at times understood as part of the patriarchal power system, cultural instruction and control of women, have been reclaimed by feminist writers. Not only have feminist historians done much to bring to light moments in history and cultures when women were empowered rather than disempowered by their relationship to food; the recipe itself, often seen as a peculiarly female form of writing, has also been seen as an opportunity for women to creatively record and inscribe individual lives and situations, for example in the many private, personalised cookbooks never intended for publication. Janet Theophano (2002) discusses the 'expressive potential' of cookbooks, arguing that cookbooks are 'opportunities for women to write themselves into being' (5, 9). Accordingly the recipe has formed part of, or has been surrounded by, other kinds of writing: letters, diaries, fictions, polemic.

Whether recipes and cookery books enforce social norms, draw together communities or provide an arena for individual expression, they evidently participate in a social world in which meals are highly significant rituals and where patterns of behaviour stretching back into the past are illustrated and re-illustrated. Ann Romines (1997) has written of the cookbooks that 'have been there all my life, a dark presence on the shelf, in my mother's kitchen and now in mine. They were not for show, like the bright pottery and the embroidered dishtowels; over the years they grew more shabby, spotted and worn. But on occasions of ceremony and necessity ... they were consulted like oracles' (75).

Equally, though, it is possible to think of recipes as defined by moments of profound change. As Stephen Mennell (1985) and others have pointed out, cookery books were amongst the earliest of printed books (65), associated at the start with the symbolism required of aristocratic feasting. Recipes, once called 'receipts', are a form that is produced by writing down what is received and agreed information. As well as linking with traditions of the invention of writing and the structures of feudalism and autocracy, this etymological origin may also be used to argue for the ambiguous position of recipes within a process of exchange. Luce Giard (1998) thinks of recipes as 'multiplications of borrowing' (178). The root of the word recipe, the Latin word *recipere*, meaning both to give and to receive, reminds us that the instructions that appear to tie down the form of a dish to be shared exist in a perpetual state of exchange.

This process of giving and taking, partaking and retaining, is a context for cookery writing which has endured to the present form of cookery writing in the best-selling form that we know it today. Mass migration from country to city and from nation to nation or colony from the early nineteenth century produced a range of cookery books to deal with the range of new social situations: cookbooks for the upwardly mobile and their servants, for emigrants, for colonial administrators and settlers. Moreover, as Jack Goody (1977) writes, the popular cookery book of our own experience is a form arising out of an urbanising scene in which the market and the shop make ingredients available (140). In the rural context, methods of cooking were transmitted orally if necessary. And for most rural dwellers, the cooking of food was scarcely an elaborate matter needing to be carefully transmitted. Asked by Giard (1998) about recipes handed down, a group of peasant women from the Jura Mountains replied: 'our grandmothers did not have culinary customs, we were too poor; they mixed everything in a big pot that cooked slowly ... above the fire, and it was imperative not to waste anything' (177).

This is not how many historians of cookery see things. For many, cookery books are a rural tradition and the best cookery books must strive to recover the tenuous traces of the rural past decimated by industrialisation. A recent review of a new edition of Maria Rundell asks: 'Where did the tenderness go that Rundell bestowed on spinach, sorrel and cabbage which were to be put in the pan with "no water but what hangs to the leaves from washing"? Buried under the bricky industrial terraces and laid, with a sprig of rosemary, in the graves of the last British peasantry and yeoman farmers' (Rule, 2000). In the terms of historical accuracy, this is close to whimsy. But cookery writing is indeed frequently involved in the work of imaginatively recreating the past, often a rural past, and sometimes an aristocratic tradition too.

Personal histories or pasts, constructed through memory, or the process of remembering with others, are often centred on food: favourite childhood dishes, special family occasions, first attempts to cook, celebration meals out and so on. The olefactory sense is often particularly acute in memory. Such clear recollections may include phenomenal elements or sensations of taste; feelings of pleasure and visual images may form a distinctive state of 'awareness we associate with remembering', thus linking food memories of taste, smell, technique and appearance with other wider, surrounding factors. This heightened memory concerning the senses has been called 'autonetic consciousness' (Robinson, 1978, 237). Just as we are what we eat psychologically, food constructs us too.

Other kinds of memory are also associated with food and the recipe. It has been argued, for instance, that food and its preparation '[require] a multiple memory: a memory of apprenticeship, of witnessed gestures, and of consistencies' (Giard, 1998, 157). It requires memory to know how to cook but, at the same time, a more pragmatic, everyday memory function is needed to put the food on the table, to think what is in the larder, to work out which recipe can be adapted, which are the family's favourite meals, who is coming to dinner and so on.

Food and recipes feed other parts of our lives too, as is clearly witnessed by the creative deployment of food, recipes and cooking in fictional narratives of novel and film. Links between literary structure and cookery have been made (Bevan, 1988; Schofield, 1989) which claim food as metaphor for many other aspects of life in its sensual and anecdotal malleability. Some works of fiction have been structured by food and recipes, others work such material into their story-lines. Food as part of our daily routine can be used to great effect in fictitious form, where it can be given a different treatment. If food has long been the subject of poetry and prose, it has also become an increasingly significant aspect of the subject matter, metaphorical message and *mise en scène* of films too (Poole, 1999), and perhaps has become something extraordinary or even bizarrely unfamiliar, to once again make us consider afresh our daily relationship with food.

It is this malleability of cooking and food, and in particular the text of the recipe, across diverse cultural, social, geographical and personal contexts which informs this collection of essays. The interdisciplinarity of the essays, their historical breadth, and most importantly, their examination of the sheer range of different forms of the recipe, each informed and interpreted by its surrounding discourse, will create, we hope, an expansion of the appreciation of this important textual and cultural form.

Our emphasis in this volume, then, has been to offer the reader a sample of the breadth of contexts through which the recipe may be understood. The contributors, drawing on a range of multi-disciplinary perspectives, offer distinctive and overlapping approaches to the analysis of recipes in their many different appearances. But we begin with readings that are suggestive of the varying ways in which we might narrate traditions of recipe writing. Margaret Beetham's essay tackles one of the key figures through whom we engage with the recipe writing of the past, Isabella Beeton. Moving beyond the well-trodden discussion of Beeton's career, this essay looks at the brand 'Mrs Beeton', at the publishing interests that used her name, and the ways in which this figure spoke for and to the British middle classes of the era. This is a discussion that links Mrs Beeton's *Book of Household Management* with the market for cookbooks produced by social mobility. At the same time, it also reaches back to the oppositions of nature and culture set out by Lévi-Strauss to consider what is made central and what is marginalised in Beeton's Victorian domestic world.

Andrea Newlyn's essay turns back to the familiar scene of the nineteenth-century home, family and community, looking at the presence of a mass of private, unpublished cookbooks produced by women. In a close examination of the composition of these cookbooks, she explores the fine grain of their negotiation of the same ideological premises about domesticity that Beetham addresses. Newlyn is particularly interested, though, in the form that these texts take. These cookbooks offer a paradigm of narrative form that has as much bearing on the discussion of women's writing generally as it does on the study of private cookbooks and indeed of the uses of all cookbooks.

Andrew Warnes's essay goes back to the question of origins to reconsider the issue of the oral communication of particular dishes and its relationship to the printed recipe. Starting from a standard argument about the close relationship between recipes, writing and printing, Warnes looks at how contemporary African-American writers have embraced the communication of recipes in what Warnes terms a 'conversational' style. For Warnes, the recipe books of African Americans are determinedly oral and, in discussing the case of Abby Fisher in the 1890s, he looks closely at how the voice of an African-American cook may be traced in texts edited for an audience uninterested in hearing that voice. And, as Newlyn places the writing of recipes at the heart of nineteenth-century women's literary expression, so Warnes finds the speaking of recipes at the heart of African-American literature.

Warnes's essay explores the relations of power and resistance between the African American, Abby Fisher, and her white middle-class editors. More generally, though, the world of 'home cooking', the domestic world itself, has come to be seen as an arena for the wielding and consolidation of power in the colonial and postcolonial as well as the national context. Susan Zlotnick's essay goes back to the mid- to late nineteenth century and indeed to the canonical texts of the period to examine how the recipe for a particular dish, curry, is understood within the Victorian home. It isn't just that the ways of cooking curry are used to express ideas about the relationship between home and empire, however. Zlotnick's essay looks at how, in the very writing of recipes, curry is brought firmly within the boundaries of the Victorian homeland.

The relationship between home and nation, and the private and public roles of cooking, lies at the heart of another important strand within the tradition of cookery writing: domestic science. Celia Kingsbury's essay on the American domestic science movement fleshes out the familiar scenes in which domestic science teachers insist on the national importance of cooking, raising its status and significance, in their own eyes at least, by the association with science. Here we see a group of writers whose work is taken up by government authorities in the US and incorporated within the patriotic propaganda of the First World War. Kingsbury charts the ways in which a strategy for making a claim for cookery's importance becomes a nationwide campaign to save food and cook nutritiously, that is, to fight the war through kitchen practice.

Kingsbury's work raises the tantalising question of whether the domestic science writers used government propaganda to further their own ends, or whether their work was appropriated by those more powerful than themselves. In our second section, we address the implications, for two privileged women with literary and high cultural ambitions, of writing about food and cookery. Talia Schaffer's essay looks at the late nineteenth-century writer, Elizabeth Robins Pennell. We have become familiar with arguments as to what it meant to be a writer of domesticity in nineteenth-century Britain and America: a Mrs Child, a Mrs Hale, a Mrs Beeton or a Mrs Acton. As a female aesthete, Pennell was attempting to elevate cookery to an art form, and recipes to rhetoric. In doing so she struggled to avoid too close an association with just those activities that might compromise her status as a writer: cooking and eating. Schaffer charts the progress of that struggle and its outcome in Pennell's extraordinary oeuvre.

Elizabeth David's status has, by contrast, seemed a much less problematic issue. In Britain, she has long been revered as a national treasure. Her cookery writing is not only routinely argued to have revolutionised England's eating habits, she is praised as a literary stylist as well. The association between recipes, cookery and food and the formulation of national identity is addressed here, for the case of Elizabeth David and her reputation raises questions about how far a cookery writer may really be said to inscribe nation.

In different ways, then, the writing of recipes 'worked' for Pennell, who apparently managed her career as a writer of gastronomy with great care, and for Elizabeth David, the *doyenne* of 'simple, honest food'. In our final section on contemporary contexts of recipe writing, we begin with Laurel Forster's essay and the arena of radical gender politics. Here we find the writing of cookery occupying a distinctly more rebellious and ideologically difficult position at the heart of the contradictions that defined the Women's Liberation Movement in the 1970s. Forster explores the significance of the recipe and wider food issues to the Women's Liberation Movement in Britain, through a close reading of liberation magazines and, in particular, *Spare Rib*.

In many ways the feminist literature of the late twentieth century discussed by Sceats in the next essay pursues questions that increasingly preoccupied Forster's magazine writers. And yet, while the relationship between recipes and cookery and the scene of eating disorders, power and control caused the feminist campaigners of the 1970s to reject recipe writing, in the novels examined by Sarah Sceats, largely the output of the period between the late 1960s and the early 1990s, recipes are repeatedly and elaborately intertwined textually and metaphorically with just the same themes and anxieties. In this essay, we see the range of ways in which recipes have been drawn into fiction in order to speak for those very anxieties of bodily, sexual and emotional control which are so difficult to articulate within the restrictive complexities and competitiveness of twentieth-century living.

With the same contentious arguments about gender and domestic politics in mind, Maggie Andrews's essay looks at how the sexualities performed by two television chefs, Nigella Lawson and Jamie Oliver, engage with tensions and debates around domesticity and gendered behaviour in the late 1990s. But where some cultural critics have seen, for example, Lawson's foregrounding of pleasure as mere 'gastroporn' or as imbricated within new and reactionary forms of domesticity, Andrews uses the insights of psychoanalytic criticism to suggest how TV chefs may offer rather different possibilities to their audiences.

Finally comes Marina Heck's essay, which looks at the recipes remembered and recreated in fine and evocative detail by the immigrant population of São Paulo. Her collection of different ethnic cuisines, imported and adapted by the immigrants according to availability of ingredients, and family requirements, and her work of writing and cooking the dishes they recall, brings together issues of food, migration and memory. It also brings us back to the origins of the recipe itself in mobility, migration and change.

TRADITIONS

Chapter 2

Of Recipe Books and Reading in the Nineteenth Century: Mrs Beeton and her Cultural Consequences

Margaret Beetham

The ingredients of this chapter are not usually served up in the same dish. I want to blend together research in the history of publishing with the history of nineteenth-century domesticity, both as ideology and as materiality. Then, to push the metaphor perhaps beyond the bounds of good taste, I want to stir these up in a sauce of theoretical work drawn from a range of academic disciplines which have investigated cooking and eating as crucial markers, boundaries and means of transformation in the relationship of 'nature' and 'culture'. My argument throughout the chapter, the ingredient which binds the whole, is that there is a relationship between eating and reading.

Eating, what we have to do to keep alive as physical beings, has figured largely in the life of the intellect and in the life of the imagination, and both these are manifest in a range of different kinds of writing and reading. From the anthropologist, Lévi-Strauss's (1987) distinction between 'the raw' and 'the cooked' to postmodern ruminations like Elspeth Probyn's (2000) on the queer politics of carnal appetites, academics have been busy exploring in print the significance of cooking and eating. At the popular end of the publishing market, cookery books are everywhere in evidence; indeed advice on cooking and eating is a crucial part of contemporary capitalist publishing and of print and television mass media. In 2001 the *Oxford English Dictionary* credited the cookery writer Delia Smith with giving a new word to the English language, and Nigella Lawson sold thousands of copies of her books to a greedy public. Meanwhile, novels such as Michèle Roberts's *Daughters of the House* (1992) and Laura Esquivel's *Like Water for Chocolate* (1993) explore the centrality of eating to our fantasy lives.

As a source of life and of pleasure, signifier of cultural difference and of a common humanity, eating has become inextricably tied up with the processes of writing and reading. Nor is this only a late twentieth-century phenomenon. Cook-books and book-cooks have a long and complicated relationship.

In this essay I want to focus on one particular manifestation of that relationship, the cookery book or book of recipes. This is the form of print which seems to mediate most directly the materiality of cooking/eating and popular reading. The 'recipe book' is such a familiar form, its generic features so utterly taken for granted, that it is difficult to remember that it has a history and indeed a geography. In what follows I concentrate on British publishing and on a short but crucially important period, roughly 1860 to 1900. My argument is that during these years the characteristics of the recipe book as we now understand it and its importance as a form of popular print were both laid down.

It is, of course, impossible to separate the history of this particular genre from the general history of the expansion of popular print and the growth of a mass reading public. Political and social movements, the shift from a largely rural to a predominantly urban population, industrialisation, the development of mass education and mass literacy, improvements in the technology of printing and paper-making, the transformation of communications, especially the postal system and railways: all these shaped the history of the recipe book as of all print forms. Within that general history, however, the recipe book occupies a particular place and has its own story.

Printed books of 'receipts' pre-dated the nineteenth century and continued well into Victoria's reign (Attar, 1987, 11). 'Receipts' in this context included instructions for the preparation of food along with detailed advice on a wide range of other household activities including enamelling, dyeing, bleaching, brewing and making varnishes. Such books of receipts might include in their assumed readership men who were amateur scientists as well as mistresses of households. As more and more households bought ready-made varnishes or bought in rather than brewed their own beer, these miscellaneous collections gradually changed in emphasis and their readership was increasingly positioned as exclusively female.

This does not mean that the recipe book as we understand it developed tidily from these older forms. In the nineteenth century a variety of different kinds of general household book became popular. These almost all included 'recipes' as we understand the term today, that is, instructions on the preparation of specific dishes, but often these were embedded in a range of advice on other aspects of household and domestic work. This might include everything from managing servants to caring for the sick, from laundry work to choosing the furnishings, and often mixed spiritual and moral advice with practical instruction. Dena Attar in her definitive *Bibliography of Household Books Published in Britain, 1800–1914* (1987) distinguishes nine different types of these general books including miscellanies, encyclopaedias, school textbooks and narratives (14–34).

Recipes were important in all these different kinds of household book but they did not only appear there. From mid-century onwards, magazines addressed to the middle-class woman began to appear and these, unlike the older aristocratic ladies' journals, included practical advice on domestic matters, including recipes. By the 1890s the woman's magazine had become central to popular journalism and within these magazines, whether up-market sixpenny monthlies like *Woman at Home* or penny weeklies like *Home Notes*, recipes were a regular feature, as important as the fiction, fashion plates or articles.[1] Other kinds of printed miscellany also incorporated recipes. For example, in 1876 Henry Southgate's *Things a Lady Would Like to Know* combined the recipe book with the almanac or diary, printing for each day of the year a biblical text and a recipe.

It was from this range of publications that the book dedicated exclusively to the preparation of food emerged as a genre. Elizabeth Driver in her *Bibliography of Cookery Books Published in Britain, 1875–1914* (1989) chooses 1875 as her starting date because she argues that around that date the 'form of the modern cookery book was set and its contents roughly drawn out' (18). Her work and that of other bibliographers and food historians confirms that between 1875 and the end of the century not only did the format of the cookery book become settled but also publishers came to realise the value of this form of print commodity. There was an outpouring of such books from commercial presses. The recipe book thus arrived at that central place in popular print which it still holds at the start of the third millennium.

The process by which the recipe book emerged out of the general household manual and in the context of a burgeoning print industry owed much to one publication, *Beeton's Book of Household Management*. First published in volume form in 1861, this was to become the most famous of Victorian cookery books. What is significant, however, is not the individual book, though at 1112 pages it was a substantial volume. It is the publishing history of the volume, its transformation into a whole series of other texts, which makes it so important in the development of the recipe book. If cooking is always a process of transforming known ingredients into something new, then Beeton's is indeed a 'cook-book'.

The publishing house of Beeton specialised in general knowledge miscellanies, encyclopaedias and what we would now call 'how-to' books, almost all of which were explicitly linked with the name of the firm, for example, *Beeton's Dictionary of Universal Biography* (1861–1865), *Beeton's Book of Birds* (1865), and *Beeton's Guide to Investing Money* (1870).[2] *Beeton's Book of Household Management* followed this pattern, though it was unusual in being explicitly attributed to a woman editor, Mrs Beeton. As its title made clear, it can best be understood as an example of the general household manual that I have already discussed. It included thousands of recipes but these were embedded in a mass of other material, including advice on etiquette, on managing servants, on children and illness, and a section of legal memoranda. Even the sections devoted to preparation of food included scientific and general information on the animals and plants being discussed, anecdotes, historical notes and a plethora of other information often only tangentially related to the particular recipe. In compiling her text Beeton drew directly on a range of sources. Some of these she acknowledges in her 'Preface'. However her modest acknowledgement of her debt to 'a diligent study of the works of the best modern writers on cookery' does not fully indicate the extent to which she drew not just on the model of general household books, but specifically on material from earlier writers including Eliza Acton and Mrs Parkes.[3] However Beeton's volume, as I have suggested, transformed what were familiar ingredients into something completely new and it was this transformation which was to make Beeton rather than Acton or Parkes into a household name for the next hundred years. The nature of that transformation was complex. We are given a clue to at least one part of it if we go back to the acknowledgements in her 'Preface'. Here she thanked the contributors to *The Englishwoman's Domestic Magazine*, 'who have obligingly placed at my disposal their formula for many original preparations'. The link between *The Englishwoman's Domestic Magazine* and the book is crucial. The magazine, launched in 1851 by Samuel Beeton, Isabella's husband, was the first successful middle-class woman's magazine in Britain. It took the formula of the drawing-room journal and adapted it to suit the middle-class woman. In particular it assumed an absolute connection between the middle-class femininity of its target readership and the practicalities of running the home. Its stated aim was to help readers to 'make home happy' and to that end it provided practical advice including recipes (*Englishwoman's Domestic Magazine* 1, 1; Beetham, 1996, 59–88). The magazine more than most cultural forms enabled negotiation between writers and readers. It was this generic characteristic which enabled Isabella Beeton to appeal to readers for help in her project of writing a volume which, like the magazine, was aimed at those responsible for domestic management.

It was not only specific recipes from magazine readers that Isabella drew on for her massive volume; it was the whole experience of working with her husband in the business of popular publishing, especially of periodicals for women. Recycling material in different forms, offering inducements to buy, advertising, and using one publication to advertise or 'puff' another: all these entrepreneurial skills developed in the Beeton publishing house were put to work in disseminating *Beeton's Book of Household Management*. The use Beeton made of the magazine to advertise the book was important. However far more significant was the way the idea of serial publication, the concept of the series as against the single volume, shaped the whole publishing history of 'Mrs Beeton'. In fact the 1861 volume was itself a compilation of parts which had already been issued serially and another series was bound into a volume and issued in 1863. That was only the beginning. Though Isabella Beeton died in 1865 and Samuel sold the firm, its name and titles to Ward, Locke and Tyler in 1874, 'Mrs Beeton' books continued to appear for the next hundred years. They came in a huge range of prices and formats. For the bibliographer the tangle of publications is difficult to unravel but I think two broad generalisations can be made.[4] Firstly, the volume was reissued again and again, often undated, though new issues include those of 1869, 1880, 1888 (claiming to be the 468 thousandth) and 1906. Described as 'revised' or 'reissued' and parading under the name 'Mrs Beeton', these kept elements of the Beeton format but changed its substance. The 1906 volume was written by a male chef and included virtually none of the original. Crucially for my concerns here, the volume was now definitely a cookery book. Secondly, throughout the period from 1860 to 1900, Beeton and later Ward, Locke and Tyler also began to publish spin-offs, extracting bits of the book to publish in smaller and cheaper formats. These booklets were also almost all recipe or cookery books. *Mrs. Beeton's Dictionary of Everyday Cookery*, *The Englishwoman's Cookery Book*, *Mrs. Beeton's Cookery Book*, *Mrs. Beeton's Shilling Cookery Book*, *Beeton's Penny Cookery Book* and other similar titles were issued and reissued throughout the rest of the nineteenth and into the twentieth century. Thus 'Mrs Beeton' not only found her way into kitchens of every class but she became identified almost exclusively with the recipe.

The Beeton volume, therefore, played a particular role in the emergence of 'the recipe book'. This was partly, as I suggested above, because of the entrepreneurial skills of the house of Beeton. But there were also aspects of Beeton's text which contributed to its popularity and made it such a milestone. Of course, 'Mrs Beeton' was not exclusively responsible for the emergence of the cookery book as an important print genre. Her work was a symptom as much as a cause. However in order to understand the significance of this print phenomenon it is useful to attend both to the specifics of Beeton's original text and to the social and psychological changes of which it was a part and which it helped to bring about. In the rest of this article I pursue this double agenda.

Beeton's volume, like *The Englishwoman's Domestic Magazine* in which it was canvassed and puffed, assumed a readership that was specific both in gender and class. It simultaneously addressed and sought to bring into being the middle-class domestic woman. The emergence of the popular recipe book was a symptom of the redefinition of femininity in relation to domesticity that characterised the first half of the nineteenth century (Hunter, 1994). It is no coincidence that it was the name of its female editor that became a shorthand for the title nor that even after her death the publishers continued to link it with her. Like that of Mrs Sarah Ellis before her and her contemporary Mrs Warren, who was famous for such titles as *How I Managed on Two Hundred Pounds a Year* (1864), Mrs Beeton's name chimed with the assumption of an absolute coincidence between (married) femininity and the domestic sphere.

The work of middle-class femininity was invisible to those who described her as a domestic angel or a vestal of the hearth. Indeed it was an important part of the masculine fantasy of the domestic that the work of maintenance was invisible. However, in magazines and manuals aimed at these women from the 1850s onwards, domestic work was made visible and its difficulties specifically addressed, *including* the difficulty of keeping it invisible. There is a steady shift away from general moralising towards practical detail in domestic manuals during the early Victorian period. Mrs Sarah Ellis in the 1830s and 1840s had been concerned exclusively with the moral management of the household but in the 1860s Mrs Warren mixed the practical with the didactic moral elements in her work. Beeton's emphasis was entirely on the practical through which she assumed the moral was enacted. She redefined the task of managing the domestic so that attention to the minutiae of daily life was not just given as a maxim to live by but was worked through in detail.

In defining the task of the middle-class woman as 'management' and in assuming that popular print was an appropriate, indeed *the* appropriate, medium for instruction in this task, Beeton was thus mobilising a series of far-ranging social shifts. Among these was the use of print. Writing down favourite recipes almost certainly existed side by side with oral and practical instruction for much of the nineteenth century. However, the systematic reproduction of cooking instructions in commercial forms of print was symptomatic of a much wider process by which oral knowledges were gradually superseded by print. This did not happen suddenly, and many young women throughout the nineteenth and into the twentieth century almost certainly learned to cook by doing it under instruction from mothers, teachers, older servants or other women. However print became increasingly important even for those who could not or did not read. In Beeton's case, for example, she assumed that the mistress might use the book to give instructions to her servants who would not read the book themselves. Printed texts thus became the crucial means both of codifying knowledge and of passing it on. Both these elements, codification and education, were important in the development of the recipe book.

Mrs Beeton prided herself in having codified a previously chaotic body of knowledge. Though, as I have suggested, she took recipes and ideas from others, Beeton transformed the material she borrowed and she did this through its systematic presentation. Firstly, her recipes were laid out in a standard format in which ingredients (by weight), method and cost followed each other. This now seems so obvious that it is worth pointing out what an important innovation it was. However Beeton's systemisation extended to the structure and layout of her *Book of Household Management*. Foods were divided into categories and each type was discussed according to a similar plan. Within these sections, recipes were arranged alphabetically (another innovation), and Beeton deployed a range of print sizes to help the reader. Recipe names were in large bold type and were therefore easy to find. The actual recipe was in smaller but clear print, often illustrated with the small line drawings that made the volume so attractive. The mass of detailed information that prefaced each section or was appended to the recipes was in smaller print. Paragraphs were numbered, as well as pages. Along with Beeton's wonderful cross-referenced 'Analytical Index', this helped the reader to find her way easily about the densely packed pages of the text. The printed format here not only elevated a seemingly humble task but also presented it as part of a systematic body of knowledge. In organising her material as she did, Beeton demonstrated the task of management which she advocated. As with her ideal kitchen, so with her book, there was 'a place for everything and everything in its place' (42). These elements of systematic organisation were retained through all subsequent volumes.

The way Beeton transformed her borrowed ingredients into something new thus clearly owed much to her own and Samuel Beeton's particular skills. However her volume was also, as I have suggested, part of a larger process. Middle-class women (like middle-class men) were called on to manage others: domestic servants and the other members of the household, particularly children. As with other branches of middle-class work which were being redefined in the Victorian period, notably engineering and medicine, traditional practices were being redefined and attached to formal methods of learning. Beeton was important here. Her aim was to produce a science of domestic management, one that could be systematically taught. By the end of the century domestic science was an established part of the curriculum in Board schools across the country and it was taught through textbooks. In schools, however, while domestic study kept its strong identification with gender (boys were barred from taking it), its class element had changed and it was aimed at producing good domestic servants rather than managers of households.

The location of women in the domestic rather than in the public sphere of men's work meant that management was inflected differently for women. Whereas men's place was in the public world of work and their economic role was production, women were located in the domestic and their role in the economy was to manage consumption. The household as the unit of consumption was crucial and became increasingly important as – in a move I have already gestured towards – domestic consumption came to depend less on the home-grown and the home-made. The woman's role was to manage her family budget but also to manage the different kinds of consumption which went on in the family, including crucially the consumption of food. It is not surprising then that not only the purchase of food but cooking, eating and serving of meals were important parts of women's work. Nor is it surprising that books addressed to this should appear as the print industry expanded.

In this respect the proliferation of cookery books should be set in the context of a general expansion of the market for household goods. Beeton's volumes were part of an increasingly sophisticated targeting of the domestic market. Every volume of Mrs Beeton's book, including the first, contained a detailed (usually illustrated) account of the huge variety of utensils deemed essential for the kitchen. As the century went on the Beeton publications included not only prescriptions in the text but advertisements for brand names of sewing machines or kitchen ranges. Then, as commercially made foods, including jams, puddings and soups, began to be sold, these too were advertised. The 1897 copy of *Mrs. Beeton's One-Shilling Cookery Book*, for example, has advertisements on its end pages for Crosse and Blackwell's Soups, Milkmaid Condensed Milk, Kilvert's Lard and other foods as well as aluminium ware and 'gourmet boilers'. The corollary of this was that the management of the household's consumption included finding a way through a proliferating range of ready-made goods, kitchen- and table-ware and, of course, the ever-expanding range of books including recipe and household books.

Although consumption cannot be separated from production, the ideological separation of the domestic world was rigorously maintained. It was crucial to Beeton's project that eating, like other intimate social relations, be conducted within the home, the domain of woman. As she pointed out in her 'Preface' to the 1861 volume:

> Men are now so well served out of doors, – at their clubs, well-ordered taverns and dining houses, that in order to compete with the attractions of these places, a mistress must be thoroughly acquainted with the theory and practice of cookery, as well as perfectly conversant with all the other arts of making and keeping a comfortable home.

Women had to work hard to ensure that what was served up to men at home was as desirable as what was offered in the promiscuity of the public eating house. Just as working-class women were admonished to make their homes attractive to ensure that men did not resort to public drinking, so middle-class women were responsible for making sure their men came home at the end of the working day to be renewed and recreated for the struggle of production. The legitimate seductions of the domestic table could not rest only on individual recipes but depended, as Beeton says, on a wider understanding of the arts of homemaking. It is not surprising then that food writers, including Beeton, gave advice on how to combine recipes into meals and to manage a range of different kinds of dining. Sample menus appropriate for each month, suggestions for how to plan for family dinners and formal entertaining, as well as general advice on presenting and serving at table, were all important elements of the advice they offered.

What was at stake here was not simply eating or even cooking but 'dining'. The distinction between eating and dining, Beeton suggested, marked the progress of different nations in civilisation. She prefaced the section of her book on menus and 'bills of fare' with the words:

> The rank which a people occupy in the grand scale may be measured by their way of taking their meals as well as their way of treating women. A nation which knows how to dine has learned the leading lesson of progress. It implies both the will and skill to reduce to order and surround with idealisms and graces the more material conditions of human existence. (905)

For Beeton the organisation of eating was a matter of the utmost cultural significance. It was, as she constantly stressed, the way of transforming the natural into the cultural. As she put it: 'Everything that is edible and passes under the hands of the cook is more or less changed and assumes new

form' (39). Her book therefore sought to produce bodies that not only ate
and were sustained but which through their manner of eating were inserted
into nineteenth-century economies of class and gender. This was not only
about the assignation of the management of consumption to women.
Dining, because it is about the transformation of nature into culture, had a
particular relationship with femininity in a cultural economy where women,
more explicitly than men, were bearers of the nature/culture paradox.
Beeton was aware of this in that she made a nation's way of eating and its
way of treating women analogous markers of progress. However the link
extended beyond such easy parallels. For the nineteenth century,
femininity, like 'dining', was both natural and always to be cultivated.

Such cultivation involved incessant labour. A close reading of Beeton's
text shows how the undisciplined forces of the natural were constantly
erupting into her ordered world. Indeed her insistence on the need for
systematic organisation was a measure of the energy of the natural, which
Beeton seemed simultaneously to celebrate and to deplore. As James
Buzard (1997) has argued in a witty essay on Beeton, the sheer exuberance
of the natural world appeared in those bits of text in small print that
prefaced each section or were appended to the recipes. Here a Darwinian
proliferation of species is evident:

> The fecundity of fishes has been the wonder of every philosopher whose
> attention has been attracted to the subject ... According to Lewenhoeck, the cod
> annually spawns upwards of nine millions of eggs, contained in a single roe.
> The flounder produces one million, the mackerel above a hundred thousand ...
> (109)

and so on for several sentences. Through proper management these
extravagances of nature could be turned to good effect. The pig was defined
as an animal whose voracious appetite simultaneously attracted and
repulsed. He is 'of such a coarse and repulsive mode of feeding' that he has
'in every country and language obtained the opprobrium of the unclean
animal'. Yet if properly managed there is no domestic animal 'so profitable
or so useful to man' (302).

Such management requires constant vigilance since nature is always
unpredictable. Not only is the pig excessive in its habits, the hunted wild
boar is capable of turning and ripping with his savage teeth the bowels of
the hunter (376). This is also the moral of the mackerel, a fish as voracious
as it is fecund:

> Pontippod relates an anecdote of a sailor who belonged to a ship lying off one
> of the harbours on the coast of Norway, who, having gone into the sea to bathe

was missed by his companions; in the course of a few minutes, however, he was seen on the surface with a great number of mackerel clinging to him by their mouths. His companion hastened in a boat to his assistance, but when they had struck the fishes off him and got him up, they found he was so severely bitten that he shortly afterwards expired. (141)

These cautionary tales are given in the minute print that Beeton used to intersperse general facts and histories between her recipes. However the small print cannot undo their disturbing power. Such stories show that the natural can disrupt or even reverse the fundamental laws of who eats and who gets eaten which underpin all 'dining'.

Though a judicious understanding of the potential of nature both for good and ill is necessary at every point, not all the warnings Beeton gives are so dramatic. Black pepper, for example, 'a well-known aromatic spice', is 'generally employed as a condiment; but it should never be forgotten that, even in small quantities, it produces detrimental effects on inflammatory constitutions' (183). Here the inflammatory quality of the spice has been transferred to the constitution of the eater, an easy elision since what we eat makes us who we are. However the important aspect of this warning about the use of pepper is that it stresses the need for restraint. The natural fecundity and voraciousness of nature is both necessary and dangerous for culture. In Beeton's volume, therefore, two key concepts are excess and restraint. These are the twin poles of the world of 'dining'. To put it in Beeton's terms, her recipes were designed to produce a way of eating (and therefore a way of living) which combined 'elegance with economy'.

By the late nineteenth century Beeton's name had become a by-word not for economy but for extravagance. The music hall joke, repeated to me in the early 1960s by my elderly auntie, was that Beeton recipes were ridiculously excessive involving such openings as: 'Take two dozen eggs and throw away the yolks.' This reputation for excess persists in the popular imagination where the enormous formal dinners and over-furnished drawing rooms of the high Victorian bourgeoisie have been the stuff of television dramas and popular novels. However much of that reputation rests on the later volumes, particularly that of 1906, which demonstrated what the American economist Thorstein Veblen (1899) called 'conspicuous consumption', a phrase he coined to describe 1890s upper-class life on both sides of the Atlantic. However it is true even of the original Beeton that its project, like that of other similar titles, was to enable the rising middle class to take part in the display deemed necessary to their social status. For example, the management of 'dining' included the provision of elaborate dinners of several courses at which you entertained friends or business contacts.

Just as, in Beeton's world, the practice of 'dining' distinguished the advanced peoples such as the British from more primitive groups, so the 'elegance' of the dinners provided by the competent mistress for 'the over-worked man of business, the statesman or the dweller in towns' was to be distinguished from the 'simplest food' of those who lived by hard physical labour (903). Although the field worker might have a heartier appetite, the middle-class diner would be offered not just more expensive but far more dishes, and probably more than he and certainly more than she could be expected to eat. A menu for 'Dinner for Eighteen Persons' laid out diagrammatically on the page opposite the quotation below gives four courses and twenty-seven different substantial dishes (904). Excess therefore was not only to be found in the natural world but was also endemic in the particular class culture in which Beeton's readers either lived or to which they aspired.

The kind of elaborate dining which Beeton assumed her readers would undertake depended primarily on a certain level of income. However, it was not enough to have the income. One had to know how to manage it and hence, of course, books like Beeton's: 'The elegance with which a dinner is served is a matter which depends of course, partly upon the means, but still more upon the taste of the master and the mistress of the house' (903). The transformation of income into 'taste' was the central project of her book. Taste here does not only signify the shift of meaning from the most physical of sensations into a mark of the highest culture. It is also in the context of Beeton about the relationship of excess to restraint. For her concept of 'elegance' was not just a code for conspicuous extravagance. Excess, whether in the natural world or in the social, needed to be restrained or it would bring destruction.

Specifically, the mistress had to learn how to manage expenditure so that the excesses of middle-class dining and all that went with it did not make the family bankrupt. The management of consumption meant producing the maximum of display while keeping at bay the threat of financial collapse. The silly young woman who cannot keep her accounts, allows her servants to cheat her and therefore brings her family to ruin was a stock figure not only in contemporary advice manuals but also in fiction. The most famous of these silly housekeepers was probably Dickens's Dora in *David Copperfield* (1850), but most such bad managers were less sympathetically treated. For Beeton therefore 'economy' was the crucial balance to what she called 'elegance'. Keeping accounts was the bedrock of housekeeping. Managing the servants was crucial and beyond that Beeton's ingenuity in suggesting ways of being economical without losing status was remarkable. There are as many recipes for appetising ways of serving up cold meat leftovers as there are for splendid dinners (xii–xiii).

The struggle between economy and elegance is well illustrated in the decision Beeton had to make about whether to recommend that dinner parties be served in the Russian or the French style. The traditional method for serving dinner was called *à la française* and involved putting dishes together on the table where they were carved and where guests served themselves and each other. By the 1860s this method was being overtaken in upper-class circles by the *à la russe* method, which meant that carving and serving were done by servants (Brears, 1994; Mars, 1994). Instead of dishes being placed on the table, there were elaborate centre decorations, and the various courses were cleared and served from the side. This method was more expensive in staff, in tableware and in table decoration, as Beeton explained when she advised:

> Dinner à la russe is scarcely suitable for small establishments: a large number of servants being required to carve and to help the guests; besides there being a necessity for more plates, dishes, knives, forks and spoons than are usually to be found in any other than large establishments. (955)

She therefore included only two examples of this method of serving as against 81 for the French method. However, it was precisely its excess that made the Russian method increasingly popular with a middle class dedicated to display. Though some elements of the French mode of serving persisted, by the 1890s the Russian had come to dominate middle-class dining and recipe books, including later Beeton editions. This may be read as evidence of that increase in conspicuous consumption on which Veblen remarked. The various editions of Beeton make clear that, while it was always seen as crucial to find a balance between excess and restraint, the point of balance could not, and did not, remain constant.

The need to reissue a revised version of 'Beeton' and of other cookery books thus arose in part from the way the culture of 'dining' was always being redefined. Also the psychological desire to be seen to consume had its roots in the very material ways in which dining was linked into capitalist consumption, whether of cookery books, of china, knives, kitchen utensils or kitchen ranges. Not only did each generation need a new version of Beeton but, as I have already indicated, each new edition recommended and sometimes actually advertised yet more kinds of cooking apparatus and cooking utensils.

As I have tried to show in this discussion, the responsibility for the preparation and consumption of food placed the mistress of the house in a position of power. Beeton opened her volume by comparing the mistress of the household to the commander of an army (1). However with that power went considerable cultural anxiety. Eating, whether in the family or at a formal dinner, was loaded with cultural meanings. These included social meanings to do with status. The mistress had to find a way between the excess and restraint of middle-class living. But eating also marked a boundary or site of exchange between nature and culture. She therefore had also to undertake the task of giving cultural meanings to bodies that eat. These difficulties were compounded for middle-class women by the cultural imperative on them to control their appetites and discipline their bodies. In the late eighteenth century it was already accepted that 'eating a great deal is deemed indelicate in a lady', and this idea persisted throughout the nineteenth and into the twentieth century (Brears, 1994, 94).[5] Managing the domestic, therefore, meant keeping in place not only material objects (kitchen utensils, glasses, flowers for the table), not only meals appropriate to the time of year and the family's income, but also her own body and the bodies of her household with their appropriate cultural meanings.

All these boundary problems relate to that most crucial set of markers which the mistress had to keep in place: those between inside and outside. At the level of the social this meant the mistress was responsible for protecting the boundary between the world of the domestic circle and the public world. In the mythology of Victorian capitalism, the world of the family represented a safe haven from the struggle of the market. The survival of the fittest in the market, as in the natural world, meant that the rules about who ate and who got eaten were liable to break down there. Outside the home men could be devoured, either whole or by being nibbled, as the sailor was by the mackerel.

Psychologically the barriers between outside and inside work at another level altogether. I began this chapter by suggesting that cooking is always about the transformation of the natural into the cultural, the raw into the cooked. However eating is even more profoundly concerned with transformation. Whatever we eat becomes us; we become what we eat. The necessity and the pleasures involved in this transformation are fraught with danger, because eating involves breaching the barrier between the world and the body. We must eat to live, yet even a few grains too much of pepper may cause problems. If we survive being poisoned or made ill, still there are the dangers integral to the crossing of that most important divide between the 'not-me' and the 'me'. No wonder that these other cultural anxieties attached themselves to eating and no wonder that books like Beeton's, which offered to allay their readers' anxieties, became so popular.

We have no way of knowing how the Beeton volumes were actually read, or even whether they were read. The 1906 volume I inherited from my grandmother was a wedding present that looks as if it has been barely opened, let alone used in the kitchen. But the transfer of the delights of eating into reading is always a complex process. Reading can set off its own cultural anxieties, as the Victorians knew well. Reading is like eating in that in both the barriers between inside and outside are crossed. In western European cultures, shaped as they are by the Christian identification of word and bread, the metaphor of reading as eating is endemic. In the nineteenth century anxieties about the reading of women and the working class were habitually explored through metaphors of 'healthy eating', through anxieties about the way undisciplined readers devoured unsavoury fictions, and even fear that certain kinds of reading could become addictive.[6] The consumption of texts, like the consumption of food, went on largely in the domestic context and Beeton assumed that the management of the household included the provision of good reading, both for the mistress herself and for others, particularly her daughters and her (female) servants.

Much of the anxiety about reading, especially women's reading, was focused on fiction, because fiction dealt not only with the 'real world' but also with fantasy and desire. Household manuals and recipe books would seem to be exempt from such concerns. However I would argue that the cookery book, like the novel, deals with more than matters of 'taste'. Beeton's book dealt with fantasy and desire at a number of levels. Most overtly it dealt with the fantasy of transforming income into taste; it offered access to the world of middle-class display to which her readers aspired. It also offered a model of femininity that seemed attainable if you followed the steps set out so clearly in the text. The fantasy here was of the truly domestic and therefore desirable woman whose husband and children are kept safe in the circle of home. Perhaps most importantly the Beeton texts presented their readers with the fantasy of an ordered cultural world that recognised but contained the exuberance of the natural. Cooking and reading alike offer us the fantasy of a transformed nature, since for the recipe writer as for the cook, 'everything that passes under her hands is changed and assumes new forms'.

Part of the success of Beeton lay in changes in the definition of middle-class femininity and the related growth in the market for household goods in which the print industry played a crucial part. But this is not all. It was also because it functioned simultaneously as a practical manual, a method of scientific education and a fantasy text that Beeton's book came to occupy a crucial role in nineteenth-century print culture.

Notes

1   I discuss these developments fully in *A Magazine of her Own? Domesticity and Desire in the Woman's Magazine 1800–1914*, 1996.

2   These are among the tens of titles attributed to the publisher S. O. Beeton in the British Library General Catalogue.

3   [Beeton, I], 'Preface', *Beeton's Book of Household Management*, 1861, (hereafter, Beeton), n.p.. In her unpublished M.A. Dissertation: 'Tradition, Innovation and Borrowing in Nineteenth-Century Household Books': *An Encyclopaedia of Domestic Economy* and *Beeton's Book of Household Management*, 1975, Rachel Goodyear of Leeds University School of English shows in detail how Beeton borrowed but also transformed borrowings, particularly from Mrs Parkes. I am grateful to Rachel Goodyear and her tutor, Professor Lynette Hunter, for giving me access to the dissertation.

4   The bibliographical history of the Beeton volumes is extremely complex and difficult to untangle. The 1861 text is itself not straightforward as it consisted of the publisher's binding of part-issues, which is what I refer to throughout the rest of this paper. Driver, *A Bibliography of Cookery Books*, 1989, pp. 101–102, has a brief account of the bibliography. See also *The Cambridge Bibliography of English Literature, 1800–1900*, 1999. I am grateful to Leslie Howsam of the University of Windsor for allowing me to read an unpublished paper 'Women's History/Women's books: Recovering the Nineteenth-Century Mrs. Beeton'.

5   Brears quotes from John Trusler, *Honours of the Table*, 1788. See also Michie, *The Flesh Made Word: Female Figures and Women's Bodies*, 1987, for a discussion of the ideological constraints on women's eating as explored in nineteenth-century fiction.

6   See Flint, *The Woman Reader, 1837–1914*, 1993. I have elaborated this argument in 'Women and the Consumption of Print', 2001, pp. 55–77.

Chapter 3

Redefining 'Rudimentary' Narrative: Women's Nineteenth-Century Manuscript Cookbooks

Andrea K. Newlyn

Cookies
2 eggs, 2 cups of Sugar, 1 cup of Milk, 1 Cup of butter[,] 2 nutmeg, 1
teaspoon of quick yeast[,] flour enough to make into a stiff dough, roll and cut
out, dampen the top with water[,] dip into white sugar, then bake in a quick
oven, From Sallie. (Mary Smith's cookbook, 1874)

We cannot assume that a text ... tells no story because it does not make its
story explicit, formally organized, and finished (that is, fully narrative); we
cannot even assume that explicitness is universally a sign of 'full' narrativity.
(Marilyn Robinson Waldman, 1980)

Cookbooks, relegated to the 'women's sphere' and the realm of domestic
economy, have long been considered inconsequential if not altogether
immaterial, and certainly have never attained the status of literary text or been
considered a part of the canon of American literature. And yet while they
seem, as Anne Bower (1992) notes, 'innocent of narrative force' (1), they
contain an implicit narrative structure and a wealth of cultural and socio-
historical material invaluable to scholars of the nineteenth century and
women's history and culture. To begin to adequately define 'women's
culture' in the nineteenth century requires a willingness to consider a variety
of texts never before contemplated as literary works, including cookbooks,
quilts, account books and other cultural artefacts. In *Mythologies* (1972),
Roland Barthes examines how culture can be read as a text, and how cultural
artefacts or 'myths' – everything from soap powder to wrestling matches to
guide books – contain a system of signs that can be interpreted and understood
both semiologically and ideologically. Barthes thus enlarges the notion of
text, extending semiological and narrative analyses into 'nonliterary' realms.

Comparable artefacts from the nineteenth century can also be read semiologically and narratively, including the more overtly literary texts accessible to women (particularly middle-class women), such as magazines, advice books, domestic manuals, pamphlets, fiction and sermons, but also forms typically defined and designated as non-literary, such as cookbooks, diaries, quilts, fashion, pottery, tapestry weaving and other 'household arts'. By extending structural, semiological and narrative analyses into these supposedly non-literary realms, contemporary scholars of nineteenth-century culture can begin to understand more fully the myriad and complex ways that women expressed themselves, created an institutionalised network of conventions, rituals and customs based in same-sex relations and, significantly, developed textual strategies that complicate modern notions of narrativity.

Nineteenth-century private domestic cookbooks are explicit emblems of women's relegation to the private sphere, maintaining, as they did, institutionalised patriarchal systems, and serving the organisational core of that system, the family. More than just a collection of recipes or 'receipts' (as they were commonly called), manuscript cookbooks comprised the literary text of the nineteenth-century housekeeper, playing a crucial role in maintaining communal structure, social ties and cultural tradition. These cookbooks inscribe a narrative which figures household protagonists as protectors of domestic sanctity able to deliver the family from disorder, disease and waste. Despite the cookbook's overtly collusive function, its makers re-appropriated the cookbook form and transformed it into a locus of female artistry, empowerment and social reform. The re-appropriation of cookbooks' otherwise domestic function demonstrates not only women's efforts toward empowering themselves and the spaces they inhabit, but also reflects their development of alternative textual strategies that contest dominant conceptions of narrative.

Nineteenth-century private unpublished domestic cookbooks are an important example of a material and socio-literary form excluded from critical scholarship by rudimentary concepts of canonicity, overly literal notions of narrativity and limited ideas about what constitutes a literary text. However their lack of academic currency is also marked by an unrelenting gender essentialism which suggests that non-literary material, cultural artefacts and literary texts that are dominated by what Ann Romines (1992) refers to as the 'rhythms and stresses of domestic ritual' (including texts written in the sentimental tradition), are specious, devoid of real value or use to critics and historians (9). This gender essentialism, which has historically pervaded criticism of nineteenth-century 'women's literature',[1] relegates the domestic to the arena of the feminine and identifies the feminine with emotion, which then becomes (re)coded as excess and, most importantly, non-literary. This gender essentialism surrounding women's artistry and literature in the nineteenth century also intersects with, and is informed by, the deprecation of popular culture. While Bower suggests, rightly I believe, that scholarship about domesticity has become a 'legitimate' critical pursuit and more readily accepted in recent decades, this chronic conflation of 'the feminine' with a debased popular culture reveals a tenacious apprehension around scholarly involvement with non-literary texts, especially those by women and/or those considered 'popular'. Although scholarship by New Americanists and feminist critics has once again reclaimed nineteenth-century women's literature, and in particular the sentimental genre, long subject to a continuous round of censure and acclaim, denigration and reclamation, there is nevertheless this persistent and problematic conflation of the popular with the feminine, and the association of both with debasement.

This denigration of the feminine and popular culture, including sentimental literature, reflects, as Cathy Davidson (1998) points out, a 'social anxiety' that indicates a 'generic wish for an unconflicted world, one where ... emotions and intimacies, are epiphenomenal' (455). It also reflects an anxiety, visible in both nineteenth-century and contemporary cultures, that by the 'last decades of the eighteenth century a more polite, feminine, weaker (both philosophically and aesthetically) version of American culture prevailed', devolving, as Ann Douglas (1977) argues, into 'the sentimental strain in American literature' (Davidson, 447). Recent efforts to reconceptualise domesticity make visible how this early criticism of 'women's fiction' further privileged and reified canonical, and inherently patriarchal, notions of what is 'great' literature. Also, while the recent endeavours to re-examine separate spheres as an appropriate metaphor for American culture in the nineteenth century make visible the limitations of such an oppositional model for understanding the socio-historical dynamics of the time period, these efforts to demonstrate the permeability of the boundaries between these supposedly dichotomous spheres address only the 'purely' literary, or narratively *familiar*, texts by women.[2]

Although private manuscript cookbooks form the literary text of the nineteenth-century housekeeper, historically these manuscripts have not been the subject of scholarly investigation not only due to their being reduced to things 'feminine' and/or popular, but because of their relegation to the realm of American material culture or ephemera. The classification of these texts is thus not only bound up with gender ideologies and the debasement of popular cultural material, but also with ideologies about what is, and what is not, 'narrative'. Traditional concepts of what constitutes a literary text or even 'narrative' exclude not only important historiographic material such as annals and chronicles, as Hayden White and others have demonstrated,[3] but other socio-literary texts and non-literary material culture. While scholars and historians have traditionally positioned (and dismissed) manuscript cookbooks as mere ephemera, and certainly not narrative, private cookbooks often do adhere to many of the organisational principles central to conventionalist approaches to narrativity. As Susan Leonardi (1989) points out, a recipe is an 'embedded discourse' that contains not only an implicit narrative strategy, but a cast of characters (the recording of recipes passed on to other women), and a central narrator or persona (340). However while these manuscript cookbooks may conform to conventional expectations of narrative proper, they also challenge fundamental beliefs about what constitutes a story, contesting dominant theoretical paradigms of narrativity. For Robert Scholes (1980), a narration involves:

> ... a selection of events for the telling. They must offer sufficient continuity of subject matter to make their chronological sequence significant ... When the telling provides this sequence with a certain kind of shape and a certain level of human interest, we are in the presence not merely of narrative but of story. (206)

According to Scholes, then, and other structuralist narrative theorists, narrative must have certain properties: continuity, linearity, temporality and 'human interest', or what other narrative theorists refer to as the 'moral voice' or 'moral centre' which is linked, structurally, with narrative. In order for a story to be fully 'narrative', then, there must be this linkage between narrativising and moralising.

While private cookbooks may conform to some of these traditional notions of narrativity, the authors of these nineteenth-century private cookbooks created manuscripts in which the narrativity or story of the text is not always readily identifiable as such. As Marilyn Robinson Waldman (1980) notes, 'we need some kind of definition of narrative that will allow us to view "rudimentary" narratives as potentially alternative strategies' (245). While Waldman is speaking specifically of annals, chronicles and other historiographic materials, her call for the need to open up the definition of narrative to encompass other textual strategies – such as those that manuscript cookbooks pose – challenges more traditional definitions of narrative, including the notion that narrative follows a certain trajectory, encompassing a chronological and linear temporal sequence and specific syntactic shape that are, in the words of Scholes, 'rule-governed' (206). It is precisely this notion of narrative as 'rule-governed' – a conception that dominates contemporary narratology and literary studies in general – that cookbooks contest in their diverse forms.

Eclectic in its composition, the cookbook provided women with a textual apparatus which enabled artistic and creative experimentation, and beyond that some claim to legitimation and public spaces. The cookbook is both literally and metaphorically a canvas (often containing actual drawings and sketches), a frame in which to situate and arrange forms to evoke both artistic and social meaning. Cookbooks not only reflect the women writing and compiling such texts and the nature of the communities in which these texts circulated, but they also record women's efforts toward legitimating themselves and authenticating the spaces they inhabit, demonstrating both the diverse mediums in which female artists worked and their attempts to control their own stories, histories and traditions. As Romines remarks, '[l]ooking at the literature of domestic ritual, we see the idea of the individual, which American culture has privileged, being tested in the context of an ongoing traditional culture, that of housekeeping' (14). Written under the aegis of patriarchal ideology, the cookbook narrative is a privileged site for examining the contradictions, tensions and conflicts surrounding not only the shifting concept of the gendered (that is male) individual in the nineteenth century, but other dominant cultural ideologies such as separately gendered spheres and idealized feminine virtues. But while manuscript cookbooks reproduce these ideologies, they also enact responses to, and resistances toward, such cultural dicta.

At first glance cookbooks appear only to reproduce the period's various competing ideologies of femininity, domesticity, motherhood, 'real womanhood' and the 'true woman', tenets derived from notions of discrete gendered spaces, the protection and care of progeny, and the protection of property.[4] All stemming from the same patriarchal imperative, these ideologies were dependent upon positioning women as caretakers of a house which legally belonged to the male, making them responsible for the welfare of a family and the maintenance of a home to which they had no legal claim. As texts reflecting this highly structured socio-cultural reality, cookbooks delineated domestic, social and even cultural responsibilities. Mapping out value systems and behavioural edicts, cookbooks inscribed paradigms that women could learn, follow and eventually pass on to other housekeepers. By providing models of proper – and idealised – values and etiquette, cookbooks were an important venue for the dissemination of domestic education. In and of themselves, then, cookbooks were explicit emblems of women's relegation to the domestic sphere: the world of the home. And yet the cookbook narrative accommodates more than just recapitulations of patriarchal ideologies. Just as sentimental novels both reproduce and rescript the discourses of domesticity and true womanhood, containing implicit critiques of patriarchal institutions such as marriage and Calvinism, if not of housekeeping itself, these private manuscript cookbooks similarly belie any 'easy alignments', to borrow Kate McCullough's (1996) phrasing (24), into reductive and overly simplistic oppositional paradigms that would relegate these manuscripts to either championing or resisting dominant ideologies around domesticity and housekeeping.

Alongside their reproduction of normative white, middle-class ideologies, private manuscript cookbooks contain a powerful, if not radical, message: that women's influence within the private domain extends beyond the boundaries of their supposedly 'separate' sphere to reform not only the individual home and family but the larger community as well. The agents of potentially significant social reform, housekeepers created narratives in which they posited themselves as domestic heroes, protagonists full of agency and promise in texts rich with possibility. As Leonardi notes, producers of cookbooks construct an 'identifiable authorial persona' who 'approaches the first-person narrator of fiction or autobiography' and, in the process, a new type of literary discourse (342). Producing narratives in which the protagonists had an effect on the home, family and by implication the nation, cookbooks became the intertextual locus of reform that ultimately affected the women whose influence they represented, a manoeuvre that ruptures the symbolic stability of separate sphere ideology.

Demonstrating women's attempts to present themselves in their own narratives not as victimised but, paradoxically, as enfranchised by their relegation to domestic spaces, cookbooks situate the kitchen as an emancipatory space in which women could transcend traditional identities and control how domestic spaces were deployed. Catherine Beecher and Harriet Beecher Stowe endow the housekeeper with similar agency and authority in *American Woman's Home* (1869), a domestic 'how-to' manual that offers instructions on everything from domestic manners and ventilation systems to the proper stacking of a woodpile. Through the delineation of a model 'family state' headed by a 'chief minister' who is, notably, the housekeeper/mother (19), the Beechers offer a vision of domestic and social reform in which the housekeeper trains her family, community and even the country to become better 'children of the Heavenly Father' (433). Although domestic guidebooks, 'how-to' manuals, and conduct books – widely popular during the mid-nineteenth century – appear only to reify a patriarchal imaginary in which women and men are 'neatly divided up according to an occupational, social, and affective geography of gender' (Davidson, 444), the Beecher sisters' *American Woman's Home* reconfigures traditional notions of gender roles and heteronormative familial structures, disrupting the separate spheres metaphor through its incorporation of pursuits and concerns that – notably – take woman precisely *outside* the home. In addition to the promotion of social reform, *American Woman's Home* includes precise architectural renderings of homes, churches, schools and city tenement dwellings for the homeless, as well as explanations – complete with mechanical drawings – on the inner workings of cooking stoves, how to build 'earth' or water closets, and guidelines for the care of farm animals. Through mini-treatises on the properties of water and air, radiation and reflection, conduction and convection, the Beechers undermine the ethos, structure and integrity of the 'Christian family' that the narrative seems to engage, subverting the very patriarchal, heteronormative logic which engendered their text's production, and destabilising the exclusivity inherent to the separate spheres model. Although *American Woman's Home* contains chapters on the care of the sick, domestic duties and manners and the ordering of the kitchen, this text complicates the conceptual categories of gendered spheres, 'women's work', true womanhood and domesticity, making visible the instability surrounding the institutions and social constructions that supposedly structured nineteenth-century American society.

Like *American Woman's Home*, nineteenth-century cookbooks reflect prevailing ideological precepts through their reinscription of normative conceptions of familial domesticity, but they also resist such ideological identifications and constructions. The primary mechanism by which private domestic cookbooks efficiently conveyed both ideology and emancipation was by inscribing a narrative in which a woman protagonist salvages a household characterised by chaos, waste and illness. Figuring the protagonist/housekeeper as an agent of reform who restores an otherwise marred domestic scene, cookbook narratives recreate the pattern described by Scholes, who argues that a story is a narrative 'with a certain very specific syntactic shape (beginning–middle–end or situation–transformation–situation), and with a subject matter which allows for or encourages the projection of human values upon this material' (206). The private manuscript cookbook often inscribes this narrative of the transformation of events into stories imbued with human values through a narrative trajectory that moves from an unhealthy, inefficient and disorderly house to an organised, productive and healthy home (situation–transformation–situation) through the management of everything from dropsy to family meals to the layout of kitchen furniture. By situating the housekeeper as an agent of, and protagonist in, her own narrative, cookbook texts such as Mary Smith's, with its recipe for sugar cookies 'From Sallie', demonstrate not only the value and function of American domestic spaces, but also represent the profound undertaking of narration. For the women writing cookbooks, to narrate the self, to narrate the home and environs, and to narrate a community in a time when women were generally disenfranchised and scripted to an identity not necessarily chosen, represents a significant socioliterary endeavour that radicalises modern conceptions of narrativity, challenging our assumptions about what constitutes a 'story' or even 'narrative'.

Not all private domestic cookbooks contain the exact same components structurally configured in an identical pattern, but they do share elements in common and the sequence of those elements often follows a similar pattern. While the recipes themselves are of interest because of what they reflect about class, region and gender, and for what they signify about female artistic expression, recipes remain only one element in a larger structural system. The other constituent pieces of private domestic cookbooks include ornamentation (including mock title-pages, graphics, drawings, dried flowers), magazine clippings (typically articles and poetry on an array of subjects), and interleaves (notes, poems, articles, recipes, accounts and other ephemera, handwritten or printed).

The ornamentation found in cookbooks takes a number of different forms and is one of the more visible signifiers of female artistry and authority. Mock title-pages, often the first type of ornamentation one encounters in a cookbook, were often quite elaborate. In general title-pages contain the name and location of the cookbook's creator, the date and, less commonly, a family history that chronicles the arrival of relatives in the United States. While Mrs E. S. Borden's cookbook (1873) merely calls itself 'The Manuscript Receipt Book and Household Treasury, Third Edition', Mrs Charles Devitt of Philadelphia lends credibility to her creation by including under her name, address and date the title of 'Profeser [sic] in the art of Cooking', even noting the tutelage: 'under instruction Phoebe. Lare Dutchy Wagner. Maggie Eduards'. In saliently acknowledging other women through an epigraph, Mrs Devitt privileges the cookbook's producers, lending credibility both to the cookbook and American cookery. But this process of acknowledging other women also makes visible the supportive network of same-sex relations that, as Caroll Smith-Rosenberg (1975) has argued, were 'institutionalized in social conventions and rituals which accompanied virtually every important event in a woman's life, from birth to death' (9). Other ornamentation found in cookbooks includes drawings (often of figures, particularly women, in period clothing) and graphics (usually designs but also representations of fruit bowls, fish, leaves or flowers, as well as bold or decorative letters that accent or emphasise a new recipe or section), and, as in the case of Mrs Fiske, complete drawings of formal table settings.

Noteworthy for its demonstration of the role of the cookbook in educating young housekeepers into the dimensions of domestic rituals and responsibilities, Mrs Fiske's cookbook (c.1810–1850) includes prose and diagrams for the young or inexperienced housekeeper that reaffirm and reidealise ideological notions of femininity. Prefaced by text which specifies where the hosts, guests and accoutrements should be situated, the author demonstrates how a formal table setting should appear in detailed drawings accompanying the text. In 'Setting the dinner table', for example, Mrs Fiske explains on one page how to set a table properly for a formal occasion and, on the facing page includes a diagram – entitled 'Table set for dinner' – which outlines the correct placement of mats, 'caucers', cups, sugar bowls, milk bowls, meats and vegetables, gravy, utensils and cutlery and of course the appropriate positioning of the 'gentleman' and 'lady' of the house. Mrs Fiske also provides a description of how to set a tea table:

> To set the tea table. at head of table lady of the house ... in front her tray have on it cups caucer spoons milk the sugar – slop bowl 2 mats one on each side of the tea tray one for tea pot one for water next in front butter knife nest butter at the right next cake. left preserves middle toast on head at the foot cold meat tonge on cheese &C.

The diagram that accompanies this text includes detailed illustration of the tea table, right down to the doilies. Mrs Fiske also includes in her cookbook text instructions on the proper methods – and order – for doing chamber work:

> ... remove all lamps or vessels to the kitchen make the bed all but the outside quilt then sweep Do something else such as filling lamp &C while the dust falls 20 or 30 minutes in all rooms after dusting put all things in ... it is best to cover up many nice things that would be injured by dust.

Following Tzvetan Todorov's (1977) notion of dynamic narratives that describe a passage from one state to another, and demonstrating his identification of a narrative trajectory that moves from disequilibrium to equilibrium,[5] Mrs Fiske's cookbook enacts the movement toward the 'ideal' state of equilibrium and 'order' through properly set tables and dust-free rooms.

As both the protagonist-heroines of the cookbook's narrative and the producers and authors of their own cookbooks, women perpetuated this narrative of domestic order and stability and idealised feminine virtue in part through the ideology found in magazine clippings, another major component of private cookbook texts. Most often a recapitulation of traditional values, these clippings, including articles (on behaviour, current events, trends, fashion, health and other topics), poems, household hints and advice, recipes and quips on domestic arts, frequently line the inside and back jacket covers of cookbooks. Popular throughout the nineteenth century, women's magazines such as *Godey's Lady's Book* (the most popular national magazine for women after the Civil War), *Peterson's American Ladies Magazine* (later merged with *Godey's*), *The Ladies Companion* and *Columbian Lady and Gentleman's Magazine*, contained articles and other miscellanea, in newspaper-like columns, that housekeepers fastened to the fronts of their texts. Demonstrating their observance of the sensibility professed to be characteristic of womanhood, housekeepers cut out these articles, poems, and prose from magazines and other materials and fastened them to the insides of their cookbooks. Serving as pointers to an unfolding narrative of domestic order and felicity, the positioning of these articles on the inside jacket covers and in between the pages signals not only the artistry with which housekeepers constructed their texts, but represents the productive reiteration of the very ideological precepts which engendered the cookbook's creation in the first place.

Maintaining wide appeal, ladies' magazines proved to be an important arbiter and disseminator of domestic ideology. While several leading ladies' magazines, including *Godey's Lady's Book* and *Peterson's* contained recipes which appear in private domestic cookbooks (*Peterson's*, for example, had as a regular feature 'Our New Cook-Book', a column that included recipes for cakes, preserves, and other foodstuffs '[hand-]tested by a practical housekeeper' that often appears in private manuscript cookbooks), it is not the recipes alone – or even primarily – that women appropriated for their own cookbook texts. Dominated by romantic plots in which the power of love assuages all ills, ladies' magazines such as *Godey's* aspired to contain in their pages only that which was 'pure and wholesome' and extended a 'sentimental and moral' sensibility. They favoured stories in which the husband and wife form an ideal union, and the wife, assuming her true vocations (marriage and motherhood) is fulfilled and content, eager to serve her family, the community and God. Espousing a narrative predicated on the heroine's demonstration of idealised feminine traits (such as chastity, purity, submission and virtue), the stories in ladies' magazines were, then, predominantly 'success stories' in which love and feminine virtue triumph. Although contributors to *Godey's*, *Peterson's* and other ladies' magazines included Stowe, Emerson, Hawthorne, Poe, Lowell and Longfellow, among others, there was, as Eleanor Thompson (1947) notes, a 'remarkable sameness about most of the "literature" ... To the writers and readers of the ladies' magazines, success meant just one thing, – marriage and living happily ever afterward' (5). Little if any conflict materialises in these stories. If it does, it is easily thwarted, overcome by the end of the narrative through the dynamic forces of feminine virtue and heterosexual romantic coupling.

There were exceptions to this standard construction, however, in marriage plots involving physical or emotional abuse or alcoholic husbands, and deprivation plots in which a young girl has to fill in for a deceased mother or care for ailing or convalescing parents. Although these stories of deprivation contain different plot lines, they resolve and attain closure similar to the romantic stories featuring the replication of conventional sexual ideologies: both end up with the re-establishment of domestic order and harmony, both figure the protagonist/housekeeper as requited, fulfilled and recontained by the story's end, and patriarchy, never really threatened, remains intact. Borne out of the same ideology, these deprivation stories can only end with the restoration of a domestic economy that privileges order, balance and strict hierarchical arrangements, a reinstatement that signals the inherent instability of those conceptual categories (feminine virtue, heterosexuality, 'order'). Many of the articles in ladies' magazines are, then, an overdetermined response to an anxiety about the stability of these symbolic categories and the coherence of these dominant social constructions. Articles such as 'Illegal Flirtations', found in Mrs Fred Patterson's cookbook (1870), seek to ensure that femininity does triumph by outlining the parameters of proper female etiquette and conduct:

> No woman can carry on a flirtation with a married man that is not criminal. No married woman can flirt innocently, even with a young man ... Many a soul has gone bloodstained, into the presence of its maker, sent thither by [a] climax of dark circumstances brought about by a woman's flirtations. Don't flirt! It is unwomanly; it is wrong against that mother whose memory you revere.

Stopping only at the invocation of a dead mother, 'Illegal Flirtations' not only identifies 'womanly' behaviour, it also presents the story of the bad – immoral, 'unwomanly' – housekeeper.

With a cautionary tone similar to that found in 'Illegal Flirtations', Mrs Fiske's 'To make our earthly paradise' reifies notions of the cult of womanhood by asserting that women should be:

> ... always of one mind, always good tempered, always industrious[,] supply your real wants[,] have no imaginary wants[,] be gentle[,] kind and loving ... modest in deportment, [and] guarded in conversation with all men.

Reproducing the very same narrative of deportment found resonating throughout ladies' magazines and other cultural material of the period, Mrs Fiske's verse, with its compensatory mimetic recapitulation of dominant ideology, suggests just how tenuous such ideological constructions and identifications are.

Despite the prevalence of articles like 'Illegal Flirtations' and 'To make our earthly paradise' that sanction adherence to traditional roles, other articles such as 'Hints to Husbands', also found in Mrs Fiske's cookbook, appear to question the hierarchical structures that governed relations between the sexes. Appearing to counter cultural norms, 'Hints to Husbands' advises men to think of their wives as equal partners through the assertion of woman's right to ownership of half her husband's possessions and her right to be informed of business and economic matters:

> Do not, by being too exact in pecuniary matters, make your wife feel her dependence on your bounty. It tends to lessen her dignity of character, and does not increase her esteem for you. If she is a sensible woman, she should be acquainted with your business and know your income ... Your wife has an equal right with yourself to all you possess in the world – therefore she should be made acquainted with that which is of great importance to both.

The prevalence of these articles in women's private cookbooks suggests that the cookbooks' creators were on some level questioning the very ideological tenets embodied in the cult of true womanhood.

And yet while 'Hints to Husbands' clearly undermines the heterosexual hegemony that marked nineteenth-century culture, and indeed the hegemony of the marriage tradition in American fiction,[6] it simultaneously embodies it, ending with advice that masquerades as feminist politicisation. 'Hints to Husbands' cautions men to remember that 'she treasures every word you utter, though *you may never think of them again*' [emphasis mine], and not to:

> ... treat your wife with inattention in company; it touches her pride and she will not respect you more, love you any the better for it ... Do not entertain your wife with praising the beauty and accomplishments of other women. Do not upbraid your wife in the presence of a third person. The sense of disregard for feeling will prevent her from acknowledging her fault ... Do not be stern and silent in your own house, and remarkable for your sociability elsewhere.

Thus although initially this article seems to advocate gender parity, such equity is understood within the parameters of the very social system that engendered the need for such assertions in the first place, demonstrating the limitations of deviations from normative ideologies which appear to collapse dominant social hierarchies. Nevertheless, the function of such articles, widely published and disseminated, reveals the extent to which the symbolic imaginary in the nineteenth century surrounding sex/gender matrices was, at the very least, contested, rife with tensions and contradictions, leaving the creators of manuscript cookbooks (who included these often ambivalent messages regarding the identificatory roles of wife, mother, housekeeper within their cookbooks) similarly questioning the stability and coherence of the same ideologies which, perhaps ironically, facilitated their texts' production.

Although private domestic cookbooks are diverse compilations, scrapbooks if you will, of women's lives, recipes were of course the ostensible reason for keeping a cookbook. Recipes reflect not only what the family ate and drank, but also attest to economic concerns ('Cheap Lemon Pie') and salubrity (cures for cough, colds, and dropsy). Often interspersed with food recipes, cures for ailments or debilitating medical conditions such as a 'cure for cholera' can be found next to a recipe for gooseberry jelly. The conditions in need of medical attention or 'cures' range in these texts from common headcolds and earaches to ulcerated sore throats, neuralgia, smallpox, hydrophobia, consumption, croup and piles. Although finding handwritten recipes for cures is not unusual, most of these cures or instructions are cut from magazines. A regular column in *Peterson's* magazine, 'Mother's Department', written by a medical doctor, regularly featured such antidotes. Housekeepers also cut out 'recipes' for an assortment of other needs, including cleaning golds and silvers, getting rid of insects, destroying mice, stopping bleeding and drying sheets. Although food recipes for jumbles, 'cauces', veal, fish and beef abound in domestic cookbook texts, the most prevalent recipes are for other 'victuals', including cakes, pies, puddings, cookies and other foods utilising the basic (and most readily available) ingredients of flour, sugar, butter and eggs. Hattie Chase's cookbook (c.1880–1890), for example, contains recipes for ten kinds of cakes: silver, feather, soda, dark, marble, sponge, pound, raised, Washington and white.

Within the economy in which recipes circulated, recipes and even entire cookbooks were appropriated, copied, altered and embellished. In an effort to overcome the compartmentalisation women often experienced living in the private sphere, housekeepers shared recipes, passed them on to neighbours, handed them on to friends. Reflecting this communal element, many recipes contain the name of a woman, either at the end of the recipe or as a title label, as a means of attribution. Hattie Chase includes recipes such as 'Mrs Wiggin [sic] Pound Cake', or 'Maggie's Lemon Molasses Gingerbread'. Many of Mrs Patterson's recipes and cures are attributed to other women: 'Jane Elliott's soft ginger cake', 'Mrs Lerner's burn salve', and 'Mrs Neals [sic] sealingwax'.

This kind of attribution is not only an articulation and reflection of community, but, more importantly, a designation that establishes a heritage of tradition and ritual in the form of recipes passed on from mother to daughter or

from friend to neighbour. Mary Smith's recipe cited in the opening section of
this essay contains a narrative structure that enables readers (housekeepers) to
recreate the events – ingredients, amounts, results – that produced and formed
the originary text. And yet each new housekeeper who used this recipe
(Sallie, then Mary in this particular example) reinscribed the narrative – either
by changing quantities or ingredients – before passing the recipe on to another
housekeeper. Mrs Keyworth's cookbook (c.1820), for example, contains
recipes that note the succession of recipients: 'Mrs Pell to Mrs Washington'.
Similarly, Anna Hadley Louise White (1880) notes the chain of inheritors next
to her recipes: 'Angel's food. (Lydia)'; 'Vira's cake. (Mother)'; 'Myrtle's
spice cake'; 'Bread cake. (Mother)'.   White's inscription 'Vira's cake.
(Mother)' indicates – as in the recipes for angel's food and bread cake – that
this particular recipe was handed down twice, first from Vira, then from
Anna's mother. Each woman who used a particular recipe was likely to
reinscribe it – either by changing quantities or ingredients – before passing the
recipe on to another housekeeper. As Leonardi notes, '[e]ven the root of
recipe – the Latin *recipere* – implies an exchange, a giver and a receiver. Like
a story, a recipe needs a recommendation, a context, a point, a reason to be'
(340). That 'reason to be' is the social community created by – and reflected
in – the sharing of recipes. Affording the opportunity to recreate triumphantly
the narrative events that produced and formed the original text, the
reinscribing of recipes permitted housekeepers some measure of individuality,
authorship and artistry, while also maintaining important communal same-sex
relations. Symbolising a prosperous and rich woman's cultural economy, the
exchange and passing down of recipes, a practice still in existence today,
enabled women to become agents of their own histories by perpetuating their
own customs and ceremonies and by creating their own unique narrative form:
the manuscript cookbook.

   Not only did recipes reflect attribution, but they also indicated the
cookbook author's own assessment of the recipe. Qualifying recipes by
adding a descriptive word or two next to the recipe, H. N. Pilsbury, for
example, noted in her cookbook (1847) the following assessment of a recipe:
'Wilson's cake   good'. Anna Hadley Louise White noted next to a one-egg
cake recipe attributed to Mrs Black that the cake was 'No good'. Other
common descriptive expressions include 'Very Nice Fruit Cake', or, as found
tucked inside an envelope in Louisa Gephard du Pont's cookbook (c.1860),
'dear Polly's recipes – very precious'. As Leonardi notes, the construction of
an identifiable authorial persona and implied reader creates a dynamic in
which the reader of the recipe 'not only *can* agree or argue but is encouraged
to agree or argue' (342). The sharing of recipes and even entire cookbooks
facilitated individual creativity and textual authority through the assessment

and/or alteration of recipes, or through the inclusion of additions to a circulating community cookbook. Sharing recipes, expressing an opinion about the merits of those recipes, passing recipes on to others, and perhaps altering recipes to suit individual tastes served several functions: it reinforced bonds among women and reaffirmed their place in the larger community, helping to maintain ties among friends and relatives, while also enabling housekeepers to observe shifts and advances in American cookery, food storage and domestic arts. More importantly this process afforded housekeepers some measure of creative sovereignty and independence. The communal structure in which recipes circulated among friends, neighbours, churches and even entire communities helped then to foster and maintain an important supportive network among women who might, for geographic reasons or class boundaries, have otherwise been isolated from other women. As Leonardi observes, the sharing of recipes creates a 'loose community of women that crosses the social barriers of class, race, and generation' (342). Louisa Gephard du Pont, a member of the wealthy and then prominent du Pont family, probably did not often cook herself, and yet she maintained her own cookbook. Attesting to the interrelationships among women, community, food and cookbooks, and to the importance of the medium as a vehicle for a female aesthetics, du Pont's keeping a cookbook suggests that the value of cookbooks far exceeds cookery and domestic economy. Encoded with meanings that reflected individual women and their interpersonal associations, cookbooks allowed women, as Romines observes, to 'see [their] lives ... as a sustaining part of a pattern' (69).

While the sharing of recipes alone demonstrates women's interactions within a broader community, the cookbooks contain other evidence – often in the form of interleaves, the other major element in cookbook texts – that speaks to the cookbook's utility in curbing isolation and to the strides women took to empower themselves in ways that undoubtedly allowed them to see themselves as integral agents in that 'sustaining' tradition that Romines identifies among women/housekeepers. Mrs E. A. Phelps's cookbook (1814) contains the following letter that demonstrates the social composition of the community and the integral place that cookbooks, recipes and cookery held in that community's discourse:

> Dear Aunt   Our recipe is not fit to eat and here
> is one Martha gave me which she says is good. If you
> could only get Hannah Kirchenbacker's recipe it is
> the best kind I can eat – I am going to try for you
> and will send it if she will tell me, Here is Martha's

Directly following this letter is a recipe for Martha's cake, and, following that, the recipe from Hannah Kirchenbacker that Mrs Phelps mentions. Similarly, Louisa Gephard du Pont's cookbook contains the following letter:

> I am at home at 2 o'clock to dinner, do come and dine with us some day – If Gilly is well enough she and I expect to go to Philadelphia on Friday afternoon – to stay until Saturday – she is better and in the library to day – I have an engagement so must stop

On the other side of this letter is a recipe for a dessert. A common practice, then, was to contain a recipe within a letter. In Louisa Gephard du Pont's cookbook, there is a recipe for blackberry wine right in the middle of a letter du Pont kept in the pages of her cookbook:

> My dear Harry,
> I send [sic] Louisa a bottle of the blackberry wine we were speaking of the other night, so that she can judge how she liked it, it is very easily made and is a very wholesome drink; it does not require much water added to it as it is – 'haf and haf' – when made, but by pouring it over some ice cooks it and weakens it sufficiently. The receipt is to one quart of juice put one quart of water, and 3 lb of light brown sugar to every gallon of that mixture, put it in a demi john cork it up – stand away for the next summer, when it is racked off and bottled.

Here recipes and cookery form the structure of the letter, as well as the basis for a letter being composed at all. This functions to expand our notion of epistolarity. That recipes are the occasion for letter writing reflects the interesting imbrication between recipes (and by extension cookbooks) and narrative structure, a relationship minimised – or ignored altogether – in traditional narratology.

Another mode through which the intricate relation between recipes and epistolary discourse becomes visible is through the ways in which recipes became the basis for other news, such as the arrival of friends or relatives. Mrs Phelps's cookbook contains a letter to a friend or family member that is an occasion for making a commitment to see the recipient's cousin:

> Dear Lizzie you are quite welcome to the recipe –
> and I wish you success in making the cake – I will come in
> and see your cousin as soon as possible.

If, as Hayden White (1987) claims, 'narrative is a meta-code, a human universal on the basis of which transcultural messages about the nature of a shared reality can be transmitted', then what is revealed (or transmitted) in these letter-recipes is both the deployment of recipes within the structures of narrative, including epistolary narrative, and the nature and extent of the network of same-sex relations in the nineteenth century (1). For the recipes became a metonymical link in a chain that joined together and sustained a set of traditions, relations, and rituals in a community of women who created new textual strategies and modes of representation via their recipes, cookbooks and letters.

While this type of appropriation and reinscription revolved around individual recipes, this practice extended to entire cookbooks as well. Demonstrating the culture of holographic copied texts, one author created a cookbook (c.1830) in which her title-page claims the name of Amelia Simmons, the author of *American Cookery* (1796), the first authentic American cookbook (that is, without English recipes or influences) published in this country (Taylor, 1991, 40). Creating an identical title-page complete with graphics, publisher, year of publication, and publication rights, the copyist even duplicated Simmons's description of herself as an 'American orphan'. However the copyist did not retain the same recipes or, if she did, she adapted and modified them to suit her own needs or tastes. Although the recipes in the copyist's text are of the same type as Simmons's (reflecting the overall homogeneity of American cookery at this point in history despite regional and class distinctions), her recipe for Spruce Beer, for example, differs significantly from that of Simmons. The practice of taking recipes and copying them in one's own cookbook was at that point already customary, as was the publishing industry's practice of reprinting published recipes.

Published cookbooks after the turn of the century left space for housekeepers to interleave loose recipes or other miscellanea. Demonstrating the importance of cookery and recipes to the community of women and the extent of the practice of interleaving loose recipes into their own texts, published cookbooks accommodated this custom as late as the 1960s. But publishers in the nineteenth century also realised that women were generating their own cookbooks, concocted not just of recipes, but interleaves (ephemera and other material) as well. In the third edition of *The Manuscript Receipt Book* (1870), the preface acknowledges precisely *how* women used printed cookbooks, appropriating them and making them distinctly their own:

Receipts, without number, are constantly given to the public by newspapers magazines, and larger works, under various headings: and yet, who is there that does not desire to retain a memorandum of familiar home-dishes, – some entirely out of date, and some unknown to compilers of cook-books, – but still savory, in the old homestead, and, perhaps, by hands made more dear by remembrance. Besides, many persons gather in, day by day, receipts used by familiar friends, and which are not to be found in print: and this HOUSEHOLD TREASURY, with its complete classification, – presented in an attractive form, – will be found admirably adapted for their reception. (Anon, 1870, vii)

Notably, the creators of *The Manuscript Receipt Book* altered their cookbook – leaving room in its volume – for women to make that text their own by inserting their own recipes or other material.

Other ephemera incorporated into nineteenth-century private manuscript cookbooks include, as in the case of Mrs Fred Patterson's text, obituaries, a list of area attorneys and a local census. An emblem of the times, Mrs Patterson's cookbook also includes pencil renderings of railroads and bridges as well as a map of coal regions of Pennsylvania. Similarly in the Rappe family recipe book (1810–1840) there is, in addition to the familiar cures for dysentery, croup, rheumatism and ringworm, and the more traditional recipes for foods like apple pudding found in other nineteenth-century private manuscript cookbooks, the Rappe family history, including details of the family's emigration to America. H. N. Pilsbury's cookbook contains, in addition to recipes for tea cakes and sugar biscuits, as well as cures for cholera, accounting information, another component inherent to many private manuscript cookbooks. The presence of this material – inventories, financial records, business and legal papers – demonstrates how the so-called 'woman's sphere' did not necessarily mean that women subscribed to those hegemonic gender roles, either in theory or in practice. That so many women's private cookbooks contain financial records for the family household *and* business demonstrates the failure of the model of 'separate spheres' to account for the complex roles that women played in the nineteenth century. The importance of the insertion of this ephemera – including accounting information, inventories, genealogies, narratives of emigration, letters, poems, drawings, obituaries, maps, legal papers and financial records, newspaper clippings or handwritten material documenting the development of railroads, canals, bridges, and household inventions like the refrigerator and stove – is twofold. It speaks to the artistry with which the overall cookbook text was composed. It also makes visible the ways in which these texts were social registers, barometers if you will, that gauged not only individual familial developments and changes, but also the modernisation of society *vis-à-vis* the creation and emergence of technological, industrial and other advancements.

By sharing recipes, changing or adding to them, writing letters which contained recipes, passing receipts down in families, and cataloguing all of this activity in their cookbooks, women secured not only the present but ensured their future by providing alternative historical texts through which to read women's lives and understand nineteenth-century women's cultural history. Thus the cookbook, with its emphasis on food, is an appropriate metaphor for women's histories, underscoring sustaining traditions, ritual and ceremony. Despite its originary site of production (the home), and its symbolisation of women's apparent geographic and psychological separation from the commercial marketplace, the cookbook nevertheless functions as a catalyst for social reform through its positing of a domestic hero: the housekeeper who can, in a narrative of domestic felicity, restore balance and order to an imperfect domestic scene and, in the process, reform her family and community and perhaps even the nation as well.

Women's private manuscript cookbooks thus not only provide us with important records of women's sociocultural history and artistry in the nineteenth century; they also compel us to consider the ways in which manuscript cookbooks are precisely 'narrative', and how such manuscripts contain textual strategies that fall outside the bounds of representation associated with narrative proper. Because these manuscript cookbooks do not necessarily follow the structural and temporal sequences associated with narrative, or contain all the constituent parts of stories that are 'fully narrative', these supposedly non-literary material cultural texts challenge contemporary scholars to (re)consider both the notion of what constitutes narrative and the process of narrativisation itself. The process of how these texts are formed, and then reformed and reshaped in their communal circulation, challenges traditional conceptions of narrativisation as private, as a teleological endeavour which progresses toward some type of conclusion, fuelled by a thousand contingencies, or as recollection, a telling of events and experiences that leads to some type of moral meaning. While cookbooks and other domestic guides and manuals circulating throughout the nineteenth century articulate the possibilities for not only familial but communal and, by extension, national reform and change, this type of 'moralising' reconfigures, in its expressions of expanded roles for women and its destabilising of separate gendered spheres, traditional notions of 'moral meaning' in narrative form. Dominant theories of narrative, which link narrativising with 'moralising', are predicated on a concept of *universality*: the notion that the moral meaning imbued in a text must contain a moral intention and significance whose interpretation is accessible to all. But of course the concept of universality in the nineteenth century was, just like the concept of possessive individualism, reducible to a highly specific corporeality: white, male, middle class, heterosexual. The 'moral' messages of individual and social change contained in these manuscript cookbooks, as well as other guidebooks and domestic how-to manuals, are often expressions that are inherently feminist and reformist in substance. What these manuscript cookbooks call attention to are the ways in which these concepts of 'universality' and 'morality' – when applied to traditional concepts of narrative and canonical literature – are ideologically laden, encoded with cultural inscriptions and assumptions that do not, despite their appeals to 'universality', cross normative gender, racial, social and cultural boundaries.

With their rich mixture of prose, recipes, personal memories and historical events, nineteenth-century private manuscript cookbooks demonstrate alternative textual strategies created by women that not only contest dominant conceptions of narrativity or what constitutes a 'story', but also reconfigure prevailing ideologies about systems of cultural and individual expression and modes of representation. Despite critical efforts (especially those in the 1980s and early 1990s) to bring to the foreground texts by women held in obscurity, the ideologically laden notion that women's private lives – or indeed, that the private itself – are of little literary interest or consequence is bound up with notions of canonicity, gender ideology, and what constitutes a literary text. By extending semiological and narrative analyses into non-literary realms such as material culture to include texts such as cookbooks, historiographic theorists, feminist scholars and narrative critics would be enacting what these nineteenth-century manuscript cookbooks themselves accomplished: taking the private into the public.

Notes

1   See, for example, Henry Nash Smith, 'The Scribbling Women and the Cosmic Success Story', 1974; Alfred Habegger, *Gender, Fantasy, and Realism in American Literature*, 1982; and Ann Douglas, *The Feminization of American Culture*, 1977.

2   Susan Strasser, in *Never Done: A History of Housework*, 1982, explains that separate sphere ideology first appeared in early nineteenth-century women's magazines, household manuals, etiquette books, religious literature, and sentimental texts, pp. 181–2. The message of the separate sphere doctrine was twofold: first, that the home should maintain certain values (virtue, morality, piety) which would provide men with a sanctuary from the demands and brutality of the commercial marketplace, and second, that women *belonged* in the home. More generally, contemporary scholarship, particularly that by New Americanists and feminist critics, questions the validity of this gendered dimorphism as a way of understanding nineteenth-century culture and women's literature and history. See, for example, a special edition of *American Literature* edited by Cathy Davidson, 1998, 'No More Separate Spheres!'

3   See, for example, Hayden White, *The Content of the Form: Narrative Discourse and Historical Representation*, 1987; Marilyn Robinson Waldman, '"The Otherwise Unnoteworthy Year 711": A Reply to Hayden White', 1980; and Louis Mink, 'Everyman His or Her Own Annalist', 1980.

4   See Frances Cogan, *All-American Girl: The Ideal of Real Womanhood in Mid-Nineteenth Century America*, 1989, for a discussion of 'real womanhood'. See Barbara Welter, 'The Cult of True Womanhood: 1820–1860', 1966, for a discussion of the 'true woman' and the four 'cardinal virtues' that a woman must adhere to or strive toward, which included piety, purity, submissiveness, and domesticity.

5   Tzvetan Todorov, in *The Poetics of Prose*, 1977, maintains that '"ideal" narratives begin with a stable situation ... disturbed by some power or force ... [that] results [in] a state of

disequilibrium; by the action of a force directed in the opposite direction, the equilibrium is re-established'. He also argues that narratives contain two types of episodes, those which 'describe a state (of equilibrium or of disequilibrium) and those which describe the passage from one state to the other. The first type will be relatively static and, one might say, iterative; the same kind of actions can be repeated indefinitely. The second, on the other hand, will be dynamic ...' , p. 111.

6   This argument is made in Joseph Boone, *Tradition Counter Tradition: Love and the Form of Fiction*, 1987, p. 20; the hegemony of the novelistic marriage tradition extended, he argues, from 1840 to 1930.

Chapter 4

'Talking' Recipes:
What Mrs Fisher Knows and the African-American Cookbook Tradition

Andrew Warnes

This essay is a consideration of the African-American tradition of cookbook publishing. It begins with a discussion of cookbooks issued in the last twenty years by a former Black Panther and a former pop singer among others, and ends with Abby Fisher's *What Mrs Fisher Knows about Old Southern Cooking*, a recipe collection which in 1881 became one of the first to be published by an African American.[1] What emerges in the course of this overview is that African-American cookbook writers very often imbue their recipes with an oral quality. As we shall see, otherwise disparate African-American cookbook writers very often infuse their prose with new coinages, with improvised formulations and deliberate informalities, that seem to sign and to simulate the distinctive patterning of black vernacular speech. But this overview also contends that the impulse and bid to capture orality is not the exclusive preserve of black cookbook writers, but rather one that draws upon and contributes to a longstanding tradition in which African-American literary artists of all types have sought new ways of writing the vernacular.

In more general terms, the discussion of orality brings with it the discussion of the cultural shift toward mass literacy: a shift which, for African Americans, was delayed by racist legislation during slavery and segregation and which began only with the tentative establishment of black schools and colleges during the Reconstruction era. From *The Domestication of the Savage Mind* (1977) to *Food and Love* (1998), the sociologist Jack Goody has looked critically at a range of examples of the cultural shift to mass literacy. In these discussions, Goody often speaks of such shifts in terms of profit and loss, and often balances what a given society gains from the advent of mass literacy against what it loses. And what a given society characteristically gains, to summarise Goody's position, is access to the metropolitan discourses that nurture national cohesion and stratification, while what it characteristically loses is the influence and genealogical pedigree of those familial and regional traditions that are disseminated via oral channels. When discussing educational developments in pre-colonial and colonial India, for instance, *Food and Love* argues that this society witnessed mass literacy's general propensity to 'divide internally as well as unify ... externally': to erode the roles of smaller familial and regional units in cultural production, and to ferment, instead, national identification (185–187).

This cautious balancing of advantages and disadvantages develops views set out in *The Domestication of the Savage Mind*, which also couches the shift towards mass literacy in positive and negative terms. For example, an explanation of the development of international cuisine in industrial Britain invokes not only improved transportation and mass literacy, but also the history of imperialism. Mass literacy, for Goody, produced new social conditions in which cookbooks could begin to record and so retain an expanded culinary vocabulary of previously unsustainable breadth. Yet Goody also recognises the threat print concurrently posed to 'regional cooking', whose 'attraction' in the age of mass literacy is 'precisely that it is tied to what grandmother did ("*les gaufres de mémé*") ... rather than to the recipes that are diffused by writing' (140). *The Domestication of the Savage Mind*, like *Food and Love*, thus views the shift to literacy as one which dissolves or at least destabilises a foregoing vernacular tradition even as it anticipates the expansive culinary enterprises of the future. It views the shift to literacy as monumental, to the point where this transformation even lays the foundations for a definition of the recipe itself:

> The point about a recipe or a receipt that emerges from ... dictionary definitions and literary usages is their essentially written character. The recipes are collected in one place, classified, then serve as a reference book for the doctor or the cook, for the sick or the hungry, as in Dryden's line, 'The Patients, who have open before them a Book of admirable Receipts for their Diseases'. For recipes, once collected, have then to be tried....
>
> The recipe or receipt, then, is a written formula for mixing ingredients for culinary, medical or magical purposes; it lists the items required for making preparations destined for human consumption. (136–137)

This definition returns throughout the following pages precisely because it is problematic and because, by examining the problems it raises, I hope to reach an understanding of the recipe form that is more malleable and applicable to African-American experience. The major problem with this definition lies in its characterisation of the recipe as an intrinsically written genre that is not transformed so much as actively produced by the arrival of mass literacy. As I suggest in this essay's first section, the corollary of this characterisation, which is that there can be no such thing as an oral recipe, is refuted by several African-American cookbooks, by their simulation of speech and by their allusions to recipes exchanged using precisely the vernacular channels which Goody claims were lost. These speculations culminate in the second section of the essay, which discusses the fact that the text at the head of the African-American cookbook tradition – *What Mrs Fisher Knows about Old Southern Cooking* (1881) – was written by a former slave who could not write. Since it required her recipes to be written down by others, Abby Fisher's illiteracy raises highly pertinent issues about the nature of the involvement of Fisher's transcribers from the San Francisco Women's Institute. Goody's definition will be tentatively endorsed as I acknowledge that the transformation of spoken into written words from which *What Mrs Fisher Knows* resulted indeed featured certain subtle and not so subtle interventions on the part of these Californian transcribers. On the other hand, I question the exclusivity of Goody's emphasis on the written status of the recipe, since such absolute terms would presumably imply that these transcriptive interventions were of sufficient scope as to *create* the recipes of *What Mrs Fisher Knows*. This emphasis is incompatible with the fact that the recipes of *What Mrs Fisher Knows* pertain to what its full title terms *Southern Cooking* and are as such manifestly attributable to its South Carolinian author rather than to its Californian transcribers. The example of *What Mrs Fisher Knows*, the clear need to reaffirm the primacy of Fisher's contributions to it, thus urge us to rework Goody's definition and so reach an understanding of the recipe genre that is less beholden to its occasional textual status as script. The following discussion, then, attributes the sense of orality within many African-American cookbooks to a desire not only to bring the immediacy of speech to the printed page but, in the process, to honour those local traditions which, despite Goody's suggestions, have long been a source of oral recipes.

Talking Cookbooks

> Now listen, folks, I have got to admit that I have never put a single brain into my mouth. I am extremely open-minded about food but I figure this way: I've gone this long without eating anybody's brains, so I can certainly go a little while longer. ... But this is a most typical dish from the deeeep deeep South and lots of people like it. So, here's how it's made. ... Now what do you think you do with the poor things? You place them in a colander and pour boiling water over them to rid any traces of blood and membrane which remain. (You

want to sort of clear the mind, so to speak.) ... When the fat is hot, but not smoking, you just throw your old brains right on in there. Lower the heat but don't stop stirring them around, oh no, or they might decide to clump up or stick to the pan. Well, now that your brains have been nicely browned, oh about 10 minutes in all, pour in your already beaten-up eggs and scramble it all up there together. (Sheila Ferguson, 1989)

Obviously, the tails have gotta be washed off, even though the fat seems to reappear endlessly. When they are pink enough to suit you, put them in a large pot full of water. Turn the heat high, get 'em boilin'. Add chopped onion, garlic, and I always use some brown sugar, molasses, or syrup. Not everybody does. Some folks like their pig extremities bitter, others, like me, want 'em sweet. It's up to you. Use a large spoon with a bunch of small holes to scrape off the grayish fats that will cover your tails. You don't need this. Throw it out. Let the tails simmer till the meat falls easily from the bones. Like pig's feet, the bones are soft and suckable, too. ... There's nothin' wrong with puttin' a heap of tails, feet or pig's ears right next to a good-sized portion of Hoppin' John, either. (Ntozake Shange, 1998)

By addressing readers individually, by importing phrases from the black vernacular and by relentlessly apostrophising and abbreviating, several African-American cookbook writers have recently presented their recipes less as acts of writing than as transcripts in which the fleeting spontaneity of speech is apparently captured. Initiated and popularised by the 1960s cookbooks of Vertamae Grosvenor, this authorial simulation of orality is maintained in texts published at the close of the twentieth century by the former Three Degrees singer Sheila Ferguson and by the novelist and poet Ntozake Shange among others. Indeed, Grosvenor supplies the foreword to Ntozake Shange's *If I Can Cook / You Know God Can* (1998). Despite Ferguson's and Shange's very different cultural backgrounds, they both strive to recreate black dialect conversations in print, to offer such oral exchanges as evidence of a broader cultural literacy which, in turn, primes the reader for the introduction of those forbidding offal cuts long associated with soul food.

Shange and Ferguson are not the only African-American writers to follow Grosvenor's example and imbue their written recipes with this distinctive and deliberate oral atmosphere. Since 1970, the literary fabrication of the black vernacular has emerged as the preferred approach of professional African-American cookbook writers. For instance, the first recipe offered by *Barbeque'n With Bobby* (1998) – a cookbook that the former Black Panther Bobby Seale conceived while a 'political prisoner in 1969', and which he eventually published in 1988 – arrives in the form of a quotation from Seale's uncle (ix). Surrounded by speech marks and represented through a literary vocabulary specifically tailored to the writerly capture of black speech, the transcribed words of Seale's uncle insist that: "'When you make bobbyque, you don't put no sauce on it till it's done. Da base makes it tenda. Taste good right down to da bone'"(3). Seale's efforts to freeze his uncle's speech into publishable prose are signalled by his use of the double negative and by his references to 'da' and 'tenda', where both respellings are clearly guided by the desire to represent their pronunciation in print. Alongside Seale's introduction of a new and playfully self-aggrandising term ('bobbyque'), such literary strategies plainly reveal that *Barbeque'n With Bobby* stands alongside Ntozake Shange's *If I Can Cook / You Know God Can* (1998) as another cookbook whose recipes represent speech and cooking simultaneously.

This broad church of cookbook writers, which numbers a former easy-listening singer and a former advocate of Marxist black nationalism among its congregation, becomes broader still due to the appearance within it of Oprah Winfrey. In a preface to *In the Kitchen With Rosie* (1994), a collection of recipes authored by her privately employed and calorie-conscious cook Rosie Daley, Winfrey similarly strives to create the impression that she is not writing so much as transcribing speech. Winfrey's introductory sentence – 'Some of my fondest early memories are of my grandmother over a stove fixin' food for our daily feast' – re-employs the apostrophising used by Shange and, in the process, directs attention away from the cerebral cookbook and back towards cookery's primary site, the stove itself (xi).

The remarkable hold that the oral sensibility retains over cookbooks recently published by African Americans grows firmer still in the work of Jessica B. Harris. The cookbooks issued in the 1980s and 1990s by Harris – who, as a Professor of English, divides her time between writing recipes and teaching writing – transform the imitation of orality into an ambition which Harris foregrounds, articulates and celebrates. In support of her conscious summoning of the orality that her writing irrevocably transforms, Harris introduces her cookbook of the African diaspora, *Iron Pots and Wooden Spoons* (1989), with an excerpt from an 1880 *Harper's Magazine* article by Charles Gayarre. In it, Gayarre insists:

> The Negro is a born cook. He could neither read nor write, and therefore he could not learn from books. He was simply inspired; the god of the spit and the saucepan had breathed into him; that was enough. (xxiii)

That an author who expresses pride in her racial identity should introduce her celebratory affirmation of diasporic foods by invoking an essentialist view which relegates the fabled culinary expertise of African

Americans to the level of basic instinct, demands immediate critical attention. Only by realising that here Harris is confirming neither Gayarre's essentialism nor his subsequent depiction of cooking as an acceptable replacement for the literacy which apparently remains beyond African Americans can we begin to comprehend this editorial decision. What Harris finds of use in Gayarre's observation is its revelation that African-American cooking traditions were maintained in the absence of mass literacy. The realisation that earlier disseminators of African-American cooking traditions necessarily operated via conversational channels immediately indicates that, if Harris's work is to continue rather than destabilise these traditions, she must achieve a newly accommodating writerly voice in which the rich legacy of orality remains apparent.

A Kwanzaa Keepsake (1995), Harris's guide to celebrating the diasporic and African-American holiday of Kwanzaa, subsequently becomes interpretable as a cookbook which is shaped by a desire to surmount the transformations orchestrated by the sheer fact of writing, and remain 'true' to a foregoing oral tradition. Implicitly and explicitly, throughout *A Kwanzaa Keepsake*, tributes are paid to what Harris calls the 'juking and jiving, talking and testifying, speechifying and signifying, preaching and teaching' of the vernacular tradition. Explicitly, the desire to protect and maintain the centrality of such oral practices yields an emphasis on *griots*, on gifted speakers, on those whom Harris terms the 'true masters of the word, … [who savour] each nuance of language … Think of the sermons of unknown ministers or the songs of the minstrels of Mali.' This celebration of the 'unknown' oral practitioner lends shape to the subsequent celebration of such published and therefore 'known' *griots* of industrial America as Maya Angelou and Toni Morrison, who, for Harris, 'capture our ephemeral words from the air and place them on paper for the future'(23). The somewhat misleading depiction of the African-American literary canon as one which not only sustains but is practically identical to an ongoing oral tradition systematically mutes the transformations wrought by publication, obscuring that shift to mass literacy which, for Jack Goody, can 'divide internally' and 'unify … externally.' Harris associates *A Kwanzaa Keepsake* itself with this reduction of literary practice to a kind of visionary transcription, presenting her holiday manual as a work that merely records pre-existing oral texts. This rather inaccurate self-portrait, which disguises the mediations and manipulations in which Harris is actually engaged, culminates with the incorporation into the cookbook of several sections of entirely blank pages that are simply entitled 'Family Recipes'. The authorial silence embodied by these sheaves of whiteness is explained by the following invitation:

One of the aims of Kwanzaa is to bring together families and friends in productive ways. To this end, each night will conclude with a project ... On the first night of Kwanzaa *Umoja*, family unity, is saluted with the creation of a cookbook of family favorites. Most of us know only too well that we never ask for the recipe for something until it is too late. When grandma's gone, we wish we knew how to make her beaten biscuits. When Aunt Dorcas moves away, we wish we had watched exactly how she fluted the edges of her pies. ... Begin this first night of Kwanzaa by making a conscious effort to write down the favorite recipes of your family. ... Start by using the blank pages in this book. Then, collect the recipes on sheets of paper to be kept in a file folder or a blank book. ... Keep the project growing and developing. It will help to keep the family together and it will preserve your traditions for another generation. (46)

This prescriptive attempt to solicit audience participation, which simply shifts responsibility for transcription from writer to reader, is the ultimate expression of the deference that *A Kwanzaa Keepsake* as a whole pays to the vernacular tradition. The ultimate tribute that it pays to orality through these white pages can also be seen as the ultimate expression of Harris's ambivalence regarding the act of publication. For the blank pages introduced by the above invitation confirm that the entire form of *A Kwanzaa Keepsake* has been determined by certain assumptions concerning publication, some of which support and some of which refute the recipe definition posited in *The Domestication of the Savage Mind*.

On one level Harris's ingenious formula for preserving familial tradition reveals that Goody's definition, and the notions of profit and loss with which it associates the cultural shift to mass literacy, retain enormous resonance for Harris among other African-American cookbook writers. After all, *A Kwanzaa Keepsake* is not an actual conversation: it *is* a cookbook. And Harris's preference for this textual status effectively concedes that, as Goody maintains, advantages are indeed bound up in publication. The process of publication facilitates the archiving and popularising possibilities that *A Kwanzaa Keepsake* repeatedly characterises as a switch from the 'unknown' to the 'known'. Nor is this all. Motivating the production of these blank pages is an equally profound apprehension of the loss of those familial formulas that Goody terms '*les gaufres de mémé*' but which Harris specifies as 'grandma's ... beaten biscuits' and the 'pies' of 'Aunt Dorcas'. Guarding against the melancholia inspired by the vanishing of such recipes, the abandonment of these pages to the reader recreates them as a ghostly space on which the actual ghosts of family and friends can be memorialised. Overall these silent white pages thus speak to a tacit endorsement of Goody's definition, since they draw from the archiving opportunities that he identifies as a key advantage of publication, while striving to avoid the homogenisation he identifies as a key *disadvantage* of publication.

Even as the blank pages of *A Kwanzaa Keepsake* reiterate the notions of profit and loss that structure Goody's analysis, however, they effectively refute his concomitant characterisation of the recipe as an intrinsically written genre. That is, these silent white pages also speak to a position that is implicit throughout Harris's cookbook oeuvre: namely that, contrary to Goody's claims, there *was* and *is* such a thing as an oral recipe. Through her simulation of orality, and through her attempts to involve readers in her transcriptive processes, Harris characterises the shift to writing less as a revolution, in which the recipe is conceived from scratch, than as an evolution that merely alters the formal qualities of extant oral texts. Nor is it that this oral recipe merely exists: for Harris this undiminished vernacular template exerts enormous influence over, and lends shape to, the production of a written version that is correspondingly presented as merely derivative of speech. What can be characterised as the aesthetic of transcription guiding *A Kwanzaa Keepsake* in this way refutes Goody's suggestion, asserting, simply, that recipes predate cookbooks.

Consider Harris's argument, though, in the light of the following anecdote:

> [My Master] used to read prayers in public to the ship's crew every Sabbath day; and then I saw him read. I was never so surprised in my life, as when I saw the book talk to my master, for I thought it did as I observed him to look upon it, and move his lips. I wished it would do so with me. As soon as my master had done reading, I followed him to the place where he put the book, being mightily delighted with it, and when nobody saw me, I opened it, and put my ear close down upon it, in great hopes that it would say something to me; but I was sorry, and greatly disappointed, when I found that it would not speak. This thought immediately presented itself to me, that every body and every thing despised me because I was black. (46)

This deceptively naïve anecdote about the enigmatic and magical interactions of writing and speaking is taken from the slave autobiography *A Narrative of the most remarkable particulars in the life of James Albert Ukawsaw Gronniosaw, an African Prince* (1770). It has recently reappeared in the preface to *The Norton Anthology of African-American Literature* (1997), which recasts it as an unconscious statement of intent to which this literary canon repeatedly aspires. In his influential preface to the anthology, Henry Louis Gates Jr uses Gronniosaw's anecdote as a springboard from which to launch his analysis of the significance of orality in much subsequent African-American literary production. Gates's argument, which develops ideas theorised in *Figures in Black* (1987) and *The Signifying Monkey* (1988), holds that African-American writers have frequently implored audiences to read not only with their eyes but also, figuratively, with their ears, thus producing 'talking' books that somehow consummate Gronniosaw's impossible vision.[2] Gates observes that the trauma of the Middle Passage, which was surely a linguistic as well as a human atrocity, coupled with educational inequalities produced by slavery and segregation, compelled African Americans to fashion a compensatory oral culture of particular vibrancy, durability and resilience. Qualities forged in the enforced void of West African languages and mass English literacy thus created a vernacular tradition which, originally defined against social inequities, became so desirable, flexible and useful in its own right that such eminently literate academics as Gates now seek to protect it. Thus Gates suggests that, while '*all* of the world's literatures have developed from an oral base', these origins in speech retain particular influence over 'our literary tradition, [where] the oral ... is never far from the written' (xxxviii).

As we have seen, the archive of recipes published by African Americans, several of whom seem motivated by a desire to produce 'talking' cookbooks, amply substantiates these claims. But materials offered throughout *The Norton Anthology of African-American Literature* also substantiate them. Prose and poetry in which the vernacular is simulated, together with statements upon the correct literary rendition of black speech such as Zora Neale Hurston's 'Characteristics of Negro Expression' (1934), generously pepper the anthology's 2665-page tour of African-American literature. Poets proclaim an intense identification with singers, momentarily puncturing the ultimately impermeable boundaries between script and performance: James Weldon Johnson's 'O Black and Unknown Bards' (1908) murmurs a tribute to those 'unknown', because illiterate, slaves who composed spirituals like 'Go Down, Moses' or 'Roll Jordan Roll' (769).[3] To Johnson's explicit poetic tribute to oral practitioners, meanwhile, there can be added the respect implicitly paid by those poets whose output refashions orality into a form consistent with the metropolitan sphere of literature by extensively borrowing from such vernacular forms as the blues, rap, spirituals, sermons and signifying. *The Norton Anthology of African-American Literature* samples much poetry, encompassing the dialect verse not only of Johnson himself but also of Claude McKay, Langston Hughes, Sterling A. Brown and others, in order to demonstrate the enduring influence that orality holds over African-American poetic practice. Yet the restrictions of space that control all anthologies mean that *The Norton Anthology* excludes as much vernacular

verse as it includes. One such editorial omission is Paul Laurence Dunbar's
1896 poem, 'Possum':

> Ef dey's anyt'ing dat riles me
> > An' jes' gits me out o' hitch,
> Twell I want to tek my coat off,
> > So's to r'ar an' t'ar an' pitch
> Hit's to see some ign'ant white man,
> > 'Mittin' dat owdacious sin –
> W'en he want to cook a possum
> > Tekin' off de possum's skin.
>
> W'y dey ain't no use in talkin',
> > Hit jes' hu'ts me to de hea't
> Fu' to see dem foolish people
> > Th'owin 'way de fines' pa't.
> W'y, dat skin is jes' ez tendah
> > An' ez juicy ez kin be;
> I know all erbout de critter –
> > Hide an' haih – don't talk to me!
>
> Possum skin is jes' lak shoat skin;
> > Jes' you swinge an' scrope it down,
> Tek a good sha'p knife an' sco' it,
> > Den you bake it good an' brown.
> Huh-uh! honey, you's so happy
> > Dat yo' thoughts is 'mos' a sin
> When you'se settin' dah a-chawin'
> > On dat possum's cracklin' skin.
>
> White folks t'ink dey know 'bout eatin',
> > An' I reckon dat dey do
> Sometimes git a little idee
> > Of a middlin' dish or two;
> But dey ain't a t'ing dey knows of
> > Dat I reckon cain't be beat
> W'en we set down at de table
> > To a unskun possum's meat! (141–142)

The work of one of the earliest published African-American poets
whose oeuvre extensively simulates orality, 'Possum' initiates a discourse
upon the best way to write black speech, a discourse to which African-
American writers of the inter-war period made particularly valuable
contributions. Inter-war poets like Sterling A. Brown inherited from
Dunbar a new sense of poetic possibility, which delegated aesthetic

responsibilities to a fictionalised black persona whose conversance with the vernacular amply compensated for his or her imagined illiteracy. Apparent in the development of this new and profoundly egalitarian poetic model was an inquiry into how best to capture and place upon the printed page the characteristic speech of this innovated folk mouthpiece. 'Possum' displays many of the conclusions that Dunbar arrived at in the course of this inquiry. Intense abbreviation, the coining of such new words as 'unskun' and 'owdacious', participate in a sustained effort to consummate Gronniosaw's vision and figuratively draw the reader's ear closer to the page. Some of Dunbar's innovations have not stood the test of time: later African-American poetry rarely if ever substitutes 'is' with 'ez', while the failure of such coinages as 'w'y' and 'w'en' to alter significantly the pronunciation of 'why' and 'when' speak to an overly enthusiastic apostrophisation. However other formulations have been so frequently reused by later African-American writers that, as elements within a vocabulary tailored to the writerly reproduction of the vernacular, they have acquired the status of a standardised spelling. *Dat*, *dey*, *git*, and *jes* – like Dunbar's consistent trimming of the gerund *-ing* to *-in'* – reappear incessantly throughout the *Norton Anthology*, re-emerging everywhere from the verse of Langston Hughes to the dialogue of Richard Wright.

These coinages also re-emerge in *Barbeque'n With Bobby*: '"When you make bobbyque, you don't put no sauce on it till it's done. Da base makes it tenda. Taste good right down to da bone."' That is to say, Dunbar's inquiry into how to write the vernacular not only influenced the official black canon, as sanctioned by academics like Henry Louis Gates, but also bequeathed its ready-made and improvisational lexicon to those uncanonised cookbook writers who sought to simulate oral recipes. Interconnections like these solidify once we acknowledge that 'Possum' is as concerned with cookery as Dunbar's even more famous 'Dinah Kneading Dough' (1899), and that the recipe at its heart energises its every line. 'Possum skin is jes' lak shoat skin; | Jes' you swinge an' scrope it down, | Tek a good sha'p knife an' sco' it, | Den you bake it good an' brown.' By delivering a soul food recipe through the vernacular, 'Possum' clearly anticipates post-war recipes produced by Grosvenor, Seale, Shange, Ferguson and Harris. Indeed if Dunbar's and Seale's recipes were placed side by side, one would quickly recognise both as drawing from approximately the same pool of vernacular formulations. And the fact that Dunbar's poetic recipe and *Barbeque'n With Bobby* so evidently belong to the same publishing tradition effectively overhauls our view of this tradition. It reveals that African Americans were producing 'talking' recipes long before the Second World War. It reveals that issues negotiated in *A Kwanzaa Keepsake*, whose blank pages result from anxieties surrounding the transformation of conversations into books, merely revisit the same vexed and complex relationship between speech and transcription which 'Possum', not to mention Gronnioiaw's autobiography, negotiate. Yet while it may be contended that the simulation of orality evident in Dunbar's 'Possum' establishes it as the first 'talking' recipe by an African American, the lines at its heart are by no means the first *recipe*. Instead, as the following pages demonstrate, the origins of the broader tradition of African-American cookbook publishing reach further back even than the writing of 'Possum', to the late nineteenth century, and to the fascination with African-American cooking in the Gilded Age that led to the publication of such pioneering cookbooks as *What Mrs Fisher Knows about Old Southern Cooking*.

What Mrs Fisher Knew

In 1880, having travelled to California by means that remain unknown to us, a middle-aged African-American woman from South Carolina stepped inside the hall of the San Francisco Mechanics' Institute Fair. Into this artisanal occasion, which evidently tolerated the idea of interracial competition, Abby Fisher placed the pickles and preserves that she had made following the same oral recipes which had earned her a diploma at the previous year's State Fair in Sacramento. This time around, Abby Fisher's pickles and preserves not only merited acknowledgement but also acclaim. Sampling her submissions for the categories of 'Pickles and Sauces' and 'Jellies and Preserves', the Institute Fair judges pronounced them the best on display. Nor did Fisher's success end there. No less impressed than these judges by this exceptional woman's culinary expertise, the Women's Institute of San Francisco and Oakland commissioned a cookbook for local publication. Under the title of *What Mrs Fisher Knows about Old Southern Cooking*, the resulting edition of 1881 established Fisher among the first African Americans to publish a collection of recipes.

Like that of Phillis Wheatley – the first African American to publish a collection of poems – the achievement of Abby Fisher was particularly astonishing given that she had been born a slave. At least this is the most plausible conclusion to be drawn from the meagre details we have of Abby Fisher's life in South Carolina before the Emancipation Proclamation of 1863. As Fisher's editor, Karen Hess (1995) speculates:

In ... 1880, precisely during the period when Mrs. Fisher must have been occupied with her cookbook, the census records list Abby C. Fisher, then 48 years of age, as living at 207½ Second Street in San Francisco. Her profession was given as "cook," and under race she was listed as "*mu.,*" that is, *mulatto*, born in South Carolina of a mother who was also born in South Carolina and a father who was born in France. ... In 1832 or thereabouts, when Abby Fisher was born, any relationship involving a man born in France and producing a child designated as *mulatto* was almost certainly that of slaveowner and slave. Any other scenario would be torturous, especially in South Carolina plantation society. I think it safe to say that she was born a slave. (76)

Like *Poems on Various Subjects, Religious and Moral by Phillis Wheatley, Negro Servant* (1773), *What Mrs Fisher Knows* can probably be counted among that astonishing archive of cultural documents authored by men and women to whom state laws and plantation codes had once assigned the status of a commodity. Fisher's preface to *What Mrs Fisher Knows* reveals that, in one crucial respect, this pioneering publication was even more remarkable than Wheatley's poetry volume:

The publication of a book on my knowledge and experience of Southern Cooking, Pickle and Jelly Making, has been frequently asked of me by my lady friends and patrons in San Francisco and Oakland, and also by ladies of Sacramento during the State Fair in 1879. Not being able to read or write myself, and my husband also having been without the advantages of an education – upon whom would devolve the writing of the book at my dictation – caused me to doubt whether I would be able to present a work that would give perfect satisfaction. But, after due consideration, I concluded to bring forward a book of my knowledge – based on an experience of upwards of thirty-five years – in the art of cooking Soups, Gumbos, Terrapin Stews, Meat Stews, Baked and Roast Meats, Pastries, Pies and Biscuits, making Jellies, Pickles, Sauces, Ice-Creams and Jams, preserving Fruits, etc. The book will be found a complete instructor, so that a child can understand and learn the art of cooking. (v)

Unlike *Poems on Various Subjects, Religious and Moral by Phillis Wheatley* (1773), *What Mrs Fisher Knows* can be counted among the problematic archive of works conceived by illiterate African Americans but transcribed by literate white Americans. Fisher's preface to *What Mrs Fisher Knows* reveals that its author was not only likely to have been born a slave but was also, to paraphrase Gronniosaw, someone to whom writing refused to speak. It reveals that, unlike those twentieth-century African-American cookbooks that are presented as transcripts, *What Mrs Fisher Knows is* a transcript. But Fisher's preface also reveals that the transcriptive processes that commit her spoken words to paper are of a particularly interventionist and transformative kind: 'I concluded to bring forward a book of my knowledge', 'upon whom would devolve the writing of a book at my dictation', 'after due consideration': this is writerly English, so aggressively styled into formality as to leave little to no trace of black vernacular speech. Indeed Fisher's confession of illiteracy is itself rather studied, and effectively asks the reader to believe that an unlettered woman would describe her husband as being 'without the advantages of an education'. And this rather implausible contention, which anticipates the string of equally implausible and equally formalised phrases lodged by the subsequent recipes of *What Mrs Fisher Knows*, opens a paradox. For it reveals that *What Mrs Fisher Knows* differs from such 'talking' cookbooks as *A Kwanzaa Keepsake*, not only because it actually *is* a transcript, but because the model of transcription that produces it strives to extinguish all semblance of orality from its text. Put another way, if *A Kwanzaa Keepsake* is a cookbook that works hard to present itself as a transcript, then *What Mrs Fisher Knows* is a transcript that works equally hard to present itself as a conventionally composed text.

An explanation of these differences lies in the issues of collaboration and conflict, of authorial ownership and control, which arise from the production of *What Mrs Fisher Knows*. For the above preface indicates that Fisher's ownership and control over her cookbook has been severely tested by her illiteracy, which has forced her to call upon transcribers whose whiteness, given the interracial inequalities then prevailing in the American publishing industry, was all but inevitable. In turn, Fisher's dependency on these Californian collaborators situates her cookbook not only as a signifier of racial progress but also as an example of the intense and often anxious fascination with blackness that filtered much contemporary white American cultural production.

The Gilded Age culture into which *What Mrs Fisher Knows* was issued witnessed an increasingly conspicuous and startling commodification of African-American cultural materials for white bourgeois consumption. Such commodification was epitomised by the marketing and publishing phenomenon of Joel Chandler Harris, who, through his recounting of black vernacular folktales in titles like *Legends of the Old Plantation* (1881), enjoyed considerable popularity. It was also exemplified by what Doris Witt (1999) terms the white cultural yearning 'for African American women to be the ever-smiling producers of food', which encouraged several food companies in the 1880s and 1890s to incorporate caricatures of smiling female and male African-American cooks into their advertising (23). The launch of the Aunt Jemima trademark by the Quaker Oats company in 1889 marked an apotheosis in this commercialisation of black caricature, although the appearance in 1893 of the 'Rastus' logo – a waiter dubbed the 'Cream of Wheat Cook' advertising breakfast porridge – arguably had equal importance.[4] Smiling, inoffensive and deferential, these caricatured creatures were part of contemporary capitalism's response to the increased bourgeois interest in black culture; a response that, effectively, fed the new consumerist appetite by carving this culture up into manageable mouthfuls of stereotype. Logos like Rastus and Aunt Jemima yielded no trace of the lynchings, destitution and disenfranchisement that actually determined African-American social experience in the immediate aftermath of Reconstruction. Their purpose was instead that of wish fulfilment – of negotiating and containing the volatile mix of fear and fascination that tended to surface when the contemporary white American gaze fell upon black culture.

My suggestion is that this explosive mix of conflicting passions is also apparent in Abby Fisher's transcribers' decision to 'cleanse' all trace of black speech from recipes like the following:

Ochra Gumbo.

Get a beef shank, have it cracked and put to boil in one gallon of water. Boil to half a gallon, then strain and put back on the fire. Cut ochra in small pieces and put in soup; don't put in any ends of ochra. Season with salt and pepper while cooking. Stir it occasionally and keep it from burning. To be sent to table with dry boiled rice. Never stir rice while boiling. Season rice always with salt when it is first put on to cook, and do not have too much water in rice while boiling. (Fisher, 22–23)

Here, the editorial conversion of Fisher's speech to standard grammar, although less relentless than that which produced the cookbook's rather staid preface, nevertheless results in an exceedingly precise list of step-by-step instructions from which the informalities of speech are once more absent. The effort not only to transcribe but to translate Fisher's speech, which eliminates the definite article along with the hesitation and sheer verbosity that typify speech, betrays a desire to shape this recipe into a conventional form. What 'Ochra Gumbo' witnesses is an aggressive moulding of Fisher's speech to fit a cast whose essential shape remains undisturbed by its carefully managed accommodation of a former slave. Strenuously reassuring the implied white reader that the cookbook canon will change Abby Fisher rather than the other way around, 'Ochra Gumbo' emerges as another gesture of containment, which, like Rastus or Aunt Jemima, effectively reinstates white authority by carving African-American culture into digestible mouthfuls. Admittedly we must remain cautious here. We must also entertain the possibility that the decision of Fisher's transcribers to convert her speech into standard American English resulted from a benevolent desire to circumvent the negative connotations of the demotic and, in the process, to avoid exactly those forms of caricature which Aunt Jemima encapsulated. Yet this possibility is hardly incompatible with a reading of 'Ochra Gumbo' that sees, in its standardisation of speech, telltale traces of the anxiety which Fisher's transcribers felt upon realising that the culinary ingredients and procedures of this problematic recipe were not only immensely gratifying but also inescapably black.

After all, this recipe imports not only its central ingredient from Africa, but also both parts of its name. As Karen Hess (1992) observes: 'Okra is native to Central Africa and was brought to the New World by way of the slave trade. The word itself is derived from *nkru-ma*, its name in the Twi language of Ghana, according to Jessica B. Harris. *Gumbo*, its other name in English, comes from *kingombo* from Angola' (111). When filtered through the dogmatically Manichean raciology of contemporary dominant American culture, which flattened the countless black Americans engaged in domestic labour into the silenced Aunt Jemima logo, such provenance could have identified okra itself as a potentially hazardous signifier of irrepressible Africanism. For Fisher's transcribers, the realisation that 'Ochra Gumbo' amounted to an unequivocally African-American handling of an unequivocally African ingredient could have been taken as unwanted evidence of black cultural autonomy. It might have been taken as a declaration of cultural independence that, among other things, eroded the comforting reliance on white assistance apparently enshrined in Fisher's dependency on transcription. To then describe a vernacular food through vernacular language, to add the further spice of the black demotic, would have been an explosive intervention indeed. In order to defuse the autonomous blackness of 'Ochra Gumbo', then, Fisher's transcribers were obliged to describe its vernacular foods through any but vernacular words. The grammaticisation and gentrification of Fisher's speech can thus be read as the product of an intricate interracial arbitration, in which her Californian transcribers appeased white hungers for soul food while easing any menace that the uncurbed indulgence of such exoticism posed to the cherished white supremacist order.

Let us compare this rather dismal situation with an example of how okra has been handled by a more recent African-American cookbook writer:

Fried Okra

Wash 1 pound of okra real well, like all other vegetables, in cold water. Then chop the top thick ends off. Discard. The rest of the okra is fine for cookin'. Chop your lovely fresh okra into slices 'bout an inch wide, including the cute little ends. They'll fry just fine. Now, you can make you a batter of 1/2 cup of cornmeal, 2/3 cup milk, and 1 egg to dip the okra in before fryin'. Or you can simply dip the okra in some milk, run it through flour or cornmeal fast as lightning, then fry. Butter is great, but you'll need a lot of it to get the okra the right color brown. So try some regular household oil like Crisco or Mazola. Before you put your okra in to fry, make sure water sizzles in the grease. Make sure that you've got a good, heavy fryin' pan, so the okra doesn't stick to the bottom and burn on one side, gettin' stuck to the metal.... There, we've got a batch of fine fried okra. (Shange, 1998, 75)

Many more differences than similarities exist between Abby Fisher's 'Ochra Gumbo' and this conversational recipe from the cookbook that introduced our discussion, Ntozake Shange's *If I Can Cook / You Know God Can.* Such differences reach beyond the simple fact that Fisher's recipe is restricted to the same official English vocabulary, authorised by dictionaries, which Shange's vernacular instructions deliberately abandon. For such linguistic devices as Shange's consistent abbreviation of the gerund merely signal a far more encompassing and abiding switch in the general compositional approach of the African-American cookbook writer. Italicisation, the trimming of the gerund, and Shange's consistent use of the inclusive 'we' signify a more ambitious declaration, which is that recipes concerning African ingredients like okra will no longer disguise this provenance behind an Anglo-American master narrative dedicated to silencing the vernacular. In the process of issuing this declaration of cultural independence, '*Fried Okra*' retrospectively recasts the way we read *What Mrs Fisher Knows* in general and 'Ochra Gumbo' in particular. For example, Shange's consistent and conscientious desire to supply a supplementary justification for every order issued in the course of '*Fried Okra*' – so that '*make sure that you've got a good, heavy fryin' pan*' immediately prompts the explanation, '*so the okra doesn't stick to the bottom*' – effectively clarifies the contrasting didacticism of 'Ochra Gumbo', the contrasting failure to explain why cooks should 'never' stir but 'always' season rice. In the same way, the resurgence of joy ('*lovely fresh okra*') and metaphor ('*fast as lightning*') into '*Fried Okra*' reveals that the sheer pleasure of cooking – which was, surely, a key motive behind Fisher's decision to enter Californian culinary competitions – is utterly absent from the starched wording of 'Ochra Gumbo'. By recasting the recipe as a joyful enterprise, and by characterising it as part of a discursive process more redolent of the seminar than the lecture, '*Fried Okra*' redirects attention to the oral recipe excluded by Jack Goody's definition. It also enlists this newly primary conversational recipe within a broader restoration of the sympathetic collaboration that Shange sees as underpinning the African-American cookery tradition. Via this return to orality, in other words, Shange, like Harris, presents black culinary expertise less as the secret knowledge that an isolated writer 'knows' than as a public archive in which writer and reader are similarly conversant. Put another way, if *What Mrs Fisher Knows* is evidently very different from what her transcribers knew, then conversational recipes such as the above assume that the expertise of writer and reader overlaps.

These differences appear to confirm rather than refute the characterisation of *What Mrs Fisher Knows* as antithetical to post-war 'talking' cookbooks like *A Kwanzaa Keepsake*. But the importance of these differences lies in their ability to lead us to a more fruitful understanding of Abby Fisher's rather curious connection to the tradition she helped to initiate. For these differences also indicate that the relationship between *What Mrs Fisher Knows* and 'talking' cookbooks like *A Kwanzaa Keepsake* is best understood not as antithetical but as that of problem and solution. They indicate that *What Mrs Fisher Knows* can be seen as a cautionary tale concerning authorial control, which outlines the problem to which Shange and Harris among other African-American cookbook writers respond. Put crudely, the problem that *What Mrs Fisher Knows* presents to later African-American cookbook writers pertains to the apparent incompatibility of the soul food recipe and standard American English. Behind this simple linguistic injunction, as a warning which later recipe writers have either consciously or unconsciously heeded, Fisher's lack of control over her words as well as her foods suggests through its very absence the future importance of the vernacular within this specific cookbook tradition. And the fact that Shange and Harris, not to mention Dunbar, arrive at the same solution – suggesting that a soul food recipe should instead be written in the vernacular – reveals that, far from sitting incongruously within this tradition, *What Mrs Fisher Knows* actually initiates its ongoing inquiry into the simulation of speech.

To clarify these concluding remarks, let us return to a recipe from *What Mrs Fisher Knows*:

Jumberlie – A Creole Dish.

Take one chicken and cut it up, separating every joint, and adding to it one pint of cleanly-washed rice. Take about half a dozen large tomatoes, scalding them well and taking the skins off with a knife. Cut them in small pieces and put them with the chicken in a pot or large porcelain saucepan. Then cut in small pieces two large pieces of sweet ham and add to the rest, seasoning high with pepper and salt. It will cook in twenty-five minutes. Do not put any water on it. (57–58)

On one level, the above instructions reveal that, to the incontestably African schema of 'Ochra Gumbo', *What Mrs Fisher Knows* adds another gumbo, or Creole, in which the international cookery traditions prevalent in the South create a new template for the infinite exchanges of a new and emphatically American cuisine. On another level, however, this text can also be read as a problem for which the later 'talking' recipe proposes a solution. It can be read, that is, as the call to which subsequent African-American cookbook writers respond. The displacement of the vernacular, the transcriptive attempt to force Abby Fisher's speech to comply with the semantic rules of standard American English, produces a recipe for a now famous Southern dish that seems somehow Othered by its saturation in formality. As such the removal of Fisher's speech from 'Jumberlie' indeed points to the need for future black recipe writers to describe their soul food culinary procedures using the vernacular.

Yet this recipe not only ushers us towards this problem but simultaneously points us in the direction of its solution. For, while this recipe, like *What Mrs Fisher Knows* as a whole, presents itself as anything other than a transcript, the volatile orality which such rigorous transcription seeks to defuse suddenly explodes into the title: 'Jumberlie – A Creole Dish'. Apparently unbeknownst to Fisher's Californian transcribers, this title translates the dish *Jambalaya* into a coinage in which their subject's South Carolinian lilt is suddenly, unexpectedly, wonderfully retained. The involuntary coining of 'Jumberlie' is thus the crisis point: the moment at which fingers slip, wires cross and the vocabulary at the disposal of Fisher's transcribers fails to accommodate the language spoken by their subject. In this unexpected resurgence of orality into the text of *What Mrs Fisher Knows*, Fisher's transcribers were clearly forced to fall back on those literary devices which have since been deliberately employed by Shange and other writers of the conversational recipe. Although the circumstances surrounding their production were drastically different, the improvisational coining of *Jumberlie* by Fisher's transcribers involuntarily initiates the sustained refashioning of a new vernacular vocabulary which, at the close of the twentieth century, has culminated in such words as Dunbar's 'owdacious' or Seale's 'bobbyque'. Furthermore, whether voluntary or involuntary, conscious or unconscious, these improvisations redirect our attention back to speech. Effectively, they subordinate script to speech, reminding the reader that the words he or she is reading are preceded by words which may not be found in the dictionary but which have long been exchanged, in the kitchen, by the vernacular cook. In this sense, then, *What Mrs Fisher Knows* not only helped to initiate the tradition of African-American cookbook publishing, but also embodied the problems that this tradition has since encountered. It also anticipates the prime motive that lends shape to this cookbook canon as it forces audiences to not only read with the eyes but, figuratively, with the ears. To the *griots*, the illiterate cooks of the nineteenth century, celebrated by African-American recipe writers as Jessica Harris, then, there should now be added the name of this most ironic publishing phenomenon, the unlettered writer, Abby Fisher.

Notes

1   The status of *What Mrs. Fisher Knows* as the first cookbook to be published by an African American is proclaimed on the front cover of Applewood's 1995 reissue of the text, to which this article refers. However, the premier status of Fisher's text is challenged in forthcoming research by Rafia Zahar, while Doris Witt notes the existence of earlier recipes by African Americans in *Black Hunger: Food and the Politics of US Identity*, 1999.

2   See: Henry Louis Gates Jr, *The Signifying Monkey: A Theory of African-American Literary Criticism*, 1987; and *Figures in Black: Words, Signs and the 'Racial' Self*, 1987.

3   James Weldon Johnson [1908], 'O Black and Unknown Bards' in Gates, 1987, and *The Norton Anthology of African American Literature*, 1997, p. 769.

4   A useful discussion of the African-American caricature in US commercial advertising can be found at http://www.ferris.edu/news/jimcrow/tom.

Chapter 5

Domesticating Imperialism: Curry and Cookbooks in Victorian England

Susan Zlotnick

Good cooking is a moral agent. (Joseph Conrad, 1923)

Domesticity, Englishness and empire

Feminist historians and literary critics have done much to lay to rest the popular image of the colonial woman as an unthinking memsahib, a 'frivolous, snobbish and selfish creature who flitted from bridge to tennis parties' (Barr, 1976, 1). By revisiting and revising the relationship between white women and British India, they have newly complicated our understanding of the real labour European women undertook as wives, mothers, missionaries and governesses in India and Britain's other colonies.[1] Equally important, they have complicated our understanding of the ideological work that gender performed in the construction of empire, from Jenny Sharpe's (1993) explorations of the allegorical use of women in post-Mutiny narratives, where violated white women became signs for the violation of imperial rule, to Sara Suleri's (1992) reading of Englishwomen abroad as 'the symbolic representation of the joys of an English home' (76). In addition to elaborating upon the ideological work of gender in the empire, recent criticism has detailed its reverse, the ideological work empire (and its imbricated discourses of race, nationhood, class and sexuality) has performed in the construction of gender. Here the empire emerges as an ideological field on which competing and even contradictory versions of womanhood can play themselves out. In Antoinette Burton's (1994) study of British feminists and Indian women, British imperial politics becomes the means through which feminists 'undermine the

Victorian construction of woman as Other by identifying her with the Self of nation and empire' (35); while for Vron Ware (1992) the empire functions as the space in which varieties of femininity are themselves mapped out, so that 'the Englishwoman abroad could be at once a many-faceted figure: from an intrepid adventuress ... to a vulnerable, defenceless piece of property' (12). Just as women did not play one role in colonial India (the mindless memsahib at tea and tennis), neither did gender remain a unitary, coherent term in nineteenth-century colonial discourse. Like all signs, it could be deployed in a variety of mutually constructing and conflicting ways to preserve and protect the always fragile, always fictional imperial state, and its even more vulnerable imperial subject.

This essay also addresses the ideological work of gender; and it does so through the medium of Victorian domestic cookbooks and the curry recipes they contain. If recent scholarship has hitherto concentrated on Englishwomen abroad in the years after the 1857 Mutiny, this essay remains resolutely domestic in its focus. It explores the tangled relationship between a potent domestic ideology and imperialism in the first half of the nineteenth century by charting the domestication of curry, which, in the words of one Victorian cookery expert, had become a 'completely naturalized' English food by mid-century (Rundell, 1851, 311). In the years before the Mutiny, when utilitarians like Thomas Babington Macaulay and James Mill were busily trying to assimilate India into the British Empire and Anglicizing it through educational and legal reforms, British women undertook an analogous task. They incorporated Indian food, which functioned metonymically for India, into the national diet and made it culturally British.

Nupur Chaudhuri (1992) has already detailed the material practices of Victorian memsahibs who helped to diffuse curry and rice into the national diet, thereby functioning as 'agents of cultural exchange between colonizers and colonized' (232). However, Victorian women were not only 'agents of cultural exchange' but were invested by the domestic ideology with the powers of moral agency (powers which Joseph Conrad mistakenly attributes to good cooking rather than to the good (female) cook) that allowed them to undertake the ideological work of domesticating imperialism. It is the 'good' Victorian woman's moral agency and figurative power to domesticate the foreign that this essay traces through the medium of cookbooks and curry recipes. For in addition to offering us an abundant crop of arcane recipes – everything from sheep head's soup to lark stew – nineteenth-century domestic cookery books are self-conscious cultural documents in which we can locate a metaphor for nineteenth-century British imperialism, and in which the Other presents itself not as a source of threat and contamination but as a source of nourishment. By virtue of their own domesticity, Victorian women could neutralise the threat of the Other by naturalising the products of foreign lands.

If women could domesticate imperialism, it was because the potent ideology of domesticity figured women as agents of domestication. Emphasizing separate, gendered spheres of private and public life, the potent ideology of domesticity emerged out of the evangelism of the Clapham Sect in the earliest decades of the nineteenth century to become, by the 1830s and 1840s, the dominant ideology of the middle classes. It figured women not merely as disembodied angels in the house but as powerful moral missionaries within the domestic realm. Women contained the potential to repair and reform not only their husbands but also the nation as long as they remained morally intact and politically aloof, isolated from the workaday world of capitalist competition and parliamentary processes. As the great mid-Victorian art critic John Ruskin famously stated in 'Of Queen's Gardens' (1865):

> What the woman is to be within her gates, as the centre of order, the balm of distress, and the mirror of beauty, that she is also to be without her gates, where order is more difficult, distress more imminent, loveliness more rare ... There is not a war in the world, no, nor an injustice, but you women are answerable for it; not in that you have provoked it, but in that you have not hindered it. Men, by their nature, are prone to fight; they will fight for any cause, or for none. It is for you to choose their cause for them, to forbid them when there is no cause. There is no suffering, no injustice, no misery in the earth, but the guilt of it lies with you. (38)

The contradictory nature of the domestic ideology – at once profoundly conservative in its configuration of women as purely domestic beings and profoundly radical in its ability to imagine them as the moral redeemers of the nation – accounts for much of its enduring power throughout the century. Even Victorian feminists, Antoinette Burton notes, deployed the ideology of domesticity in their struggles for a larger role in Britain's political life, believing as they did 'that women's special qualifications as national mothers and homemakers automatically gave women an imperial role' (51). Domesticity, then, remains central to the construction of middle-class identity as well as a developing national identity as both eminently bourgeois and absolutely imperial: imperialism and domesticity are distinctive, core values of the Victorian middle classes that slowly disseminated through Victorian society and emerged as 'national' values by mid-century, an emergence that marks the bourgeois ascendancy in

Victorian Britain. Sarah Stickney Ellis (1844), a leading domestic ideologue, declared that 'it is the domestic character of England – the home comforts, and fireside virtues for which she is so justly celebrated' (5). And while all women were essentially domestic in this universalising discourse, 'the ideal Englishwoman's special quality', Jane Mackay and Pat Thane (1986) point out, 'was that she practised these virtues in a fashion superior to women of other countries' (191). Englishwomen's domesticity became one of the most visible and remarked upon signs of their – and their nation's – superiority.

Figuring themselves as essentially domestic at heart helped the English in allaying the inevitable anxieties produced by their colonial encounters. If Edward Bulwer Lytton could proudly proclaim in his *England and the English* (1833) that 'we … are becoming Citizens of the World' (34–35), it is because Sarah Ellis, at roughly the same cultural moment, was just as loudly praising England's domestic character. The domestic nature of English national identity needed to be formulated precisely at the time that it appeared most vulnerable. England's domesticity develops as a distinguishing feature of Englishness when the English noticeably and regularly begin to abandon their firesides for colonial destinations. If the fixity of Englishness is a fiction 'designed to mask its uncertainty', as Robert Young (1995) contends, then the fiction of England's domestic character conceals the reality of its imperial status and effaces the fact that Ellis's homebodies are also Bulwer Lytton's 'Citizens of the World'; moreover, the figure of the domesticated Englishwoman helps to constitute and stabilize an Englishness that is always 'estranged from itself, sick with desire for the other' (2–3). But that desire for the other, and the fear of hybridity it unleashes, could be deactivated through the metaphors of domestication. Middle-class women, as morally regenerative and utterly domestic figures, could take into their homes a hybrid like curry, the mongrelised offspring of England's union with India, and through the ideological effect of domesticating it, erase its foreign origins and re-present it as purely English.[2] So alongside the trope of hybridity (the self becoming Other) we can place the trope of incorporation (taking the Other and making it self) as one way in which early Victorian England imagined its relationship with India.

Incorporating India

Before detailing the role played by Victorian women and their cookbooks in domesticating imperialism, this essay will first sketch out the issues surrounding the incorporation of India in the first half of the nineteenth century. The most self-conscious novelistic deployment of the metaphor of incorporation – of both India and Indian curries – for the act of imperialism appears in *Vanity Fair*, William Thackeray's 1848 epic satire of British life.[3] If the empire seems very far off in other Victorian novels, a place to exile redeemable reprobates like Mr Micawber, *Vanity Fair*, written by the Anglo-Indian Thackeray, exposes London's status as an imperial capital and exults in displaying the spoils of empire, everything from white cashmere shawls to black footmen, that littered the Victorian domestic scene. Thackeray's London also contains figures like the extremely corpulent Joseph Sedley of the East India Company, the novel's most visible (and sizeable) representative of British imperialism in Thackeray's self-illustrated text: growing fat and rich in Bengal, the Boggley Wollah tax collector consumes vast quantities of Indian food and wealth. Like the imperial project of which he remains a loyal but not terribly efficient servant, Jos engages in, as Thackeray puts it, 'the delightful exercise of gobbling' (29).

The metaphor of incorporation, of delightful gobbling, exists along with – and in fact is the other side of – the much-excavated trope of self and demonized Other. Both originate in the oral phase of development when the infant begins to realize that the world, which has hitherto provided food and warmth, is not an extension of the self and hence not under the child's control. As Sander Gilman argues in *Difference and Pathology: Stereotypes of Sexuality, Race and Madness* (1985), the child compensates for this loss by splitting 'the self and the world into "good" and "bad" objects, the "bad" self is distanced and identified with the mental representation of the "bad" object. ... The deep structure of our own sense of self and the world is built upon the illusionary image of the world divided into two camps, "us" and "them." They are either "good" or "bad."' Thus, for Gilman, stereotypes become 'palimpsests on which the initial bipolar representations are still vaguely legible. They perpetuate a needed sense of difference between the "self" and the "object" which becomes the "Other"' (17–18). Othering, or projecting negative attributes onto the colonised subject, is a basic tenet of post-colonial studies, and one that has been criticised for its dichotomising view of the imperial world as an agonistic struggle between self and Other. By returning to the first half of Gilman's formulation, to the 'good' self and the 'good' object (the object which nurtures), one can recapture this alternate colonial trope, localised in early Victorian cookbooks, that depends not on an absolute, dichotomised split between self and Other but on the assimilation of Other into self.

Victorian Britain, in which national identity struggled with imperial ambition, contained a dialectical tension always in play between eating and the fear of being eaten. For, as Maggie Kilgour contends in *From Communion to Cannibalism* (1990), 'imperialism is a form of cannibalism' (185–186). Always lurking behind the desire for incorporation is the fear of being incorporated, which can rightly be read as a response to the culture's own 'desire to assimilate and possess what is external to the self' (5), and which frequently entails the projection of its own cannibalistic desires onto the colonized Other. At the level of popular culture, the desire to eat can be represented by the cookbook writers of the 1830s and 1840s, and the fear of being eaten by the locus classicus of late Victorian anxieties about imperialism, Bram Stoker's *Dracula* (1897), in which an undesirable alien from the East arrives on Britain's shores and starts feeding off the natives, transforming them into versions of himself in an act that is represented as the cannibalistic ritual of blood sucking. This 'narrative of reverse colonization', as Stephen Arata (1990) identifies it, recurs frequently in fiction and non-fiction texts at the end of the century and expresses the fear that the 'civilized' world might be overrun by 'primitive' forces from Britain's far-flung possessions (623).

While both tropes – eating and being eaten – co-exist throughout the century, the former seems to predominate in the decades before the Indian Mutiny of 1857, an uprising by the Indian recruits in the East India Company's armies that led to a re-evaluation of Victorian England's complicated theories of race and empire.[4] For example, in *Vanity Fair*, written a decade before the Mutiny, Thackeray raises the spectre of Indian cannibalism only to dash it. When Mr Sedley reviews the marital prospects of his son Jos, the Boggley Wollah tax collector, with Mrs Sedley, he declares that the boy 'is destined to be a prey to women . . . It's a mercy he did not bring us over a black daughter-in-law, my dear. But mark my words, the first woman who fishes for him, hooks him' (36). Sedley's parental anxieties, particularly directed at the possibility that his son, the proverbial good catch, might be reeled in by an Indian woman prove unfounded, or more precisely, inappropriately focused. At the conclusion of the novel, a woman does eat Jos alive, but this is as a result of Jos taking out a life insurance policy naming as beneficiary the novel's husband-hunting heroine, Becky Sharp, who has been figuratively transformed into a siren, one of those 'fiendish marine cannibals revelling and feasting on ... wretched pickled victims' (813). Jos's fate, to eat and be eaten, enacts in its trajectory our twinned imperial metaphors; but it is not a 'black daughter-in-law', as his father feared, who destroys him, but a white woman. In fact, Dobbin, the hero of Thackeray's 'novel without a hero', even counsels Jos to return to India, where he could safely elude Becky's rapacious appetite. For Thackeray, writing the late 1840s, the real threat comes not from abroad but already exists at home in the form of Becky, an unscrupulous and greedy representative of the rising middle classes.

To the extent that even the text's mulatto heiress – a 'Hottentot Venus' (259) – can be incorporated into London society under the matrimonial signifier 'Mrs McMull', *Vanity Fair* enacts the Utilitarians' basic principle of assimilation, even if the novel remains largely untouched by the enthusiasm for the rationalising reform that dominated English thinking on India before the Mutiny (Brantlinger, 1988, 90–91). 'The missionaries of English civilization in India', Eric Stokes (1959) argues, 'stood openly for a policy of "assimilation". Britain was to stamp her image upon India. The physical and mental distances separating East and West were to be annihilated by the discoveries of science, by commercial intercourse, and by transplanting the genius of English laws and English education' (xiii–xiv). This early moment of Victorian imperialism, when Britain could fearlessly imagine assimilating India and Indians, perhaps gets its clearest articulation in Macaulay's famous 'Minute on Indian Education', which formed the basis of The English Education Act of 1835, denominating English the language of instruction in India.   In the 'Minute' Macaulay intervenes in the debate between Anglicists and Orientalists, and on the side of the Anglicists who favoured giving Indians a solid British education and discontinuing support for the study of Arabic and Sanskrit. Underlying Macaulay's proposals is the assumption that 'it is possible to make natives of this country thoroughly good English scholars', by which he means scholars who could speak, read and write good English, but also scholars who would thus be transformed into 'good' Englishmen. So important is the double meaning of 'English scholars' to Macaulay that he does not leave his readers the pleasure of the ambiguity; instead, he offers a clarification in the next paragraph: 'We must at present do our best to form a class who may be interpreters between us and the million whom we govern: a class of persons, Indian in blood and colour, but English in taste, in opinions, in morals and in intellect' (249). Apparently, unlike poets, Englishmen could be made, or at least they could be in the mid-1830s. The 'Minute on Indian Education' offers Macaulay's recipe for preparing the raw ingredients of the Indian to fit into the mould of an Englishman, and in this regard it imagines and even anticipates transforming educated Indians into the naturalized products of the British Empire.[5]

However Macaulay's cheerful and unclouded vision of the Anglicized Indian fades after the Indian Mutiny, which marks the turning point in the discourse of incorporation. In a letter sent during the height of the Mutiny,

Queen Victoria confesses 'that my heart bleeds for the horrors that have been committed by people once so gentle' (Hibbert, 1985, 137). Her shock and sadness are not unique, for as Thomas Metcalf (1964) notes, 'Once betrayed by those whom they had trusted, the British could no longer bring themselves to trust anyone with a brown face: all alike were tainted' (290). Remarkably Queen Victoria's Mutiny correspondences also capture the destabilising effect of the rebellion on the metaphor of incorporation. Writing to Lady Canning, wife of the Governor-General of India, for confirmation of some of the rumours then abroad in London, Victoria requests 'any reliable evidence of eye-witnesses – of horrors, like people having to eat their children's flesh – and other unspeakable and dreadful atrocities which I could not write' (Hibbert, 138). In her ambiguous phrasing – it is unclear whether she attributes these cannibalistic acts to Britons or Indians – the metaphoric apparatus of nineteenth-century imperialism hangs suspended in air. For here we have the future Empress of India unable to recognise the real figure of cannibalism In the colonial drama, a momentary confusion that allows the imperial state both to acknowledge its own cannibalistic desires and transpose them onto an Other.

Cookbooks, curry and the commodity

In *Good Things in England, A Book for Everyday Use, Containing Traditional and Regional Recipes Suited to Modern Tastes, Contributed by English Men and Women Between 1399 and 1932* (1932), Florence White informs us that the English have enjoyed curry, a highly spiced stew, ever since the reign of Richard II. 'Two "receipts" for curry powders', she notes, 'are given in the roll compiled by his master cooks about the year 1390' (178).[6] While culinary historians contend that the heavily seasoned concoctions of medieval court chefs did resemble Indian cuisine (Sokolow, 1991, 96), the similarity between medieval cookery and the contemporary Indian diet is not the point White aims to make. For the two recipes she then offers up as examples of this authentic English food are for Madras Chicken Curry and Ceylon Curry, borrowed from 'the greatest modern authority on curries and curry making' (178), who of course turns out to be an Anglo-Indian, Colonel Kenney Herbert, famous for his late nineteenth-century treatise, *Culinary Jottings for Madras* (1878). Whatever Richard II's royal chefs may have served up, it was not Madras Chicken Curry; but, by the early twentieth century, curry is so much a part of the British national identity that cookbook writers can even begin that eminently British activity of discovering spurious medieval antecedents for it.

As one can imagine, curry was not always so readily identified with the British Isles. Near the beginning of *Vanity Fair*, published in 1848 but set during the Napoleonic Wars, Becky Sharp determines to pursue the gourmandising Jos Sedley, who has briefly returned to England to cure himself of a liver complaint. To ingratiate herself, Becky feigns an enthusiasm for all things Indian, including the exotic Indian curries that Jos Sedley has his mother prepare for him. Having 'never tasted the dish before', Becky is encouraged to try it by her host, Jos's father, who thoroughly enjoys the tortures the upstart governess suffers as a result of a palate unaccustomed to generously seasoned dishes (29). Thackeray's juxtaposition of Becky Sharp, an outsider to the Sedleys' prosperous world of middle-class domesticity, with an exotic curry is not accidental: on the eve of Waterloo, curry was as foreign to the middle-class British table as was Becky, the poor, orphaned governess who had yet to make a place for herself in society.

Becky's culinary ignorance helps Thackeray situate his mid-Victorian readers back into the Regency world of the novel. Commercially available in London as early as 1784, curry was not extensively enjoyed until East India Company officials, like the hapless Jos Sedley, began to filter home on leaves during the first few decades of the nineteenth century. Becky's unfortunate encounter with curry suggests that it remained in 1815 a relatively unknown quantity outside of Anglo-Indian circles (Chaudhuri, 1992, 238). However by mid-century it had become a staple in the domestic cookery of the urban bourgeoisie. If memsahibs returning to England integrated curry and rice into the dinners they served family and friends, middle-class women like Eliza Acton and Isabella Beeton introduced curry to an even wider audience through the medium of their best-selling domestic cookery books. Domestic cookery, which came to be defined not only as home cooking for middle-class families but as plain English fare, stood in opposition to the French-influenced cookery found in restaurants, at court and in the great houses of the aristocracy. Professional chefs, men like Charles Elmé Francatelli and Alexis Soyer who occupied the aristocratic end of the cookbook market, provided their readers a French-inflected haute cuisine and scorned the plebeian fare offered up by their female competitors.[7]

The three most influential domestic cookery books written by and for the Victorian middle-class woman – the various reprints and revisions of Maria Rundell's 1807 *Domestic Cookery*, Eliza Acton's 1845 *Modern Cookery in all its Branches* and Isabella Beeton's celebrated 1859 *Book of*

Household Management – all contain chapters on curry. *Modern Domestic Cookery*, a revision of Mrs Rundell's popular cookbook, informs its middle-class readership that 'Curry, which was formerly a dish almost exclusively for the table of those who had made a long residence in India, is now so completely naturalised, that few dinners are thought complete unless one is on the table' (Rundell, 1851, 311). *Modern Domestic Cookery* can claim curry as a 'naturalised' dish in part because it ignores the origins of curry in Indian – not Anglo-Indian – culture. However *Modern Domestic Cookery* is not alone in its insistence on curry as a naturalised element of British cooking. Like the updated versions of Mrs Rundell's *Modern Domestic Cookery*, Eliza Acton's *Modern Cookery* also quite explicitly represents curry as a naturalised food. In her introduction, Acton advises her readers that, along with English dishes, 'we have intermingled many foreign ones which we know to be excellent of their kind, and which now so far belong to our national cookery, as can be met with commonly at all refined modern tables' (xii). To allay any doubts about which foreign dishes truly belong to the national cuisine and which do not, she offers an entire chapter on 'Foreign and Jewish Cookery'. Acton's Indian recipes are to be found here. The categorical imperative of *Modern Cookery* intermingles curries with traditional British fare in an unappetising chapter entitled 'Curries, Potted Meats, etc.'. By the 1840s curry has so thoroughly become a standard ingredient in the British kitchen and consciousness that the Duke of Norfolk can even recommend (and suffer much public derision for it) that the starving Irish might want to consider curry powder as an excellent and nutritious substitute for their rotting potatoes.

The Duke apparently took the figurative phrase, 'the natives of India live on curry', and literalised it; but the incident, in which politics, curry powder and potatoes collide, points to a larger truth about Victorian Britain: it was a culture that understood cooking to be a highly politicised act. The Victorians were, after all, heirs to the philosophy of the great French gastronome Jean-Anthèlme Brillat-Savarin, whose monumental *Physiology of Taste, or Meditation on Transcendental Cookery* (1826) declared that you are what you eat and that the destiny of nations depends on their diets (xxxiii). Victorian cookbook authors frequently call attention to the relationship between a nation's fate and its fare, so that, for example, Mrs Beeton begins her *Book of Household Management* by reminding readers that 'as with the commander of any army, or the leader of an enterprise, so it is with the mistress of a house' (4). And when Charles Pierce, author of the *The Household Manager* (1857), expresses concern that 'there is nothing else in which England is so much behind the rest of the civilised world as in her eating', he immediately compensates for this perceived inferiority by fabricating a distinction between rational, Western cooking and the passionate, seductive foods of the Orient. Pierce distinguishes Oriental cookery, which 'consists in the combination of the most far-fetched and incongruous materials, with the strongest, the most *quin*-t-essential sauces, and the most fiery spices', from Analytic, or Intellectual Cookery, which 'embraces the preparation of that which is not only most pleasing to the palate, but most salutary to the stomach, and beneficial to the constitution; its objects are pleasing and rational, and its forms elegant' (15–17). By figuring the 'incongruous' and 'fiery' food of the East against the classically rational and fundamentally sound cookery of the West, Pierce easily reproduces the Manichean oppositions of colonial discourse and projects them onto national cuisines.

Perhaps the conflation of a nation's diet with its destiny reaches its apogee in 1923, with the publication of Jessie Conrad's *A Handbook of Cookery for a Small House*, complete with a preface by her husband, Joseph Conrad, the great modern explorer of colonial themes and himself a naturalised British subject; although given the traditional British fare Mrs Conrad cooks up – everything from 'Bubble and Squeak' to 'Beef Tea' – one might forget (or, one might be invited to forget) that the Polish-born Conrad's origins lie in Eastern Europe. Jessie Conrad's cookbook acutely reminds us that women played a leading part in the process of incorporating and domesticating the Other. For with the Englishness of its cooking, an Englishness of which her husband is the 'Living Example' (v), Mrs Conrad's *Handbook of Cookery for a Small House* effaces Mr Conrad's alien origins and thus culturally naturalises the (already) legally naturalised novelist. In the preface to his wife's English cookbook, Conrad follows Brillat-Savarin and connects good cookery to the greatness of nations, offering the readers of *A Handbook of Cookery* a theory of dyspepsia and cultural decline:

A great authority upon North American Indians accounted for the sombre and excessive ferocity characteristic of these savages by the theory that as a race they suffer from perpetual indigestion. The Noble Red Man was a mighty hunter but his wives had not mastered the art of conscientious cookery. And the consequences were deplorable. The Seven Nations around the Great Lakes and the Horse-tribes of the Plains were but one vast prey to raging dyspepsia. The Noble Red Men were great warriors, great orators, great masters of outdoor pursuits; but the domestic life of the wigwams was clouded by the morose irritability which follows the consumption of ill-cooked food. The gluttony of their indigestible feasts was a direct incentive to counsels of unreasonable violence. Victims of gloomy imaginings, they lived in abject submission to the wiles of a multitude of fraudulent medicine men – quacks – who haunted their existence with vain promises and false nostrums from the cradle to the grave. (vi–vii)

Conrad's explanatory scheme for the 'savageness' of America's indigenous population becomes intelligible in a discourse that politicised cooking.

Given this self-conscious politicisation of food, it is not surprising that while repatriated memsahibs could introduce the culinary artefacts of their Indian experiences into their resettled British homes, Englishwomen in India had to reproduce England in India. Colonial wives and mothers, when stationed with their husbands in India, functioned as the living symbols of English culture. The most popular domestic manual, Flora Annie Steel's *The Complete Indian Housekeeper and Cook* (1888), advised memsahibs on how to keep a British house and cook a British diet despite the hardships of doing so in an alien environment. Indian food (in India) was left to cosmopolitans and connoisseurs, men like Colonel Kenney Herbert. Recreating domestic space on foreign soil is clearly the purpose Mr Sedley, Jos's concerned father, attributes to the memsahib. Although the marriage between Becky Sharp and Jos Sedley never comes off, the elder Sedley, despite his rude treatment of the governess, gives his tacit approval to the union because in contemplating the alternative, a black daughter-in-law and a parcel of 'mahogany grandchildren' (62), he chooses class over race as the less objectionable category. Thackeray proves that Mr Sedley's anxieties about the dangers the colonial enterprise represents to his family are misplaced, but Sedley nevertheless willingly embraces the socially marginal Becky Sharp in the hope that she will return to Boggley Wollah and serve as a buffer between Jos and India, or more particularly, between Jos and the Indian woman who might induce him to produce a mahogany grandchild. For Mr Sedley, the memsahib protects the British race from the contaminating influence of India precisely because she can reproduce – literally and figuratively – Great Britain in Boggley Wollah.

Like her more adventurous sister abroad, the Englishwoman at home could remake the foreign into the domestic by virtue of her own domesticity. She not only imported foreign items into the home, but she could transform them from foreign delicacies into local specialities. In being brought back to England and located within the domestic sphere, which for the Victorians would have been the realm of 'natural' relations, curry could be naturalised, converted from the exotic into the familiar (and the familial) through its association with the woman's domain of the home and kitchen. In *Vanity Fair*, when Jos returns from his ten years in India, he transfers all his curry-making expertise to his mother, who with much maternal affection prepares 'a fine curry for her son' (29). This process converts Jos's foreign curries into his mother's home cooking, with all its emotional and symbolic resonances: the Sedleys induce their son to stay at home and join in a family meal by tempting him with 'a pillau ... just as you like it' (25), as if he had been dining off his mother's Indian entrées all his life.

The middle-class Sedleys were not the only imperialists enjoying home-cooked curry in the nineteenth century, for by the mid-century curry began to work its way into the daily diets of the more prosperous members of the working classes.[8] In 'Curry' (1857), which appeared in *Punch*'s 'The Poetical Cookery-Book', the poem's anonymous speaker, the 'Samiwel' of the fourth line, describes a scene that is thoroughly domestic and English, localised in the world of lower-class London:

> Three pounds of veal my darling girl prepares,
> And chops it nicely into little squares;
> Five onions next prepares the little minx
> (The biggest are the best her Samiwel thinks).
> And Epping butter, nearly half a pound,
> And stews them in a pan until they're brown'd.
>
> What's next my dexterous little girl will do?
> She pops the meat into the savoury stew,
> With curry powder, table-spoonfulls three,
> And milk a pint (the richest that may be);
> And when the dish has stewed for half-an-hour,
> A lemon's ready juice she'll o'er it pour:
> Then, bless her! then she gives the luscious pot
> A very gentle boil—and serves quite hot.
>
> P.S. Beef, mutton, rabbit, if you wish;
> Lobsters, or prawns, or any kind of fish
> Are fit to make A CURRY. 'Tis, when don,
> A dish for emperors to feed upon. (474–475)

Here a silent wife dutifully prepares an evening meal for her unhelpful husband, a recognizable London 'type': 'Samiwel' is literary cockney for 'Samuel', as in 'Samivel' Weller, the streetwise London servant in Dickens's *The Pickwick Papers* (1836). In fact the only thing that might seem out of place in this quintessentially Victorian piece is that the meal made for a king has been upgraded into a 'dish fit for emperors to feed upon'. But then Indian curry belongs to the Victorian interior as much as tea and crumpets; and that belonging points to ways in which the Victorians understood India to be theirs. The budding imperialist Samiwel, who has already been initiated into domesticity, is now being initiated into imperialism, whereby 'the domestic "under classes" could become the imperial "over classes"' by virtue of their Britishness (Mackenzie, 1984, 254).

Ultimately curry became so 'completely naturalised' that it could be given back to India. Curry, which began as an English fabrication of Indian food, was domesticated by middle-class Victorian women in the first half of the nineteenth century and then commodified and returned to India as the gift of its 'civiliser' in the second half. Writing of the various imperial exhibitions held to display and celebrate the spoils of empire, beginning with the Great Exhibition held in London's Crystal Palace in 1851, Thomas Richards (1990) notes that 'the commodity looked like a dutiful civil servant of the Empire. Torn from the colonial world, abundance was everywhere; yet, by an astonishing reversal the English believed not that they had stolen the fruit of the earth from colonial countries but that, in taking it, they had bestowed it on them' (166). Curry, first appropriated from India and later bestowed upon it, is just such a commodity; and the way it was marketed at the end of the century underscores its ideological function. Curry advertisements publicised and popularised the image of the British as indulgent, openhanded masters. Those sponsored by J. Edmunds, sole proprietor of 'The Empress' brand curry powders, pastes and chutneys, which bore the motto 'The sun in her dominions never sets' on every bottle and tin, are a prime example. In the Edmunds advertisements, figures ranging from the former Viceroy of India's chef to natives of India are called on to bear witness and offer thanks to J. Edmunds for the excellencies of his curry. The Maharaja of Kuch Behar testifies that he prefers Mr Edmunds's curry powder 'to any other he had tried', while three Indians from Shahpore, brought to England to execute the wood carving for the 1886 Colonial and Indian Exhibition, announce that since their arrival they 'have used no other CURRIE INGREDIENTS but those supplied by Mr J. Edmunds, Stonefield Terrace, London, and we found those same excellent' (Edmunds, 1903, vii–x). In all of these testimonials, England emerges as a beneficent nation, dispensing curry powder and pastes to grateful Indians. Moreover, these Indian subjects are not merely testifying to the superior qualities of Mr Edmunds's curry products, but they are thanking Mr Edmunds – and by extension the British public – for bestowing 'The Empress' upon them, both the curry and the Queen.

In this exchange between the (male) Indian consumer and Mr Edmunds, the British merchant, the figure of the female has also been reduced to a commodity ('The Empress') functioning as the token of exchange that bonds one man to another in the homosocial union of commerce and empire. However, it is important to remember that Mr Edmunds can offer his curry powders to his Indian customers as the product of England's shores only because Mrs Edmunds – and thousands of women like her – had already domesticated curry, thus making it available for their husbands and sons to bestow on the Indian peoples. As figures of domesticity, British women helped incorporate Indian food into the national diet and India into the British Empire; and this process of incorporation remains etched on the pages of the domestic cookery books written by middle-class women like Eliza Acton and Isabella Beeton. If a later, more aggressively masculinist imperial discourse tries to erase them from the annals of empire – an effacement revealed both in Mr Edmunds's advertisements and Conrad's tribute to good cooking – early Victorian cookery books attest to the important ideological function women performed in the construction of Victorian imperialism. At both the symbolic and the practical level, Victorian women domesticated imperialism.

Notes

1   For example, see the essays that were first published in a 1990 volume of *Women's Studies International Forum* and which later reappeared in Chaudhuri and Stroebel, *Western Women and Imperialism*, 1992. In particular, Ramusack's 'Cultural Missionaries, Maternal Imperialists, Feminist Allies, British Women Activists in India, 1865—1945' details the different positions taken up by Victorian women in India.

2   Narayan's chapter 'Eating Culture' in *Dislocating Cultures*, 1997, points out that 'British curry powder is really a "fabricated" entity, the logic of colonial commerce imposing a term that signified a particular type of dish onto a specific mixture of spices, that then became a fixed and familiar product', p. 164. She goes on to read curry powder as a metaphor for the way India as a fabricated political entity was incorporated into the British Empire.

3   Of course, as Edward Said notes in *Culture and Imperialism*, 1993, 'the novel, as a cultural artefact of bourgeois society, and imperialism are unthinkable without each other', pp. 70–71. The relationship between the British novel and imperialism has been traced out in a series of recent critical works in addition to Said's *Culture and Imperialism*, including Perera's *Reaches of Empire*, 1991; and Azim's *The Colonial Rise of the Novel*, 1993.

4   Robert Young argues that the conjunction of the 1857 Mutiny, the American Civil War and the Jamaica Insurrection at Morant Bay in 1865 'altered the popular perceptions of race and racial difference and formed the basis of widespread acceptance of the new, and remarkably up-front, claims of a permanent racial superiority', 1995, p. 92.

5   Cynthia Eagle Russett points out in *Sexual Science: The Victorian Construction of Womanhood*, 1989, p. 25, that nineteenth-century enthnology, a 'kind of progenitor of anthropology more interested in cultural than biological diversity', considered races to be 'not the cause but the result of cultural and environmental diversity, and their

inferior status could in principle be remedied'. In other words, a cultural hierarchy predominated until it was superseded after mid-century by the racially determined hierarchies emerging from the new fields of evolutionary biology and anthropology. It is clearly ethnological thinking, which emphasized the primacy of cultural differences over racial ones, that underpinned utilitarian reformist principles.

6   For additional information on Florence White, an early twentieth-century food folklorist intent on preserving the vanishing 'English' cookery tradition, and the importance of *Good Things in England*, 1932, as a part of that preservation movement, see Chapter 8 of Stephen Mennell's *All Manners of Food: Eating and Taste in England from the Middle Ages to the Present*, 1985.

7   Mennell observes that by the nineteenth century 'French cookery captured the social commanding heights in England more decisively than it had in the previous century, and national differences in cuisine became entangled with class differences in Britain' p. 200. This resulted in what he labels the 'decapitation' of English cookery, whereby professional cookery was largely done in the French style, leaving English cookery no 'elite models of its own to copy, and this probably contributed to the mediocrity which both contemporary and subsequent observers remarked on in English cookery in the Victorian era', p. 206.

8   While the cuisine he offered the upper classes remained resolutely French, Charles Elmé Francatelli, the chief cook to Queen Victoria, included several curry recipes in his *A Plain Cookery Book for the Working Classes*, 1861. *A Plain Cookery Book* also instructs its readers on the proper method for cooking a rabbit, if it so happens that 'considerate gentlefolks who possess game preserves' may give them one, p. 46.

Chapter 6

'In Close Touch With her Government': Women and the Domestic Science Movement in World War One Propaganda

Celia M. Kingsbury

From the spas of Battle Creek to the cattle industry's lawsuit against Oprah Winfrey, Americans have a history of politicising food. Perhaps nowhere does that politicisation become more apparent than during America's involvement in World War One. When America entered the war in 1917, one of the main concerns was maintaining control of an already unstable system of production and distribution. With the hope of controlling the consumption and distribution of food both in the US and abroad, Congress passed the Food Control Act (Lever Act) on 10 August 1917. On the same date, the United States Food Administration was created by Executive Order to oversee implementation of the newly enacted laws.[1] It was in this context that Herbert Hoover, director of the new agency, turned to the domestic science movement for help in spreading the word regarding conservation. Already bent on changing the habits of American housewives, domestic scientists eagerly joined the war effort, creating their own propaganda and utilising that of the Food Administration to promote conservation and at the same time, to urge modernisation.

Food historians Laura Shapiro, in *Perfection Salad: Women and Cooking at the Turn of the Century* (1986), and Harvey Levenstein, in *Revolution at the Table: The Transformation of the American Diet* (1988), both briefly address the efforts of the Food Administration. In a chapter titled 'Food Will Win the War', a slogan that appeared on everything from posters to baking powder recipe pamphlets, Levenstein acknowledges the working relationship between the domestic scientists (or home economists, as they became known), and Hoover and the Food Administration, and their shared faith in the scientific approach to food (139). Both Levenstein and Shapiro also suggest that the domestic scientists' involvement in the war effort further elevated the status of the women who laboured to spread the scientific approach to housework in general. According to Shapiro, the 'new relevance' that the movement achieved through the war effort, allowed it to 'make a spectacular surge to legitimacy and emerge from the war effort as a nationally recognized profession', albeit a profession ghettoised in college and university home economics departments (218–219).

Shapiro's examination of the history of 'domestic science' is indeed thorough. In the infancy of the movement, as she explains, domestic scientists sought to educate women in the new science of nutrition, to engage industry to produce labour-saving, nutritious food products, and to establish, in Shapiro's words, 'the link between science and housework' (4). That their goals involved, in Shapiro's view, a 'profound mistrust of women', does not detract from the movement's missionary zeal, nor from the intensity of its belief that, competent to the task or not, women were responsible for the moral wellbeing of the American character (235). Old-fashioned housewives who refused to take advantage of modern conveniences, she maintains, 'bore the responsibility for the failings of the American home, failings that seemed to lead directly to poverty, disease, alcoholism, unemployment, and all the other social miseries apparent at the turn of the century' (4). By contrast, the woman who understood the importance of calorie and nutrition charts, the woman who used scientifically tested recipes, held the keys to the nation's future. According to Shapiro, the movement never sought taste or pleasure as an end in cooking, but 'dietary standardization', an agenda that both paralleled and served the Food Administration's cause. Rather, food reformers pursued, in the germ-free modern kitchen, the cure for the nation's ills, and subsequently the path to the nation's victory in the war.

Missing from both Shapiro's and Levenstein's studies is an examination of the rich body of propaganda that links the domestic science movement and the Food Administration, without which neither would have achieved their aims. In this essay, it is with the enhancement of their respective agendas through propaganda that I am concerned. Magazine and newspaper articles, housekeeping guides, textbooks, cooking classes, recipe booklets, posters and the ubiquitous pledge card: all bore the evangelical stamp of leading domestic scientists. Thetta Quay Franks, Ida Bailey Allen, Janet McKenzie Hill and many others involved in the Domestic Science movement contributed recipes, books and articles to the war effort. Their goal was both to help 'win the war' and to increase the efficiency of the American household by enlisting American women in war service. The militancy of these domestic scientists dovetails nicely into the war effort.

As Levenstein suggests, 'the home economists and reformers had been preparing the appropriate lessons for years' (138), but the range and diversity of textual interactions between domestic science and the war effort went well beyond those examined by Levenstein or Shapiro.

In the pre-war work of Franks, described and explained in *The Margin of Happiness: The Reward of Thrift* (1917), we can see the work of a domestic scientist foreshadowing Hooverisation, the popular name given to Hoover's plan to conserve food without the use of rationing.[2] Insisting that women have vast powers in matters of national importance, Franks asks, 'How many women realize the dignity and value of their position as guardians of the national health, spenders of the national wealth? Much of the power and influence of a nation lie [sic] within the keeping of its women. How many American women have learned to think nationally?' Among what Franks lists as 'some of the nation's most urgent problems' which she believes women can solve are 'the high cost of living, the increasing death rate from organic disease, and the rising divorce rate' (Franks, 1917, 3–4). Poor housekeeping, in fact, according to Franks, is responsible for the increase in the divorce rate in the US (22–23). To substantiate her assertion, she cites an article from the *Newark Evening News* of 28 March 1916 which states 'Women's ignorance and neglect of homemaking arts were pointed out as a leading cause of family desertion, at a conference yesterday afternoon of social workers.' The 'proof' for this conclusion is a statement made by a Mr Gascoyne, who declares, 'much of the blame for the delinquent husband rests on the undesirable home conditions caused by the presence of an untrained wife' (27).

To avoid the inevitable disgrace of incompetence, Franks goes on in her book to instruct women in the ways of intelligent housekeeping by suggesting, among other things, that all packaged food be stored in glass jars with etched or painted labels and that a grocery list be prepared on the typewriter and maintained in alphabetical order. As to the arrangement of the kitchen itself, all utensils must be hung from hooks for easy access, and all similar utensils must be 'placed together in orderly fashion and each has its allotted hook and must be replaced after it has been used' (118, 134). Since many women were also responsible for managing the family budget, Franks details specific suggestions for shouldering that responsibility and, at the same time, repeats her belief that homemaking is a 'social service'. A budget allotment for 'betterment', including books and the theatre, she believes, 'has ethical as well as economic values', because 'love of home and all that home stands for is the only safeguard for the nation against the growing tendency to evade the responsibilities of home life' (114). In this interesting example of circular reasoning, Franks links national interests and national security with morality and the home. In the American context, the Victorian ideal of progress reverberates in the connection with science and invention: Franks's work intimates that the up-to-date kitchen range could save the world.

In the chapter 'Cooking as a Science', Franks suggests just that. Here she links, in some cases correctly, improper diet with diseases such as heart disease. Using charts to compare the death rates in the US with death rates in England and Wales, Franks concludes that Americans eat too much meat, too much sugar, 'twice as much … as Europeans do', and too little whole grain flour (149). While we might applaud what sounds like a sensible and modern approach to eating, we cannot overlook the militancy with which she presents this 'scientific' material, as well as her strong connection between food and morality. Eating too much meat, according to Franks, 'overworks the liver and kidneys in their effort to eliminate the poisonous products produced by the excess' (148).

In Franks's hands, statistics become ammunition and food, well organised and well prepared, fights against a multitude of sins for which Franks has no tolerance. Her ultimate goal is to reach the American woman, to convince her that the application of scientific methods to cooking is a patriotic duty, and that ultimately the responsibility for the wellbeing of her family and her country is hers.

The war serves Franks's purpose by providing an incentive for women to comply. In what amounts to a manifesto at the chapter's conclusion, Franks asks, 'must we not conclude that cooking must be practised as a science in order to guard the future health of the nation? … How long will American women leave the deciding of the national eating habits to chefs and cooks in whom this wealth of valuable knowledge is lacking?' (152)

In terms of practical application, Franks details the organisation of Classes in Cooking and Household Efficiency through the Civic Committee of the Women's Club of Orange, New Jersey. Cooking Lesson 2 includes instruction in the preparation of scalloped cabbage, cauliflower *au gratin* and boiled carrots, illustrating domestic scientists' love of the simple and assumption of students' ignorance, in this case, forty-four housewives and twenty-two housemaids. A number of details are striking here. The twenty gas burners available in the Domestic Science Department of East Orange High School, rented for the sessions, could not meet the enrolment demands, so two women looked on each week rather than working directly with the recipes. US government publications supplied the recipes for every session. And finally, the women were dressed in identical uniforms that included 'a very becoming cap like those worn by professional nurses' (212). This uniform, or one very much like it, would soon become the uniform of that literal 'Army of American Housewives', the 'soldiers of the kitchen', that is, any woman who mailed in her pledge card to the US Food Administration, a card which signalled her acceptance of government intervention in the kitchen.

Once America entered the war in 1917, the values of domestic science became the values of the government war effort, and the campaign for scientific cooking became a campaign linking food conservation with military victory. Using the language of domestic science, the propaganda of the Food Administration brought women into direct contact with the war by urging them to enlist in the 'Army of American housewives' (*Selected Recipes for Wartimes*, 1918, 1). As culinary soldiers, women were held responsible not only for the moral salvation of the country through housekeeping, but, through food planning, responsible for its military salvation as well. Posters, books and magazine articles all ask women in the name of national security to conserve food, to once again prepare food at home, to use 'foods obtainable near home', and to see that 'large quantities of perishable foods [were] preserved for later use' (Hoover, 1917, 25). The labour-saving products, canned goods and pre-packaged foods that they had for the past decade been encouraged to use in their food preparation were earmarked for foreign shipment.

The duties of the patriotic housewife were well defined. Hoover, in an appeal published in the August 1917 issue of *Ladies' Home Journal*, 'What I Would Like Women to Do', speaks directly to American women about food shortages in Europe and ways to rectify them at home: 'Every woman', he writes, 'should feel herself definitely engaged in national service in her own kitchen and in her own home.' Alluding to the aspirations of the new domestic science, Hoover goes on to insist that 'the intelligent woman of America must make a proper study of food ratios, so that the most nutritious foods will appear in their proper proportions on the home table.' Hoover's entreaty combines the language of domestic science with a more direct government instruction for the new wartime circumstances. It is followed by an article on baking bread from wheat substitutes. Wheat was one of the most needed commodities in war-ravaged Europe, making conservation of wheat flour at home a top priority. In case the housewife might take lightly the appeal to her sense of patriotic duty, the *Journal* feature included a pledge card to be snipped out and sent to Hoover and the Food Administration. The American woman was thus drawn into the war effort, brought, as the subtitle for both articles proclaims, 'in Close Touch With Her Government' (25–26).

Women who did not subscribe to the *Journal* could find pledge cards everywhere. David M. Kennedy, in *Over Here* (1980), a study of American culture during the war, reports that over half a million volunteers went from door to door distributing pledge cards (118). According to Hoover himself, fourteen million families signed and returned pledge cards, along with seven thousand hotels and restaurants (1917, 12). For women whom the canvassers missed, the Food Administration placed pledge cards in other likely places. *War Cookbook for American Women* (1917), a Food Administration publication, includes a pledge card as well as an explanation of what the pledge entails. Beyond staying in close touch, the American woman is asked to 'remember the needs of the nation as told to them by the Food Administration'. Obedience is the key here. Agreeing to perform 'war service in the home' removes much of the element of choice and autonomy from questions of homemaking. Signing the pledge 'is not a promise to [do] some particular thing, but an agreement to follow directions' (5). The Food Administration's Home Card, sent in response to the pledge card (along with a window card to let neighbours know the family 'belonged' to the Food Administration), gives very specific instructions for compliance. The Home Card of 1918 asked 'every loyal American to help win the war by maintaining rigidly, as a minimum of saving' a programme of two wheatless days a week, every Monday and Wednesday, a meatless day on Tuesday, and porkless days on Tuesday and Saturday. Sugar and fats were to be saved every day and vegetables used 'abundantly'. To drive the point home, the card stated: 'DISLOYALTY IN LITTLE THINGS GIVES AID TO THE ENEMY.'

Still, the introduction to the *War Cookbook for American Women* also emphasises availability, paying attention to 'conditions that vary from day to day', and goes on to explain: 'In the spring, for example, when the stock of potatoes ran low, the directions said: Eat rice; but when the potato crop was harvested, the directions said: Eat potatoes, the rice is wanted for the Army.' While civilian needs will generally take a back seat to those of fighting forces and food shortages were a constant reality, especially in Europe, the tone of this appeal, issued on behalf of the 'cause of honour and democracy', is that of Orwellian Newspeak. The implication is that the housewife does not have the necessary tools to plan menus based on availability and therefore she must be guided and continually reminded of her patriotic duty.

Hoover and the US Food Administration targeted school children and college students in much the same vein. Textbooks such as *Food Saving and Sharing* (1918), sponsored by the National Education Association, were written for use in 'the instruction of American children' (v). Among its contributors were the editor of the *Journal of Home Economics* and a professor of food chemistry at Columbia University. *Food Saving and*

Sharing asks children to contribute to national security and world health by saving food, specifically to 'prove your Americanism by eating less'. According to what was then most recent knowledge on nutrition, the five food groups – fruits and vegetables; meat, eggs, milk and cheese; cereals and grain; sugar and sweets; and fats – are represented by imaginary booths at a food market which intelligent children visit with shopping baskets. In this way, children are instructed in domestic science and world politics and, most obviously, engaged directly in the war effort.

On the college front, *Food and the War: A Textbook for College Classes* (1918) also provides lessons in basic nutrition. Written for students of both genders, *Food and the War* begins with an appeal to each from Hoover. While the letter to 'college men' does carry the request to 'obey the food regulations', it also implores young men 'by every legal means [to] prevent their violation by others' and finally to 'be aggressive agents of the Food Administration wherever you go'. University women, on the other hand, are firmly admonished in the introduction to pursue domestic science:

> All our questions now center in food; its production, its distribution, its use, its conservation. The more you know about these things, the more valuable you will be, and the greater will be your service to humanity. We urge you to pursue those studies which deal with food, and to train yourselves for real leadership.

Texts such as *Food and the War* were prepared with the advice from professors from many of the nation's top universities, including an Associate Professor of Food Chemistry from the University of Chicago and an Associate Professor of Social Ethics from Harvard. The text itself reads much like a textbook in domestic science and is undoubtedly designed to produce those with 'real leadership' like Franks, and more authors of war recipe books. In the back, 'A Laboratory Manual' includes chemical experiments involving food items, instructions for food preparation including recipes using substitutes for wheat flour and sugar, and a detailed assignment for a student demonstration of one of the cooking processes involved. Suggested topics include the preparation of cheese soufflé for meatless meals, wheatless biscuits, and white sauce made from a wheat substitute (372–374). Thus students are themselves prepared to pass on these techniques to other culinary soldiers.

Many did so. The Woman's Council of National Defense, New Hampshire College of Agriculture and the Mechanic Arts in co-operation with the Food Administration published a series of leaflets 'in behalf of the food emergency work'. The first leaflet, Extension Circular No. 21 (1917), deals with the use of fats. And in a preliminary note, the Federal Food Administrator for New Hampshire, Huntley N. Spaulding, presses the women of New Hampshire to take up the call to culinary arms when he declares: 'There is no greater opportunity and responsibility before the women of New Hampshire households than that of helping to conserve food supplies for our country and for our allies. ... The lessons ... are worthy of your earnest attention and observance' (2). Recipe 8 in this first leaflet is a formula for making soap from fats and lye (4), a practice we might have suspected vanished from the American home, except perhaps from the most rural, by the end of the nineteenth century. We can only guess how many New Hampshire households actually resorted to the use of lye soap, but we can assume the leaflets contributed to the already large body of propaganda directed at women and devoted to food conservation through domestic science.

Ladies' magazines were also quickly responsive to demands for sounding the call to culinary arms. *Ladies' Home Journal* brought the demands of Hooverising into every middle-class American home. But the more specialised domestic science journals also responded to America's need to conserve. *American Cookery: Formerly The Boston Cooking-School Magazine of Culinary Science and Domestic Economics* promotes the appeals of the Food Administration by including wartime recipes and menus and patriotic vignettes and poems alongside its articles on home decorating, such as the August–September 1918 feature, 'Harmony in the Breakfast Room'. The bound volume of the journal for 1918, through its articles and advertising, reflects changes in food shortages and Hoover's efforts to influence consumption in the home. In a news release of 27 May 1918, Hoover had asked that 'all those whose circumstances permit shall abstain from wheat and wheat products in any form until the next harvest'. In the August-September issue of *American Cookery*, the editor, Janet McKenzie Hill, herself the author of a recipe book, *War Time Recipes* (1918), ponders the 'word from the United States Food Administration', which also asks for further limitations on the consumption of meat and chicken (124). The request to abstain from the use of wheat flour results in the inclusion of bread, cake and cookie recipes using everything from rice flour to rye flour. In the 'Queries and Answers' section, Hill, extolling the virtues of rice flour, questions the patriotism of housewives who fail to conserve wheat. Instead of using half rice and half wheat flour in recipes for white cake, Hill maintains that 'If one's desire to serve her country is of more importance than the color of the cake served, use barley or rye flour to replace the wheat flour' (135). Hill had already been suggesting such changes: in the February issue, in the section 'Seasonable and Tested Recipes', she includes a formula for Corn Flour Parker House Rolls and Barley Biscuits, as well as for sandwiches made of cream cheese and decorated with crossed strips of pimento to remind diners of the Red Cross (500–502).

The patriotic woman was expected to comply. If not, she ran the risk of censure or ridicule. In the same February issue of *American Cookery*, an article called 'The Basis of Victory' by Ladd Plumley once again places the burden of victory on the American housewife when it asserts the idea that 'well-cooked food ... is what will bring quick and complete victory to America'. Because of the food problem, Plumley demands that women and girls must become more absorbed in cooking than they have been in the past. And there is no room for failure, for incompetence. Plumley staunchly maintains: 'If she is not an efficient cook, cannot make good bread, cannot make good pie, cannot make good cake, she should blush for herself. If she is not a good cook, she should take up cookery, and, as a serious study.' Plumley goes on to say that trained nurses should be able to cook because a 'well-fed patient has many times the chance of recovery than the wounded soldier who is served with ill-prepared food or has an insufficient diet' (484).

An editorial from the March issue agrees with Plumley. Reporting news that 'the girl students in six hundred American colleges' are going to be taking classes in cooking, no doubt using *Food and the War* as a text, the editors laud the plan and assert that 'thousands of bushels of wheat and other foodstuffs will be saved by this campaign, it is estimated' (575). And, beyond war-related benefits of these courses, the editors echo Thetta Quay Franks in suggesting that the introduction of domestic science as a serious course of study for women will have a more general result in the form of 'vastly improved and healthier conditions of home life throughout the land' (575–576).

If the editorials, articles, recipes and menus are not sufficient to convince the readers of *American Cookery* to conserve food, the magazine also includes poems and vignettes demonstrating the need for compliance. The March issue, furthering the argument for domestic science education, includes a vignette, 'On "Having a Case"' by 'The Wiser Person'. In this little story, an inexperienced housekeeper, faced with the problem of her 'girl's' day off and hungry men to feed, relies on eggs and bread. Confiding to her neighbour, The Wiser Person, the young wife admits her panic. Versed in domestic science, The Wiser Person enumerates, in enough detail for readers to duplicate, the emergency dishes the untrained woman could have prepared had she had a case of canned soup on hand in her pantry. All the recipes involve either stretching canned soup by diluting it, mixing it with stale bread for a 'scallop', or using it to add variety to egg dishes and soufflés. Convinced, the young wife rushes off to order a case of soup from her grocer (588–590).

Beneath the vignette, however, a more explicitly propagandist message appears in the form of a 'poem' to Herbert Hoover. 'A Hoovercessional!' by Caroline Louise Sumner proclaims:

> But since this is the edict stern,
>   If we would conquer Kaiser B,
> To disobey we'll quickly spurn!
>   We'll all respond to Hoover's plea!
> O Mr. Hoover, we're won o'er,
> We'll starve for 'FREEDOM EVERMORE!' (588–590)

Popular sheet music of the day also reflected Hoover's call to conserve food. Printed on red, white and blue sheet music embellished by a large eagle, the song, 'Hoover Hooverize' by Mrs Melrose Scales of Dallas Texas declares: 'We'll Hoover Hooverize/ We'll cut out cakes and pies/ Have bread Puddin's/ O they're good uns/ We must all economize.' The song is, of course, dedicated to Herbert Hoover and approved by the US Food Administration.

The task of Hooverising American women was embraced by many American businesses and in much the same terms as those outlined above. Manufacturers of food products assisted the Food Administration in drafting women into home front service through their advertising campaigns. Calumet Baking Powder along with other manufacturers of baking powder published recipe booklets containing recipes using alternatives to wheat flour. In addition, the booklets published letters and manifestos written by leading domestic scientists of the day. Calumet's booklet opens with a message signed by Maude Marie Costello, who was 'of the Domestic Science Branch of the University of Chicago', Costello invites housewives to '"Enlist" in the Army for the conservation of food and not … wait to be "Drafted"'(*Selected Recipes for Wartimes*, 1918, 1). Royal Baking Powder dedicates its recipe book to 'the housewives of the United States who are assisting the Government in its work through the Food Administration' (*Best War Time Recipes,* 1918).

Commercial publications such as the Calumet recipe booklet closely followed the directions on the Food Administration Home Card, urging housewives to plan two wheatless days on Monday and Wednesday of every week, one wheatless meal every day, one meatless day on Tuesday and one meatless meal every day, as well as other culinary sacrifices. 'If'', the recipe booklet admonishes the housewife, 'we are selfish or even careless, we are disloyal, we are the enemy of the home' (9). And again in copy which parallels a Food Administration poster, the booklet asks citizens to 'remember that every flag that flies opposite the enemies' is by proxy the American flag' (11). The poster itself depicts the flags of the Allies and asks Americans to 'Support Every Flag that Opposes Prussianism – Eat Less of the Food Fighters Need.' For commercial companies, self-interest and patriotism could correspond. Janet McKenzie Hill, in *War Time Recipes*, explains in her introduction that the 'U.S. Food Administration allows the name of "Victory Bread" to be applied to any bread containing twenty percent or more of wheat substitute' (4). Copyrighted by the Procter & Gamble Company, manufacturer of the then new butter substitute, Crisco, *War Time Recipes* uses Crisco in every recipe. As Shapiro points out, even before the war, the 'best-known cooks of the day happily identified themselves with the manufacturers and processors who were applying scientific techniques to food on such a dramatic scale' (192). Ida Bailey Allen's 1927 cookbook, *The Modern Method of Preparing Delightful Foods*, was endorsed and distributed by Corn Products Refining Company. Allen's recipes call for Mazola, Karo and Argo, all of which products are advertised in outlined text boxes throughout the cookbook. The policies of the Food Administration gave certain commercial companies the opportunity to advertise their own product and remain patriotic at the same time.

Food manufacturers, however, were not the only businesses that advertised and provided war recipes at the same time. Dr D. Jayne & Son of Philadelphia, makers of Dr D. Jayne's Family Medicines, published booklets instructing housewives in 'The Preserving of Fruits', 'How to Do Pickling' and, related to the wheat shortage, preparing 'War Breads'. Adjacent to an advertisement for 'Jayne's Expectorant,' cooks could find recipes for Rice Bread and Arcadian Valley Bread made of cornmeal and rolled oats (*Recipes for War Breads*, 1918, 6–7). In the short preface at the beginning of the booklet, Dr D. Jayne's Family Medicines admits that the goal of the publication is to 'bring again to your notice the merits of our preparations'. But since there is a war on, the flyleaf explains, 'it has been our unremitting effort to supply much needed information of such a kind, and in such a manner, as would be worthy of a business which has seen four great wars in its lifetime'. On the cover of the recipe book, a rosy-cheeked housewife in a white apron hands a loaf of home-baked bread to Uncle Sam, who holds her in a fatherly embrace and regards her with a kindly expression.

Profit motives notwithstanding, commercial companies were also apparently prepared to sacrifice advertising space in favour of the war effort. In a supplement to *The North American* of Philadelphia on Sunday 14 April 1918, Mrs Anna B. Scott, 'cooking expert and food economist', proposes what she calls her '50–50' plan. This asks housewives to use 'in every recipe that calls for wheat flour only one half the amount stipulated, substituting for the remainder something that will admirably take its place'. According to Mrs Scott, the '50–50' plan uses less wheat than 'even seven wheatless meals a week' without depriving diners of bread. This sixteen-page supplement includes copies of six Food Administration posters, including Henry Patrick Raleigh's graphic 'Hunger' printed in a position where, in other publications, advertisements might appear.

The Food Administration's poster campaign, in urging conservation and participation, damned the wasteful female consumer. Paul Stahr's 'Be Patriotic' shows Lillian Gish, or a Gish look-alike, as Miss Columbia, arms outstretched, asking the American woman to 'sign your country's pledge to save the food'. By contrast, a Food Administration poster portraying the careless woman shows the woman who does not do her bit as not only the enemy, but as the mythic devourer of men. The woman in this poster is not a champion of domestic science, nor is she in close touch with her government. In one corner of the poster, opposite a black cloud labelled war, a smartly dressed woman who is larger than life sips from a soda glass which merges into the ocean and becomes a vortex into which ships, some bearing the label soldiers, threaten to slip. 'Sugar Means Ships', the poster warns. 'For your beverages', it continues, ships that should be carrying soldiers and supplies would be required to carry sugar. Women should therefore reduce their consumption of sweetened drinks. In the corner labelled war, a soldier summons the ships to 'Hurry!' before, we assume, they are sucked up by those careless and thirsty women who may not heed the call to duty.

Munitions workers and a number of YWCA volunteers were literally involved in the war both in the US and Europe. But one War Garden Commission booklet, *Home Canning and Drying of Vegetables and Fruits* (1919), directly involves the housewife in the violence of war by asking her to 'Can the Kaiser', to 'Back Up the Cannon By Use of the Canner' (1). The booklet, innocuous enough itself, contains instructions for the latest and safest methods of canning and drying the produce from the Victory Garden. But the cover of the book employs an image, also used in other propaganda, of Kaiser Wilhelm stuffed into a pickle jar. Ludicrous enough on the surface, this pickled effigy calls up images of cannibalism, of which the Germans were in fact suspected. Foreshadowing the grim reality of the

Second World War, a famous atrocity story which became part of World War One propaganda was of a so-called corpse factory where bodies of German soldiers supposedly emerged as glycerine for weapons and food for hogs and poultry. According to Paul Fussell (1975), a similar rumour, not necessarily German, placed the factories on the British side. Fussell believes the story grew out of a mistranslation – probably deliberate – of the German word *Kadaver*, a word most often used to refer to the corpses of horses, which were rendered for fat and by-products in German rendering plants (116). In spite of German protests that the word was never used to refer to human remains, *The Times*, citing dictionaries to show that it was, continued to publish articles on the subject, and the British government allowed the rumours to be spread to the allies (Ponsonby, 1928, 103). In an article in the 20 April 1917 issue of *The Times*, two weeks after America's entry into the war, a British sergeant claimed that a German prisoner had told him about the factories. The British soldier stated that '[t]his fellow told me that Fritz calls his margarine "corpse fat" because they suspect that's what it comes from' (108–110). Arthur Ponsonby, in his analysis of propaganda stories *Falsehood in War-Time*, suggests the story was fabricated by Brigadier-General Charteris, who continued to deny responsibility for the story as late as 1925 (108–110). Regardless of its origin, the corpse factory rumour fired the patriotism of citizens on both sides of the Atlantic. The 'Can the Kaiser' image further employs this rumour by appearing to make a joke of implied cannibalism, this time of course with the German leader as the by-product.

Already established as a way of admonishing women, the domestic science movement provided a resource through which the US Food Administration and other patriotic organizations could reach the housewife with their pleas for conservation, their demand for patriotism and their insistence on participation in the war effort. Through posters, cookbooks and ladies' magazines, women were recruited as surely as if they were called to battle on the front lines. For so long the moral torch bearers of the nation, women were asked to win the war with food, in Hoover's words, to 'bring to a successful end the greatest national task that has ever been accepted by the American people' (1917, 25). Given the habit of holding the housewife responsible for the physical, moral and fiscal health of the nation, it should come as no surprise that she might have been held responsible for the outcome of the war as well.

Notes

1 For the history of the Food Administration, see Merritt, *War Time Control of Distribution of Foods: A Short History of the Distribution Division of the United States Food Administration, its Personnel and Achievements*, 1920; and Mullendore, *History of the United States Food Administration, 1917–1919*, 1941. Merritt lists the objectives of the Food Administration as follows: to save food and prevent waste, to distribute food equitably and at the lowest possible price to the consumer, to prevent hoarding, to save transportation, to encourage production, to facilitate the largest possible shipments of food to the Allies with the necessary shipments to neutrals and none to the enemy, and to provide for the growing needs of our army and navy, pp. 2–3.

2 Despite pleas from the European Allies, Hoover resisted the idea of food rationing, depending instead upon 'the spirit of self-sacrifice of the American people ... to accomplish the necessary results upon a voluntary basis', *History of the United States Food Administration*, 1941, p. 12.

INDIVIDUAL INTERVENTIONS

Chapter 7

The Importance of Being Greedy: Connoisseurship and Domesticity in the Writings of Elizabeth Robins Pennell

Talia Schaffer

> I think, therefore, the great interest of the following papers lies in the fact that they are written by a woman – a greedy woman. ('Introduction', *The Feasts of Autolycus*, 1896)

In 1896, an art critic named Elizabeth Robins Pennell published one of the strangest books to appear during what was admittedly a decade of unusual publications. *The Feasts of Autolycus* was a compilation of articles on food and cookery that Pennell had previously published in the *Pall Mall Gazette*.[1] In these articles, Pennell aimed to reconfigure meals as high art, turning eating into an act of intellectual appreciation. She wanted to contest the prevailing assumption that an interest in food denoted a debased bodily greed. At the same time, however, Pennell hoped to reclaim women's appetite as a natural and valid bodily response. *Feasts* therefore tries both to transcend hunger and to justify it. The language that allowed Pennell to work both sides of this divide was aestheticism. By treating food as art, Pennell exalted its status; by constructing herself as a sophisticated connoisseur, she excused her love of eating. Indeed Pennell's artful language makes her book an exemplary text for elucidating just how well aesthetic discourse served women writers in the late nineteenth century.

The 'female aesthetes', the loose coalition of women writers in which Pennell was involved, also included Una Ashworth Taylor, 'John Oliver Hobbes' (Pearl Mary Teresa Richard Craigie), Mary and Jane Findlater, Alice Meynell, 'Michael Field' (Edith Cooper and Katherine Bradley), 'Elizabeth von Arnim' (Mary, Countess Russell), 'Lucas Malet' (Mary St Leger Kingsley Harrison), Ella D'Arcy, Ella Hepworth Dixon, Netta Syrett, 'Vernon Lee' (Violet Paget), and Rosamund Marriott Watson.[2] Between roughly 1870 and 1910, they wrote novels, stories, essays, poems and plays in an aesthetic style that used archaic vocabulary and epigrammatic dialogue. Critics generally approved of the female aesthetes because they were apparently content to produce light, comic, apolitical literature (especially when compared with their much more controversial contemporaries, the New Women novelists). But the female aesthetes' frivolity was often a deliberately self-protective strategy; their obvious self-parody and oblique and artificial descriptions deflected critical scrutiny in an era when most critics believed that women's writing was entirely autobiographical. Moreover using an aesthetic vocabulary to rethink the women's sphere enabled these writers to treat traditionally female occupations with the respect usually reserved for high art. Thus female aesthetes presented themselves as knowledgeable connoisseurs, offering instructions for reconstructing the private spaces of the home, garden and body to accord with the new artistic revolution.

However most aesthetic prose writers tended to avoid the subject of cookery. Two of the central terms of aestheticism are 'taste' and 'consumption', and, in the study of food, these terms are interestingly literalised. Cookery stripped 'taste' and 'consumption' of their mystified auras and reduced them to mere synonyms for ignoble greed. Cookery, then, insisted on the physical sensation of pleasure as the basis of consumption and the meaning of taste. Not only was food ignobly material, it was also dependent upon a kind of labour that aesthetes had trouble idealising: the labour of working-class female cooks.[3] This form of production, associated with disputes over wages and hours, involving tedious and backbreaking labour, and occurring in a hot dark cellar usually infested with black beetles, seemed entirely unromantic. Cookery therefore offered powerful gender and class resistance to aesthetic ideals. It stood for an uncompromising set of categories: woman, working class, labour, physical needs, and the sordid present. Aesthetes preferred to identify themselves with an opposing set of categories: male, aristocratic, intellectualism, abstruse knowledge and the romantic past.

Another reason most aesthetes avoided the topic of food was that Victorian food prided itself on its plainness, and simplicity is a difficult category to accommodate within an aesthetic of connoisseurship. If an entrée was composed of a joint of mutton with no seasonings or sauces, there was precious little to analyse. Heavy, meat-based and monotonous, Victorian meals were supposed to be practical rather than pleasurable. At the mid-century all classes of British society preferred 'honest' food to those dangerously tasty but fundamentally unsound 'French kickshaws'. One observer recalled that a typical festive dinner in the 1840s and 1850s consisted of boiled salmon, boiled calf's head, pie, roast beef, cutlets, stewed beef and joints, followed by game and sweets (D'Avigdor, 1885, 17–19). Sarah Freeman's admirable cultural history, *Mutton and Oysters: The Victorians and their Food* (1989), reveals how déclassée cooking was in the nineteenth century: 'Nobody ... dared to suggest that higher-class women should actually cook' (147). Food preparation was almost entirely relegated to servants and, although mistresses were supposed to oversee the kitchen staff's activities, some never went into the kitchen at all. As Freeman points out, women's fashions contributed to the problem: the enormous crinoline would have attracted kitchen dirt and would have made it nearly impossible (not to mention dangerous) to approach the kitchen fire (148). The combination of an overworked cook and an indifferent mistress virtually guaranteed that meals would have to be the plainest, easiest type possible, especially when that plainness was endorsed by patriotic rhetoric. However Elizabeth Langland makes a persuasive case for the managerial competence of middle-class women in *Nobody's Angels* (1995). In Langland's description of Victorian domesticity, middle-class housekeepers are constantly overseeing cooking and cleaning, hiring and firing servants and keeping the household accounts. The stereotype of the bored, languid middle-class woman reclining on the sofa while the household degenerates into chaos around her may well have been a fiction propagated by the popular press.

During the 1880s and 1890s, new culinary choices emerged, making food preparation a more fashionable hobby amongst middle-class women. The Sale of Food and Drugs Act of 1875 significantly improved the purity of food, reducing fears of dangerously adulterated products.[4] New techniques for food distribution allowed late Victorians to vary their diet. Commercial canned and bottled food appeared, while freezing technology and faster transport made fresher foods available. Growers had also developed new breeding techniques, producing better apples and more palatable tomatoes (although tomatoes still could not be eaten raw) (Freeman, 73). Electric cookers replaced the wildly unreliable gas stoves. As it became easier to cook, cooking became a fashionable way for upper-class and middle-class women to fill their leisure time. Dishes became increasingly complex, since elaborate small meals not only provided pleasurable challenges for these genteel women, but also separated them from the déclassée 'plain cook' (Wilson, 1994; Hunter, 1994; David, 1994). 'The private housewife responded to social and domestic isolation with a series of gestures related to food. Her life revolved around a proliferation of small meals, a snack culture that places enormous emphasis on the significance of food preparation and presentation' (Hunter, 69). It is not surprising, therefore, that in the 1880s English home cooking began to be thoroughly influenced by French cuisine, with its complex sauces and its combinations of herbs. This alteration began to make it possible to view cookery as a mysterious art which could only be performed or interpreted by trained experts.

Pennell was well positioned to bring the gospel of aestheticism to food, for she was one of the central contributors to British aesthetic culture. She was married to Joseph Pennell, an artist who drew for *The Yellow Book*, and co-authored several books with him, including biographies of their friend James McNeill Whistler. The Pennells also held a kind of aesthetic salon on Thursday nights, where prominent figures met and talked, including Whistler, W. E. Henley, Henry Harland, Edmund Gosse, Aubrey Beardsley, John Oliver Hobbes, John Lane, Max Beerbohm, Henry James, William Archer, George Moore, Rosamund Marriott Watson, Alice Meynell, Violet Hunt, Oscar Wilde, and George Bernard Shaw. It was at the Pennells's flat that the idea for *The Yellow Book* was born. Pennell's literary style bears the imprint of this rather flamboyantly artistic circle, as in this description of salad in *The Feasts of Autolycus*: 'Make it of tomatoes, scarlet and stirring, like some strange tropical blossoms decking the shrine of the sun' (16).[5]

However Pennell suffered from doubts about her fitness to associate with so many spectacular writers. She rather humbly perceived herself as an overworked amateur journalist amongst a crowd of literary artists, and later she even regretted that she had conversed with them instead of transcribing their words for posterity (*Nights*, 172). Pennell's own writing tended to the autobiographical. She wrote with unusual facility and loquacity, producing books about her travels, meals, servants, friends, uncle and husband.[6] This continuous account of Pennell's life reveals a sensibility more attuned to the women's magazine custom of printing everyday domestic details than to the aesthetic ideal of carefully selected and rarefied moments. The number of her memoirs also indicates an anxiety to shape the story of her life herself, rather than allowing critics to speculate.

Like other aesthetes, Pennell collected rare antiquities but it was cookbooks that she bought. The collection, perched warily between *objets d'art* and useful household guides, between great works by famous names and anonymous hand-written compilations by household cooks, exemplified her attempt to bridge domestic and aesthetic life. Describing the growth of her collection, she writes: 'Gradually they spread out into an imposing row on my desk; they overflowed to the bookshelves; they piled themselves up in odd corners; they penetrated into the linen closet – the last place, I admit, the neat housekeeper should look for them' (*My Cookery*

Books, 3). In this account, her connoisseurship not only competes with, but actually harms, her domestic instincts. It is interesting to note that she assigns agency to the books, as if they had independently decided to pile themselves up in these inappropriate locations, thereby relieving herself of the accusation of unhousekeeperly practice. Her cookbook collection is unruly and slightly threatening in its invasive force, a sign of her uneasiness at aligning herself with 'real' collectors rather than with 'neat housekeepers'.

Pennell was not the first to apply aesthetic criteria to cookery. In 1885, 'A Wanderer' (Elim Henry D'Avigdor) published *Dinners & Dishes*. 'A Wanderer' describes some of the ludicrously bad fare he experienced on voyages through Russia, India, Roumania, Italy and Germany. D'Avigdor's introduction declares that 'dining as an art is superior in importance to music and painting' (11). In typical aesthetic fashion, he demands the establishment of professional training to create knowledgeable connoisseurs, including a 'culinary academy' along with 'an academy of arts' and culinary journals offering 'a gastronomic education' (10–14). After all, 'a connoisseur of paintings, a good art critic, a good *diner*, is not what he is without education and study' (27). D'Avigdor imagines the trained cook as a misunderstood male artist, and assumes that he wishes to cook for a cosmopolitan male diner. This future body of expert male French chefs will eventually replace the present group of ignorant, amateur female English cooks. In a chapter entitled 'British Atrocities', D'Avigdor compares English food to medieval torture, the Sudan battlefield, the Boers' usage of the Africans, the measures used to suppress the Indian Mutiny and the uprising in Jamaica. The toughness and stodginess of British pastry, the tasteless overcooking of British greens and the mangled hacking of British meat, together form a damning indictment of the female cook's misdeeds. *Dinners & Dishes* pioneers an aesthetic reformation of cuisine by emphasising the need for connoisseurship in both cooking and consuming food.

It is not surprising that Oscar Wilde reviewed *Dinners & Dishes* almost immediately upon its publication. Wilde praises D'Avigdor, agreeing that food is the ultimate art and approving of his demolition of the British female cook. But Wilde outdoes his subject by giving epigrammatic versions of D'Avigdor's philosophy: 'In this little handbook to practical Epicureanism the tyrant of the English kitchen is shown in her proper light. ... For the British cook is a foolish woman who should be turned for her iniquities into a pillar of salt which she never knows how to use.' Wilde also establishes his superior cosmopolitanism by pointing out that D'Avigdor had entirely neglected American food (194).

Wilde's review was published in the *Pall Mall Gazette*, the same journal that ran Pennell's cookery columns a few years later. Pennell may have read it there; her diaries show that between 1884 and 1891 she read the *Pall Mall Gazette*, was friendly with its editors and contributed various articles (Waltman, 1976, 287). D'Avigdor had done the important preliminary work of establishing that food was art and that professional training and thorough travel were requirements for anyone who wished to take food seriously. These are the basic ingredients from which Pennell would mix her columns.

Like D'Avigdor, Pennell decided to treat food as a serious artistic topic but, because she was a woman, she had to be more careful than her male predecessors. Wilde's and D'Avigdor's gender made readers assume they were diners who judged food created by someone else. They were already allied with the critics. But Pennell's gender would make readers assume that she was already allied with the cooks, that she was offering a practical manual with intimate information about domestic preparations, necessities and customs.[7] This expectation meant that she had to work much harder than either D'Avigdor or Wilde to create a connoisseur's role for herself. At the same time, however, Pennell had to exhibit some knowledge of practical minutiae, since readers would assume she was a bad household manager if she wrote solely from a diner's perspective. Thus Pennell worked out a style which compromised between the cookbook and the critique, teasing the reader with partial recipes withdrawn at the last moment in favour of artistic effusions about food. Cookbook historian Jacqueline Bock Williams (2000) sees this decision as a major innovation in food writing: 'Elizabeth's decision to replace the recipe formula cookbook with a series of lively and informative essays made a significant contribution to culinary history' (x). The invention of the food essay paved the way for writers like M. F. K. Fisher, Elizabeth David and Jane Grigson (xxi).

Given the multiple negative discourses swirling around British food, Pennell also had to find a vocabulary that could reconfigure food as a subject for serious admiration. Hunger was seen as a distinctly unfeminine appetite, related to desires for sexuality and power (Michie, 1987, 13). On the other hand, the popular press often ascribed ridiculously extravagant culinary effusions to aesthetes, making it hard to imagine a food discourse that would not be vulnerable to satire.[8] In response, Pennell adopted a quite outrageously flamboyant style, a deliberate performance of self-abandonment that both participated in, and parodied, aestheticism. Pennell treats food as art in the most artful of ways. She insists that the love of food is a serious, admirable emotion. However, as we shall see, she sometimes repudiates her belief in the nobility of bodily pleasure and rejects 'greediness' with real horror. This ambivalence about female appetite shapes both her view of food and her political beliefs about women's roles.

The Feasts of Autolycus resembles *Dinners & Dishes* inasmuch as it establishes its author's authority by emphasising the range of dishes she had encountered through extensive travels. Hungarian chicken is: 'the clash of the Czardas captured and imprisoned in a stew-pan. With the Racoczy's wild drumming stirring memory into frenzy, stew the fowl, already cut into six willing pieces, with butter, a well-minced onion, pepper – *paprika* by choice – and salt; ten minutes will suffice – how, indeed, endure the strain a second longer?' Her references flatter the reader by assuming he or she has shared her experiences of 'wandering across the plains and over the mountains of song-bound Magyarland' (39). Pennell generally prefers food from less popular corners of Europe, for although she shares the Francophilia that preoccupied her culinary counterparts, she also looks to Hungary, Italy and Spain for alternative models of cooking. This southern influence gives her an unusual tolerance for different food items; for instance, Pennell is eloquent in praise of onions and garlic, which were normally 'treated with great caution by anyone with any social pretensions' (Freeman, 70–71).

Pennell frames her sandwich chapter in *Feasts* with travel narratives. A mutton sandwich transports one to the Alps; thin ham sandwiches recall pleasant picnics by the Cam; pâté in a baguette brings the eater back to French railway journeys. She advises the reader to visit Budapest, she recalls 'the Russian railway station' and she recommends German '*Delikatessen*' food (18–22). This is her way of sublimating food's physicality: like Proust's madeleine, the sandwich is valuable not for its sturdy material self but because it resurrects the evanescent, subtle pleasures of memories of vanished times.

Pennell's book had to compete against the Francophile school of cookery led by Mrs A. B. Marshall, whose cookbook was in around its sixty-fifth thousandth printing by 1890. (Indeed when Pennell began collecting cookbooks, she was exasperated by the way in which friends kept offering her copies of the omnipresent work of Mrs Marshall (*Feasts*, ix).) Marshall not only authored several cookbooks but founded a School of Cookery, produced a magazine called *The Table*, and sold a variety of products under her own brand name, ranging from sugar to refrigerators. The other great name in cookbooks of the latter half of the nineteenth century was, of course, Mrs Beeton, whose *Book of Household Management* (1861) and *Dictionary of Cookery* (1864) became two of the best-selling cookbooks in British history (Spain, 1948: 164, 226). Beeton offered mainly practical, simple, sturdy recipes for everyday household needs. The *Book of Household Management* consists mainly of recipes contributed by readers and is thus a fairly reliable compilation of British middle-class women's food practices and aspirations. Nicola Humble (2000) points out that Beeton expresses a typically mid-century pride in industrialism, as she praises new labour-saving machines, breaks down tasks to their component elements and itemises costs, although Beeton also expresses nostalgia for an older agricultural tradition that was swiftly vanishing (xvi–xix). In these respects, Beeton is a paradigmatic mid-Victorian writer. She emphasises efficiency, ease and thriftiness in the kitchen rather than the food's flavour or appearance. Marshall (1890), on the other hand, gave recommendations for fashionable dishes for fancy occasions, and the difference between these two writers shows how cookery's image had changed by the end of the century. Where Beeton explains how to make Irish Stew, Marshall described 'Gibelotte de Mouton: Etuvé à l'Irlandaise' (234). Marshall's cookbook represents not actual, but aspirational, late-Victorian cookery. Dishes that demanded enormous skill and time to prepare were extremely popular, since they showcased the leisure, wealth and artistry of the lady of the house.

Almost all of Marshall's recipes were designed for elaborate dinners. A typical example of the kind of work involved can be seen in 'Ballotine of Pheasant with Cherry Salad'. This involved boning a pheasant leg, then pounding together pheasant meat, ham, egg yolks and mushroom with seasonings and passing the mixture through a sieve. This mixture was forced into the leg. In the centre of this stuffing, the cook made a little hole to insert strips of *pâté de foie gras*, then covered the whole leg with the skin of the pheasant and cooked it in stock. The leg was garnished with aspic mayonnaise, tongue, gherkin, truffle and cherry salad, and served on a bed of aspic (Marshall, 193). Most of Mrs Marshall's recipes are based upon transforming meat into creams which can then be forced into elegant receptacles: a boned fowl, tomatoes, pastry cups, aspic or even olives. The ideal was to make food neat, to encase it. And clever 'containers' within other 'containers' (like the meat holding the stuffing which in turn holds paté) became testimony to the cook's skill at disciplining food, itself perceived as an innately messy substance (Shapiro, 1986, 102). Interestingly reporters at Marshall's cooking demonstrations marvelled at how clean the cooks remained, for cleanliness and control were much more important ideals than taste. A review in *The Leeds Mercury* (17 August 1887), reprinted in Marshall's book, enthused that: 'There is no litter behind to clean up. She believes in sending out a meal from the kitchen as neatly as she serves it in the dining room, and in leaving the kitchen as orderly at the end of her operations as at the beginning. She works, in fact, without fuss and without stain. The aprons she and her assistants wore may do for any number of "Pretty Luncheons"' (Marshall, 20–21).

Marshall was not alone in this focus on containing the disorderly potential of food, as Laura Shapiro points out in *Perfection Salad*, her fascinating study of the food industry at the turn of the century. During the 1890s, cooking began to be treated as a science, and in cookbooks caloric units replaced taste as a measure of success; measurements became specified and standardised, and a pretty meal was better than a tasty one. 'In this view, raw food was a foreign, slightly menacing substance that had to be brought under strict control' (Shapiro, 91). Raw food was associated with savagery; cooking was the sign of culture. 'The object of scientific salad making was to subdue the raw greens until they bore as little resemblance as possible to their natural state' (96). The eponymous 'perfection salad' is a salad of finely chopped vegetables bound in aspic, 'the very image of a salad at last in control of itself' (100).

Marshall also offers a vegetable dish entirely encased in aspic: 'Green Salad à la Batelière' (obligingly translated into French as 'Salade verte à la Batelière'). The cook lined sandwich moulds with aspic jelly and sprinkled them lightly with pepper or tarragon, then covered this layer with more aspic, sprinkled the new aspic layer with finely shredded beans or lettuce and covered it with jelly again. These gelatine cubes were set atop a salad and garnished with chopped aspic. The 'salad' base was actually a purée of boiled herbs, olives, cooked vegetables, gherkins, anchovies, oil and mayonnaise, and the whole thing was submerged in 'a pint and a half of liquid aspic jelly'. Leftover green material had to be mixed with mayonnaise and deposited in a 'neat pile' in the centre of the dish, where it would be safely surrounded by the retaining walls of aspic cubes (Marshall, 203–204). 'Green Salad à la Batelière' reveals a real terror of food in its natural state and an almost heroic indifference to the question of food's actual taste.

Tastelessness, in fact, was fashionable. At the turn of the century, taste was seen as a vulgarly body-based desire, and the copious use of flavourless white sauce, the excessive cooking of vegetables, and the employment of cream or gelatine to cover food, were deliberately intended to blanch out flavour and thereby prove the delicate palates of those who consumed them (Shapiro, 91–93). Delicacy and diminutiveness were ideal qualities for food. In terms of taste, Marshall's food oscillates between the two extremes of the utterly bland (as in the gelatine salad above) and the extremely spicy (as in a recipe for olives stuffed with fish paste and covered entirely with gherkins, red chillies, truffles and egg white, set in aspic) (Marshall, 43–44). The gelatine salad neither pleased the palate, nor satisfied the stomach, nor built up the body, which was precisely what made it appropriate for the Victorian lady who wished to demonstrate that she had neither appetite, nor hunger, nor other bodily needs.

Nicola Humble argues that 'cookery books are always interventions in the nation's diet, rather than accurate reflections of its current state' (xvi). Both Pennell and Marshall tried to redefine British cooking on their own ideological basis. While Marshall moved British food towards elaborate Francophilic compositions, Pennell worked to create an often startlingly modern, simple, healthy, flavourful cuisine. Pennell's aesthetic sensibility is strongly opposed to Marshall's culinary code. Pennell stresses, above all, the sensual pleasure of food's strong flavours. Her emphasis on the joy of eating was sixty years ahead of its time for English gastronomic writing.[9] For instance, she praises the taste of *gazpacho* although its cheap, simple water-and-vegetable composition had made it a (literal) laughing-stock for English cooks, who were accustomed to soups based on meat stocks and enriched with cream (*Feasts*, 142–144). In this chapter, Pennell urges a philosophy that is at odds with the labour-intensive, elaborate recipes of Marshall and her peers: 'never be guilty of any work when others may do it for you, is surely the one and only golden rule of life' (143). She approves of *gazpacho* precisely because it is simple and cheap. The dish also reminds her of Andalucia, with its 'strumming of guitars and click of castanets' (142). In this passage, we can see how Pennell's aesthetic tenets allow her to value a dish her peers despised. *Gazpacho* is exotic and therefore confirms her cosmopolitanism; it is simple, thereby agreeing with current artistic preferences; and it is associated with a life of lazy, leisured ease, a favourite mode of the aesthetes, particularly Wilde, who famously disliked earnestness.

We can vividly see the extent of Pennell's departure from Marshall's type of cuisine by contrasting their treatment of macaroni. Both offer recipes for *macaroni à la napolitaine* and *au gratin*. But whereas Marshall gives explicit instructions for preparing the dishes, Pennell focuses on the sensory experience of eating the food. Marshall directs: 'mix [the macaroni] with two ounces of fresh butter, half a pint of tomato sauce, six or eight cooked button mushrooms, a quarter of a pound of cooked lean ham or tongue and two or three truffles' (279). Just like Marshall, Pennell instructs her reader to boil the macaroni in salted water for twenty minutes, but then enthuses: 'to court perfection, rely upon mushrooms for one of the chief elements in this admirable concoction, and the whole world over you may travel without finding a dish worthy to compete with it. *Maccheroni* can yield nothing more exquisite ...' (126). Where Marshall writes detailed instructions for a producer, Pennell writes quick hints for a consumer. Marshall's reader wants to make macaroni; Pennell's reader aims to impress fellow diners by explaining which secret ingredient makes the macaroni so tasty.

Pennell's sense of the meaning of food is also quite unusual, further distinguishing her from Marshall. In the Victorian imagination, to hunger for strongly flavoured food implied that one also had an appetite for sexual activity. Etiquette manuals frequently used food as a euphemism for such experiences, describing the dinner table as a scene of 'seduction' and 'temptation' (Michie, 16–17). As we have seen, Marshall negates the dangerous threat of food's flavourfulness by rendering the whole dish tasteless. But Pennell associates purity with single ingredients and regards cooking as a process of degradation.[10] She tries to preserve food's natural state as much as possible. Unlike Marshall, who concentrates on elaborate concoctions of different foods blended together, Pennell devotes much space to praising individual food items: tomatoes, mushrooms, onions, strawberries, oranges, cheese and coffee each get their own chapters. To cook strawberries is to 'defile the delicate fruit'; 'eat [the orange] as it is, unadorned, unspoiled' (159, 165). The onion example is particularly telling, for earlier etiquette writers had regarded the onion as unspeakable. 'The onion is the forbidden fruit of the modern Eve,' wrote one in 1869 (Michie, 13). But Pennell claims that 'the little delicate spring onion' has a 'tender virginal freshness', and a 'graceful maiden form' (*Feasts*, 114). Pennell manages to transform the onion from the site of unfeminine sexual knowledge to the very emblem of idealised, virginal femininity.

However *Feasts* reverses this pleasure in natural food when it begins to cite antiquarian authorities. When Pennell instils the aesthetic love of archaic language into food discourse, reading becomes better than eating. A chapter on 'The Partridge' is a kind of anthology of historical writing on the topic, offering more literary styles than recipes, as Pennell cites Daudet, Aristophanes, Aristotle, Chamæleon of Pontus, Hannah Glasse and the medieval 'Master Cook, Giles' (77–82). We are consuming language rather than real recipes here. And thus the unacceptable physical labour of cookery gets sublimated into the superior intellectual pleasure of reading about cookery. She offers 'fantastic' and 'quaint' dishes because of their charming diction, although their taste is, she freely confesses, unappealing (one dish combines mustard with sweetmeats) (80–81). Instead of describing the glorious taste and texture of food, she slips into praising the more rarefied emotion of historical nostalgia, and thereby evades the imputation of gluttony.

At times, however, *The Feasts of Autolycus* uses history to argue for a more liberatory view of consumption. Pennell's book begins with a historical disquisition arguing that the hermits of the Dark Ages began a tradition that victimised women:

> With time, all superstitions fail; and asceticism went the way of many another ingenious folly. But as a tradition, as a convention, somehow, it lingered longer among women. And the old Christian duty became a new feminine grace. And where the fanatic had fasted that his soul might prove comelier in the sight of God, silly matrons and maidens starved, or pretended to starve, themselves that their bodies might seem fairer in the eyes of men. And dire, indeed, has been their punishment. ... And thus gradually, so it is asserted, the delicacy of woman's palate was destroyed: food to her perverted stomach was but a mere necessity to stay the pangs of hunger, and the pleasure of eating she looked upon as a deep mystery, into which only man could be initiated. (1–2)

This revisionist history reverses at least three accepted truths about women and food. First, Pennell makes women's decorous disdain of food into the survival of a barbarous medieval superstition. In fact Pennell reverses the usual terms by claiming that whereas women's natural palates have 'delicacy', the modern woman's stomach is 'perverted'. Second, whereas women's preference for sweet food was usually seen as an irreducible biological attribute, Pennell presents it as a mere 'convention'. Third, the figure of the angelic lady wasting away is treated not as romantic, but as a 'dire' 'punishment'. The semi-medical language of the passage lends her authority, especially as Pennell uses a commanding passive voice ('so it is asserted') to make herself appear to speak for the experts. This daring history is what Helena Michie alludes to when she explains that 'in what is essentially a cookbook, Pennell humorously and categorically explodes the central myths of Victorian femininity' (17).

If medieval Christian history is posited as a bad body-destroying history, there is an alternative period from which women can draw, an era which actually celebrated female appetites. When she wrote *The Feasts of Autolycus*, Pennell quoted a few seventeenth-century texts but she adapted most of her recipes and language from the writers of eighteenth-century food, Jean-Anthèlme Brillat-Savarin and Hannah Glasse. Pennell's admiration for the eighteenth century is characteristic of female aesthetes, who tended to reconstruct that era as a period of playful, sportive, virginal, fresh girlhood and regard the Victorian woman as distressingly sober, domestic-minded, dutiful and maternal (Schaffer, 2000, 96–102). In *Feasts* Pennell cites Brillat-Savarin to claim that the eater can actually physically transform herself into a more girlish model of female beauty: 'A succulent, delicate and choice regimen ... gives more brilliancy to the eye, more freshness to the skin' (4). This eater casts off her hard-working, strenuously sober Victorian character and becomes a brilliant, cheery young thing, the ideal lady of the eighteenth century. In the act of eating, the gourmet becomes pretty: 'her eyes sparkle, her lips are glossy, her talk cheerful, all her movements graceful' (*Feasts*, 4). If mainstream historical accounts show an unhealthy history of female fasting, Pennell sets up an oppositional past in which women consume food with gleeful, sensuous indulgence.

Women's cooking is just as praiseworthy as women's eating. Pennell wants to place them both in a lofty artistic process of creativity, achievement and appreciation, thereby liberating cookery from its ignoble situation as the bodily underside of 'taste'. This view offers a new kind of respect to the women who prepare meals. By ascribing antiquarianism, simplicity and exoticism to food, Pennell lends food the status of art, even, sometimes, of the highest form of art: 'Set your wits to work. Cultivate your artistic instincts. Invent! Create! Many are the men who have painted pictures: few those who have composed a new and perfect sandwich' (22).

But Pennell's intention in such invocations is difficult to fix. Her chapter on the strawberry is entitled 'A Study in Green and Red', an allusion to her friend Whistler's paintings. It begins:

You may search from end to end of the vast Louvre; you may wander from room to room in England's National Gallery; you may travel to the Pitti, to the Ryks Museum, to the Prado; and no richer, more stirring arrangement of colour will you find than in that corner of your kitchen garden where June's strawberries grow ripe. From under the green of broad leaves the red fruit looks out and up to the sun in splendour unsurpassed by paint upon canvas. (157)

The exaggeration of these comments makes them seem close to self-parody. On the other hand, their constant recurrence suggests some serious content. Furthermore Pennell's own position as a member of the elite artistic world of England (an art reviewer, the wife of a famous artist, and the friend of Whistler) and the authority given to her by her travels (here invoked by her familiarity with European art museums) lend a real weight to these comparisons. This language is deliberately, carefully, ambiguous. Her narrator's excited, excessive rhetoric could indicate the author spinning out of control, or it could show the author exercising a cool, sophisticated control of language in order to parody other, less controlled aesthetic enthusiasts. This indeterminacy keeps Pennell safe. It is impossible to accuse someone of excess when one suspects she may be doing it on purpose.

At moments, however, Pennell's adoption of an art vocabulary suggests real innovations in the analysis of cookery. She is able to reveal how prominent artistic movements have also influenced the household arts, and it is perhaps the most radical aspect of her argument to say that cookery and painting and poetry are *already* connected: 'The modern gourmet, or artist, is a romanticist, whether he will or no. No screaming red waistcoat marks the romantic movement in the kitchen, and yet there it has been stronger even than in art and literature.' Cooks value 'the picturesque'. For instance, grilled mushrooms seem simple, 'and yet when, ready to be served, its rich brown beauty is spread upon the paler brown of the toast, and above rests butter's brilliant gold, have you not an arrangement as romantic in conception as the "Ernani" of the master, or the pastoral of Corot?' (96). The romanticism of this dish was deliberately planned and produced by a 'master' in a moment of artistic inspiration equivalent to Verdi's or Corot's.

However, in spite of the apparently feminist message, this newly empowered artistic chef is not necessarily a woman. In Pennell's history, the great artists of the kitchen have been men and, like D'Avigdor, she assumes that female cooks are largely incompetent. The introduction to *Feasts* explains:

> For centuries the kitchen has been [woman's] appointed sphere of action. And yet, here, as in the studio and the study, she has allowed man to carry off the laurels. Vatel, Carême, Ude, Dumas, Gouffé, Etienne, these are some of the immortal cooks of history: the kitchen still waits its Sappho. ... Woman, moreoever, has eaten with as little distinction as she has cooked. It seems almost – much as I deplore the admission – as if she were of coarser clay than man, lacking the more artistic instincts, the subtler, daintier emotions. (v)

The conditional tense ('it seems almost ... as if') modifies the bleakness of this judgement. Furthermore, Pennell places agency with the women. It is they who have 'allowed' men to dominate, and they who can change this situation. Finally, by comparing the prospective female cook to Sappho, Pennell places her above Dumas or Ude in genius. In subtle ways, then, this introduction implies women's potential superiority while bemoaning their present inferiority.

Feasts is motivated in part by the necessity to justify itself as literature, just as it redefines its subject matter as art. In the concluding chapter, 'Enchanting Coffee', Pennell ends by recommending that the reader travel to Hungary and 'return to preach the glad gospel of good coffee to the heathen at home. A hero you would be, worthy countryman of Nelson and of Wellington; and thus surely should you win for yourself fame, and a niche in Westminster Abbey' (*Feasts*, 179). In other words, by following Pennell's own example, one could become a 'hero'. This unexpectedly blatant self-praise has a comic effect, as if Pennell is brazening out her real originality by grotesquely exaggerating it, as if she can only acknowledge her own innovative writing by making it into buffoonery.

Pennell's 'niche in Westminster Abbey' depends upon her ability to depict herself as a guide to Beauty rather than a cookbook author. She begins: 'The collection, evidently, does not pretend to be a "Cook's Manual" ... It is rather a guide to the Beauty, the Poetry, that exist in the perfect dish, even as in the masterpiece of a Titian or a Swinburne' (vi). This introductory statement sets up two contradictory missions for *Feasts*. First, *The Feasts of Autolycus* wants to exalt food to the level of art, thereby recalibrating the value of women's work. Through this aesthetic treatment Pennell can present female cooks (and diners) as worthy of respect. But if Pennell depicted herself as a cook, she would become déclassée, losing the audience of cultured writers and art critics she had been pursuing. Thus she has to keep proving that she does not labour in the kitchen herself – a task which somewhat undercuts her initial impulse to exalt the status of labourers.[11] Finally, Pennell's admiration for, and dislike of, cooking labour get channelled into two different discourses. When she is defending cooking, she often adopts the practical language of cookbooks and household manuals. When she is repudiating cooking in favour of a vaguer but more splendid Art, she uses the rhetoric of aestheticism. These competing motivations and styles provide much of the tension in the text, as Pennell tries to exalt cooks while avoiding cooking, to praise the labour she disavows.

The rhetorical sleight-of-hand required can be seen in the following passage, which establishes art as the antithesis of the cookbook: 'The plodding painter looks upon a nocturne by Whistler, and thinks how easy, how preposterously easy! A touch here, a stroke there, and the thing is done. But let him try! And so with *sauce Soubise*. Turn to the first cookery book at hand and read the recipe.' After transcribing part of the recipe, Pennell exclaims: 'but why go on with elaborate directions? Why describe the exact quantity of flour, the size of the potato, the proportions of milk and cream to be added? ... In the actual making, only the artist understands the secret of perfection, and his understanding is born within him, not borrowed from dry statistics and formal tables. He may safely be left to vary his methods...' (111). This passage depicts art in Romantic terms, as unbridled creativity that cannot brook rules and requires the hand of a genius. To prove oneself an 'artist', one must ignore 'dry statistics and formal tables'. Yet Pennell is in the uncomfortable position of needing to give her readers some indication of how to make '*sauce Soubise*', since that is presumably why they are reading her chapter. She resolves the dilemma by coyly offering the first part of the recipe and mentioning the primary ingredients, yet withholding the vital information that would allow the reader to produce the finished dish. The same kind of slipperiness trickles through Pennell's account of salad dressing:

> Only the genius born can mix a salad dressing as it should be mixed. Quantities of pepper and salt, of oil and vinegar for him (or her) are not measured by rule or recipe, but by inspiration. You may generalize and insist upon one spoonful of oil for every guest and one for the bowl ...and then one-third the quantity of vinegar. But out of these proportions the Philistine will evolve for you a nauseating concoction; the initiated, a dressing of transcendental merit. (132)

Here Pennell gives the recipe but couches it in such general and ominous terms as to negate its function as a recipe. Indeed, her cooking advice is often rather perilously impractical, as, for instance, she asserts that no matter what one puts in *sauce Soubise*, stirring it with a wooden spoon will guarantee 'a godlike sauce' (111).

When Pennell does allow a real recipe to enter her text, she mitigates its practicality by excluding quantities and by describing the recipe in a rhetoric associated with the arts. We have seen how she invokes the Romantic artist. In this startling fish recipe, she adopts the tone of a novelist describing a happy bride:

> Take your sole ... and place it, with endearing, lover-like caress, in a pretty earthenware dish, with butter for only companion. At the same time, in a sympathetic saucepan, lay mussels ... and let each rejoice in the society of a stimulating mushroom; when almost done, but not quite, make of them a garland round the expectant sole; cover their too seductive beauty with a rich white sauce; rekindle their passion in the oven for a few minutes. ... Joy is the result. (*Feasts*, 59–60)

Like the bride, the sole is robed in rich white, garlanded and caressed, with only one perfect companion. The matched pairs of mussels and mushrooms surround her, like the paired groomsmen and bridesmaids at the wedding. Pennell even adapts the postnuptial wish, 'I give you joy.' Nor is the romance of the table always so decorous. Pennell could utilise the language of contemporary decadent writing too:

Another weird salad there is, with qualities to endear it to the morbid and neurotic. Let it be explained briefly, that lurid description may not be thought to exaggerate lurid attraction: drop your tomatoes, brilliantly red as the abhorred Scarlet Woman, into hot water in order to free them of their skins; place them whole, and in passionate proximity, in a dish of silver or delicate porcelain; smother them under a thick layer of whipped cream. For the sake of decoration and the unexpected, stick in here and there a pistachio nut, and thank the gods for the new sensation. (120–121)

The appetite for food is metonymically associated with the sexual greed of the 'abhorred Scarlet Woman'. By consuming this dish, the 'morbid and neurotic' eater can participate in the forbidden, 'lurid' 'new sensation' that the meal both arouses and represents.

'Recipes' like this tomato salad passage are actually creative amalgams of the cookbook and the language of literary art. When Pennell writes 'stick in here and there a pistachio nut' in the same sentence as 'the abhorred Scarlet Woman', she yokes these two genres by violence together, creating a comically exaggerated version of the female aesthetes' characteristic desire to reorganize domestic culture according to the newest artistic standards.

If *Feasts* is written by both a cook and a connoisseur, it also slides between two different positions on the Woman Question. Pennell insists that women's work in the kitchen deserves respect, but also asserts that women ought to go back to the kitchen where they belong. Sometimes she treats women as artists who choose, control and discipline the raw materials of pure creativity. She prescribes eating with gusto and applauding the strong physical body. Sometimes, however, Pennell reverts to traditional ideals of femininity, as in her description of the 'the little delicate spring onion', with its 'graceful maiden form' (114). This ambivalence regarding feminist issues is eminently characteristic of the female aesthetes. Indeed, many identified themselves with aestheticism because they could not wholeheartedly endorse either the New Women or the Angel in the House, and they liked to choose and combine elements from both roles via the permissive medium of aesthetic prose.

In Pennell's text, the New Women's politics displace the 'truly' feminist achievement of homemaking. 'Why clamour for the suffrage, why labour for the redemption of brutal man, why wear, with noisy advertisement, ribbons white or blue, when three times a day there is a work of art, easily within her reach, to be created?' (3). Working for suffrage and reform are equated with 'noise', not with creativity. Loud, vulgar and allied with 'advertisements', they represent the polar opposite of the exquisite realm of art. According to Pennell, food, rather than legislation, will solve the social problems that worried the New Women:

> Let men and women look to it that at table delicious sympathy makes them one, and marriage will cease to be a failure. If they agree upon their sauces and salads, what matter if they disagree upon mere questions of conduct and finance? Accept the gospel of good living and the sexual problem will be solved. She who first dares to write the great Food Novel will be a true champion of her sex. (5)

Contemporary readers would have recognized this passage as a parody of New Woman discourse, with its characteristic glance at the Marriage Question, its brave naming of 'the sexual problem' and its demand for a daring new novel. But Pennell's irony is difficult to place. If it is exercised at the expense of the New Women, then other passages about art might be equally satirical towards aesthetes. Because Pennell treats all these different 1890s discourses with the same levity, it is impossible to say where she stands herself.

In this section, art is not constructed according to the Romantic canons of the unfettered genius, nor according to Ruskin's ideas of simplicity, but according to the Paterian dictum of living one's life in, and for, art:

> All his life a Velazquez devoted to his pictures, a Shakespeare to his plays, a Wagner to his operas: why should not the woman of genius spend hers in designing exquisite dinners, inventing original breakfasts, and be respected for the nobility of her self-appointed task? For in the planning of the perfect meal there is art; and, after all, is not art the one real, the one important thing in life? (3)

Notice how Pennell avoids the verb 'cooking' and instead adopts 'designing', 'inventing' and 'planning', words which ally cookery to architecture or painting and play down its physical labour.

Pennell ends this introductory chapter with a vision of Utopia: 'When food is given its due ... [t]he old platitudes will fade and die. The maiden will cease to ask "What do you think of the Academy?" The earnest one will no longer look to Ibsen for heavy small-talk' (5). This is an unexpected comment from a professional reviewer of 'the Academy' and Ibsen's plays. Not only will food divert women from being art critics and drama critics, it will also displace them as artists: 'The sensation of the day will prove the latest arrangement in oysters, the newest device in vegetables. The ambitious will trust to her kitchen to win her reputation; the poet will offer lyrics and pastorals with every course; the painter will present in every dish a lovely scheme of colour' (6). In other words, cookery becomes the women's art. It replaces poetry, paintings, even millinery (signalled by the fashion-column clichés, 'latest arrangement' and 'newest device'); it provides an outlet for women's ambition, earnestness and reformist capacity. Pennell's use of cookery to replace feminist activism and artistic involvement reassures her readers that women can be channelled into the kitchen, keeping the more high-status fields of art free for men.

At the same time, however, Pennell's idea of the artistic value of cookery is so exalted that it undermines her attempt to save high art for men. If cookery is the ultimate form of art, if food is far more beautiful than anything that could be painted, then cookery is no substitute sphere but actually the superior sphere. If *Feasts* begins with this enthusiastic recommendation for women to stop protesting and start designing breakfasts, it ends with the statement that the woman who knows about coffee deserves 'a niche in Westminster Abbey'. In that respect, Pennell's flamboyant praise of cooking actually ends up downgrading the male-dominated arts.

Pennell's confusion about the rightful status of cooking reveals how much food preparation was caught in a mesh of conflicting ideologies at the turn of the century. Cooking was a high art practised by geniuses but it was also a base labour performed by menial servants. Cooking was traditionally part of the women's domestic realm, but it was also dominated by highly respected male chefs. By describing favourite dishes, one could demonstrate one's aesthetic qualities of cosmopolitan experience and historical sensitivity or reveal an unfeminine greediness. In short, cookery was the dark side of aestheticism, for it was the place where art met the body. *The Feasts of Autolycus* works both sides of this divide. Pennell's prose is shaped by the bodily shame associated with food, an unbecoming gluttony that she must either reclaim as virtue, or sublimate into art.

In 1923 Pennell republished *The Feasts of Autolycus*. Initially, she had meant to edit the chapters, but she discovered so many memories of the 1890s in its pages that she found herself unable to touch it. The only words she changed in this edition were the title words. She renamed her book, strangely enough, *A Guide for the Greedy, by a Greedy Woman*.

This self-derogatory title denies Pennell the very status she had tried so hard to achieve. It claims that she was not producing great art, but only penning a 'guide'. She was just 'a greedy woman', not a real connoisseur, and not even a lady. Nor did she write for cultured readers (they, too, were 'greedy'). Unladylike, uneducated and unable to shape her experiences into fiction, this 1923 title half-comically names herself as the very figure that Pennell was terrified of seeming in 1896. When Pennell renames herself this way in 1923, she contemptuously characterises her own earlier persona. With twenty-seven years of cookbook collecting behind her, described in detail in her new introduction, Pennell now has real claims to be considered a connoisseur of cookbook language rather than a practical cook, and from that august height she views her younger self with something like real distaste.

In the 1896 edition, Pennell worked so hard to make her language so flamboyant, so excessive, so poetic because she was using aestheticism to compensate for the fear of being greedy. In her memoirs, Pennell recalls how that fear haunted her during the inaugural dinner for *The Yellow Book*:

> I kept on emptying [my plate] in self-defense, to pass the time, wondering if, in my rôle of the *Pall Mall*'s 'greedy Autolycus,' my friends would now convict me of the sin of public eating as well as what they had been pleased to pretend was my habit of 'private eating,' for not otherwise, they would assure me, could they account for the unfailing flamboyancy of my weekly article on cookery. (*Nights*, 186)

After all Pennell's work to legitimise food, it is sad to see how her friends' insistence on finding an autobiographical origin for her flamboyant language makes them accuse her of shameful private pleasures, and how Pennell's fear of public eating inhibits her pleasure at the banquet. The 'diary of a greedy woman', the personal memoir of a female body out of control, is the figure that haunts this text. And it is that figure, so entirely anti-aesthetic, that gives the 1923 edition its uneasy status as a text whose title announces its failure to meet its own standards.

In the 1896 *Feasts of Autolycus*, however, Pennell succeeded in setting up a figure that combined what she considered the best attributes of the artistic connoisseur and the domestic woman, a figure that might provide a new model for women in the 1890s. We have seen how Pennell's arch tone manages to negotiate between numerous competing and contradictory discourses: greed and art, practical cookery and connoisseurship, serious aestheticism and parody, female emancipation and masculine high art. Pennell managed to construct a female identity that permitted all these behaviours; and she *was* 'a greedy woman' inasmuch as she managed to stir all these ideologies into one discourse. As a true female aesthete, Elizabeth Robins Pennell wanted to have her cake and admire it too.

Notes

1 Pennell's articles appeared in the *Pall Mall Gazette*'s 'The Wares of Autolycus' column, a special column reserved for women writers who wrote anonymously on different days. 'Wares' authors included Alice Meynell, Rosamund Marriott Watson and Violet Hunt: some of the most prominent and critically acclaimed women writers of the 1890s. 'The Wares of Autolycus' derived its name from the liar and rogue, Autolycus, in *The Winter's Tale*, who sells ribbons and ballads to distract his victims while he picks their pockets. This character is named after the son of Hermes, a thief who concealed his booty by changing its shape or rendering it invisible. Thus the very name of the column establishes the expectation that these women's words are ruses to cheat the reader, an odd name which undermines the women's real interest in offering important texts. A pleasure in elaborate trickery does, however, inform *Feasts*, as we shall see.

2 I have discussed female aestheticism more fully in *The Forgotten Female Aesthetes: Literary Culture in Late-Victorian England*, 2000, and *Women and British Aestheticism*, 1999.

3 Mrs A. B. Marshall's 1890 cookbook reveals how unromantic food preparation could be. In a chapter on 'marketing', she advises the reader: 'in choosing veal always examine the suet under the kidney; if this be clammy and soft, with a faint smell, the meat is not good, and always reject any that has greenish or yellowish spots about it', p. 532. Even when the cook had bought her materials, the work was not over: 'Much more work than today was entailed by groceries, since grit and pieces of stalk were left in rice and dried fruit, which had to be picked and washed before use; raisins needed stoning, candied peel chopping, and mace and nutmeg, and often ginger and cinnamon pounding or grating ... . Making a cake was thus not a matter of minutes but a prolonged operation' (Freeman, 1989, 113).

4 Freeman gives interesting details about the scandal of dangerously adulterated bread and poisonously dyed sweets, 1989, pp. 77–78, 92–93. In 1887, one writer in *The Westminster Review* announced, in an article called 'The Adulteration of Food': 'there is scarcely an article of food in which some poison or fraud does not lie in ambush for the ignorant and innocent purchaser'. Up to 30 per cent of tea might be composed of iron filings; commercially sold pepper, when tested, was found to contain no real pepper whatsoever but was composed of gypsum, mustard-seed husks, and even sand; pickles were laced with poisonous copper and the equally poisonous red lead was intermixed with curry powder.

5 All references to *The Feasts of Autolycus* refer to the edition reprinted as *A Guide for the Greedy* in 1923. There is now a modern reprint of a 1901 American edition available, under the title *The Delights of Delicate Eating*.

6 See *Nights*, 1916, and *Our House*, 1910, for instance. She also published a two-volume biography of her husband, *The Life and Letters of Joseph Pennell*, 1929, and the Pennells co-authored an account of their vacation travelling on the Thames, *The Stream of Pleasure*, 1891. Pennell also wrote two biographies of her dear friend Whistler, for which she is probably best known today, and a biography of her uncle, Charles Godfrey Leland.

7 Although her articles were published anonymously in 'The Wares of Autolycus', readers still knew she was female, since the column was reserved for women writers.

8 George du Maurier's drawing of Maudle dining off a lily and Gilbert and Sullivan's patter in 'Patience', 1881, about the aesthetes' 'vegetable passion' both appeared in the 1880s. In 1893 Ada Leverson parodied *Salome* with a description of food: 'It is

mayonnaise of salmon, pink as a branch of coral which fishermen find in the twilight of the sea, and which they keep for the King', *Punch*, July 15, 13.

9   According to Stephen Mennell, it was not until after the Second World War that English cookery writers began to describe the sensual pleasure of food, 1985, p. 244.

10   She also preferred single courses. For instance, Pennell recommends serving a large bowl of macaroni with butter and Parmesan cheese. 'Defy convention, and make it the first and last and only course. It may seem meagre in the telling. But to treat it with due respect and justice much may be eaten ...' p. 125. Such an idea would have been anathema to Marshall, whose recommended dinner menus have seven or eight courses, and two or three dishes in each course, pp. 467–469.

11   Part of Pennell's complicated attitude towards her servants can be gleaned from the book she wrote about them, *Our House and the People in It*, 1910. The book presents a memorable account of the desperate neediness of Victorian servants, who bring their history of illiteracy, abuse and poverty to confront Pennell's middle-class liberal sympathies and guilt.

Chapter 8

Simple, Honest Food: Elizabeth David and the Construction of Nation in Cookery Writing

Janet Floyd

Elizabeth David is a cookery writer accorded national significance in Britain. This essay is a reconsideration of the writing of French and Mediterranean cookery on which her reputation was built. It is also an attempt to contribute to a wider debate about cookery writing and the construction of national identity. The links between cookery, food and nation are scarcely obscure. The most cursory glance at any kind of catalogue of cookery books makes evident how many are engaged in a very explicit attempt to fix, codify and describe the traditions of nations and regions by reference to practices of preparing and consuming food. Such books of recipes seem to mount a claim that the choice, cooking and consumption of food allow us to reconnect in a quite straightforward way with national and regional tradition. This may easily be observed in books of 'farmhouse' or 'homestead' cooking in which national pasts of rural stability or frontier self-sufficiency are evoked in wholesome baking and preserves. Equally cookery books may seem to assert the possibility of preservation of identities that are compromised in other contexts. As the cookery writer Claudia Roden remarked in a recent interview, describing her own and her family's exile from Egypt: 'We couldn't preserve our wealth, but we could preserve our food.'[1] Cookery books are generated as much by experiences of exile and migration as by the impulse to conserve a shared national past.[2]

Of course the definition of national identity in cookery books is not confined to the writing of tradition and the encouragement to revivify or hold on to the foodways of a life left behind. As Arjun Appadurai (1988) has made evident in an unusually detailed discussion of the elaborate ideological work of cookery books, while some of these texts may be caught up in nostalgic fantasies of the past, others formulate authenticities with a view to casting the nation in a new image. Others still use recipe books to construct Other less 'developed' regions for the consumption of a post-colonial audience well accustomed to situating their own national cultural identity in opposition to the primitive, the exotic or indeed the authentic. However if the cookery book may be understood as involved in the familiar processes through which nation is constructed, I want in this essay to use the example of Elizabeth David to suggest how cookery books may not always work to recall, affirm or collate national identities, new or old, but rather may offer an arena in which a less coherent experience and a less confident definition of nation may be explored.

The peculiar interest of Elizabeth David in this context is twofold. Firstly, as I shall argue later, a complex sense of national identity is traced and refracted in her work. This quality of David's writing, however, has been obscured by a very different understanding of her meaning in terms of construction of nation, and it is with this second aspect that I want to begin. There is, in the largely journalistic commentary about her, an extraordinary consensus about David's status as a writer whose work reformed British eating habits and changed the nation in some profound way. Her cookery writing is agreed to be 'monumental in [its] influence on the way this country regained its appetite after the Second World War', 'one of the most important influences on the way we live in Britain' (Prince, 1997, 12; Channel 4, 1998). Elizabeth David's position as an iconic British cookery writer is strongly identified with a highly critical view of the post-war British culture of the late 1940s and 1950s, a view that she herself expressed and which is foregrounded in writing about her. Her work is argued to have drawn the British towards the recognition that her judgement of what was bad in Britain and of what was good in the Mediterranean was not only justified but an inspiration to national improvement. Through her cookery books, David is said to have introduced the post-war British to a new respect for and love of good food and even, more generally, to have reminded them of the importance of pleasure at a point when English culinary and, by association, cultural life was mired in drabness and mediocrity.

Crucial to this understanding of her work is David's expression of a lack in British cultural life. This is usually illustrated in commentary about her by the story she told of a visit to a hotel in rural Ross-on-Wye at the heart of the exceptionally cold winter of 1946: the food 'was worse than unpardonable even in those days of desperation' and 'produced with a kind of bleak triumph which amounted almost to a hatred of humanity and humanity's needs' (David, 1986, 21). Likewise, David's descriptions of the horrors of nursery food in the upper-class British household of her childhood serve a similar purpose in tracing a core of coldness and distance, even a kind of malevolence towards others in the British way of life. The clear implication is that the nation 'was' what it ate.

That the catalyst for a profoundly important cultural change in the British attitude to food and cooking should be David's writing of the very different cuisine of a wholly different culture is not regarded as problematic as far as the formulation of her national contribution is concerned; indeed it is her early books, *A Book of Mediterranean Food* (1950), *French Country Cooking* (1951), *Italian Food* (1954), *Summer Cooking* (1955), and *French Provincial Cooking* (1960), rather than her later writing of English food in the 1970s that define her reputation and meaning. This may in part be attributed to the British tradition of regarding its own cuisine as hopelessly inferior to that of the French, and to the tendency to lionise French or Francophile chefs prepared to engage in the improvement of the national diet (Mennell, 1985). David's impact on British cookery is not positioned as an embrace of the foreign. Rather it is understood as exemplifying a laudable strain of British individualism in which rejection of the dull, incurious mainstream of national life is justified. This rejection is often explained by reference to David's intense friendship with the British hedonist and gastronome Norman Douglas, a British exile portrayed as equally individualistic and as justifiably in flight from a national scene of pedestrianism and joylessness.[3] The immediate cause of Douglas's restless exile – his attraction to boys – is erased, as are the impulses which prompted David, as a young woman, to lead a rather more Bohemian existence than was expected of a young woman of her background (Chaney, 1998; Cooper, 1999). Instead we read of the friends sharing an intensely committed pursuit of a truth and simplicity traduced in twentieth-century Britain, and finding them in the 'simple, honest food' of the Mediterranean. David's achievement, so the story goes, was to bring back to a culturally listless Britain this prize of what was essential and true.

The argument about David's motivation for writing is set in the period between the late 1940s and the mid-1950s. The discussion of her influence, however, reaches beyond the post-war period into the 1960s. Claims such as Allison James's (1996) that 'since Elizabeth David first published her book about Mediterranean cooking in the 1950s, there has been a marked change in English food preferences' are common (81) It would seem, however, that they are not offered in an attempt to trace David's impact on the nation in any precise way, but rather to summarise a development that gathered steam over the late 1950s and 1960s as her work was reprinted for a mass market by Penguin Books (81). In the wake of a consumer boom, her books matched the fashion for more widespread Mediterranean travel.

They chimed in with the influence of such figures as Terence Conran in popularising a style of domestic living linked with perceptions of rural Mediterranean life. They echoed the strain of complaint about British catering that gathered steam as the practice of eating in restaurants mushroomed. Much of what Raymond Postgate had to say in *The Good Food Guide*, for example (first published in 1951 and, by the mid-1950s, available in a pocket-sized edition), was consonant with David's gloomy view of restaurants in Britain. Thus, while in the context of the early 1950s David's work appears as a lone light shining in cultural darkness, looked at in the context of the 1960s it comes to epitomise rather than drive significant national change. David remains throughout, however, a figure to whom a powerful influence is attributed.

Although the part played by David's writing in influencing consumption practices in relation to food is still widely considered pre-eminent, it is not exclusively with respect to cooking that her influence is argued to have operated. Lisa Chaney (1998), David's first and most thorough biographer, suggests that David's primary message was to '"Lift up your eyes to the Continent and take an interest in exotic ingredients"'(374), a sentiment that resonates with Cynthia L. White's (1970) interesting suggestion that the glossy magazines aimed at the wealthier class during the period between 1956 and 1965 (including those for which David wrote) were apparently more concerned to encourage people in *collecting* food rather than preparing it (161). Her work supplied those who bought her books with the 'signposts' that John Urry (1995) describes as structuring the practice of tourism (139). Jill Norman (1993) argues that *French Provincial Cookery* 'drew many English enthusiasts to France to explore the foods of the countryside' (139). Certainly in so far as David dealt with her readers' domestic experience, it was often to advise them on how to buy food and equipment rather than to shepherd them through the process of cooking. In this light, it is interesting to find that in the 1960s David herself put aside the writing of cookery books and in 1965 set up a shop in Chelsea, selling French and traditional kitchen equipment, a project that lasted until 1973.

This, then, is the substance of the claims made for Elizabeth David, claims that have raised her to the status of national icon within British cookery. As soon as we begin to examine the arguments about David's importance as an influence on perceptions of national life, however, they seem to fall apart in our hands. That her reputation should remain unexamined is perhaps unexceptionable in the case of a cookery writer: this is not a genre that has received the same level of attention as other forms of domestic instructional text, nor has the work of cookery writers generally been subjected to critical analysis. Yet the most cursory look at David's writing and the circumstances of its production takes us immediately to a major difficulty within this triumphant narrative of David's transformative intervention, or even in the positioning of her work as part of a shift in national aspirations and practices of consumption: namely, the issue of the narrowness of the audience for her writing. There is an unwillingness, in the frankly hagiographic field of commentary on David, to acknowledge that this national treasure, apparently bent on a mission to wake the nation up to what they were eating and what they had become, actually showed little interest in appealing to or engaging with an audience outside a social élite. Certainly, there has been, within some of the discussion of David, some recognition of the difficulty in attributing national influence to one whose work was read by a small highly privileged minority. A process of osmosis is sometimes proposed by way of justifying the national importance attributed to David: in a recent public 'conversation' about David's work between the journalist Paul Levy and David's editor, Jill Norman, vague assertions were made about a trickle-down effect through which the nation as a whole began to buy, cook and consume food differently.[4] But such arguments sit uneasily with the very writing that it seeks to celebrate.

Exclusive, largely inaccessible experiences of food were at the heart of David's writing. Indeed she built her career on writing for the wealthy audience for magazines such as *Vogue, Harper's Bazaar, House and Garden* and *Wine and Food*, as well as for the High Tory *Spectator*. She had no association with such mass circulation weeklies as *Woman's Own,* even when such magazines began to carry recipes for French cooking (Mennell, 250–261; Chaney, 347). And, as commentaries on David frequently point out (by way of illustrating her daring as a principled writer of good food), she wrote, in her books and in her journalism, of ingredients of a type and in quantities altogether unavailable in Britain at the time of publication: Norman (1993) cites the much-repeated story of how her first publisher's reader was 'beguiled by the recipe for "Turkish stuffing for a whole roast sheep" when the meat ration was only a few ounces a week' (33). In 1963, David herself wrote of 1946, a period of some national crisis in economic terms, as a period of deprivation sufficiently extreme that: 'No-one ever came to a meal without bringing contributions ... A wild goose, snails from Paris, mock liver pâté from Fortnum's, a hare' (David, 1986, 19). The scarcity of 'good' ingredients in Britain is a given in David's work.

The link that has been made between David's work and new practices of tourism in the 1960s is also a vulnerable one. Akhtar and Humphries's

(2000) account of post-war British tourism suggests that provincial France (one of the regions central in David's work), and certainly Provence, 'retained [their] more exclusive patronage' until the 1980s and the appearance of Peter Mayle's best-selling accounts of expatriate escapades in Provence (1989, 1991, 1993). Akhtar and Humphries describe visitors to rural France in the 1960s as 'overwhelmingly the more aspirational and adventurous middle classes ... following in the footsteps of the jetsetters, the elite, the chic trend-setters and the creative set' (101). Again, David's France is an exclusive zone. She was prone to mock those tourists who searched for the authentic by reference to the writing of more experienced travellers.   She writes wryly of 'those humble-little-auberge-with-an-unrecognised-genius-in-the-kitchen stories', she scorns 'tourist haunts' (David, 1986, 67–68). She belittles the provincial ignorance of British tourists:

> The meat of the young kid is much appreciated all over the Mediterranean especially in the more primitive parts of Corsica and the Greek islands. It is hard to say why there is such a prejudice against this animal in England, and it is only the gastronomically ignorant who, the moment they go abroad, suppose whatever they are eating is disguised horse or goat. (David, 1950, 81)

The very exclusivity of David's subject, French and Mediterranean food, provides us, however, with a good point from which to start our consideration of her writing of food, nation and place. In so far as David's work can be characterised as the literary description of the viewing, preparation and consumption of the exotic and the exclusive by the privileged connoisseur for the privileged reader, then that writing can be understood at least partially within the context of generic practices related to but not the same as cookery writing: gastronomy.[5] David's witty advice about making locust bread in a review published in *The Sunday Times* in 1955, for example, shows her writing squarely in the gastronomic vein: 'Anyone who wants to taste locust bread, a delicacy available only when the locusts make their visitation every nine years, may start planning now, for they are due next year' (1986, 143).   David's writing of such recipes does more than simply amuse her readers with the obscurity of the gastronome's desires; it positions them in a particular way in terms of notions of home and 'abroad'. A triangular relationship is created between the reader at home, the writer and the 'foreigners' whose food is observed and described. On the one hand, she foregrounds the distance between the exclusive and very different experience described by the daring connoisseur and the reader left dully at home; on the other, she makes a pact with that reader whereby writer and reader may enjoy a shared perspective on those who are observed and described as indeed extraordinarily foreign. Here, in *Mediterranean Food*, for example, David describes the unpretentious dish of kebabs in terms that seem to confirm her own privileged experience and the refined sensibilities of her readers:

ARNI SOUVLÁKIA
Eaten on the terrace of a primitive Cretan taverna, favoured with wood smoke and the mountain herbs, accompanied by the strong red wine of Crete, these kebabs can be the most poetic of food. Exquisitely simple, they are in fact of Turkish origin, like many Greek dishes, although the Greeks do not always care to admit it. (71–72)

Writer and reader twist towards and away from the attractions of home and Britishness, and of 'abroad' and foreignness. The choices are impossible ones: the comfort of being 'at home' and the confirmation of shared views (of the false pride of Greeks), against the sense of the possibilities of self-fulfilment in a life lived with intensity in 'primitive', fragrant places far away.

There is certainly wit in David's gastronomic writing of food and, as the quotation above shows, she is skilled in evoking moods of relaxed pleasure. But such moments generally exist at the sidelines of an oeuvre in which the search for good food and the description of it is a very serious matter in intellectual, cultural and artistic terms. This is in part attributable to the way in which, as Stephen Mennell (1985) points out, gastronomic writing characteristically signals the engagement of the writer in literary expression as well as in the study of food (270–272). The concentration of the writer as she strains for accuracy is always before our eyes, whether in terms of the recipe, the context or the scene of eating food. The high seriousness with which David invests the work of evoking place and experience through food is signalled in a number of ways. Firstly, she repeatedly cites the recollections of literary antecedents, quoting canonical figures bearing the highest cultural capital, such as Henry James and Gertrude Stein, and travel writers with high artistic aspirations, such as Robert Byron and, of course, Norman Douglas. Secondly, her writing insistently brings her own scholarship in arcane fields to our attention, a scholarship redolent of a lifetime of reading and a commanding cosmopolitanism:

MELOKHIA
Melokhia is a glutinous soup much beloved by the Arabs, particularly in
Egypt. Melokhia is a kind of mallow (Greek *malakhe*, Latin *malva*) ... Wash
the melokhia well and drain it dry. Take the green leaves only and chop them
finely – this is done with the two-handled chopper called a *makhrata*
(Footnote: *Hachoir* in French, *Mezzaluna* in Italian. These instruments can
now be bought at a few good kitchen stores ... Once you have used one it is
unthinkable to be without it). (David, 1950, 19)

This is not a recipe that we are encouraged to make, nor a preparation of
food over which we are invited to salivate vicariously. Rather it is the
expression of accumulated knowledge and an invitation to imagine the
practical achievement of a forbiddingly unattractive dish.

David also practised a form of recipe writing of a spareness and
austerity that implied the triviality of alluring details or even helpful advice:

ICED CUCUMBER JELLY SOUP
Grate 2 large cucumbers with the peel. Add half a small onion grated, lemon
juice, salt, pepper and some very finely chopped mint. Stir in some melted
aspic jelly (see p. 134) or 2 sheets of gelatine and leave to set. Garnish each
cup of soup with a few prawns. (David, 1950, 20)

Jill Norman (1993), in describing David's obsessive practice of engaging in
an apparently endless series of drafts, evokes the figure of the artist
eschewing the superfluous and pretentious and (subjecting herself to a
stricter trial of truth than most writers) testing her prose again and again
against the dish it was supposed to produce (42).

If David approached writing food with such seriousness, what was she
being so serious about? Certainly some element of the answer to this
question lies in David's apparent desire to emulate Norman Douglas's
connoisseurship and the outlook on philistine, repressed Britain and the
sensual Mediterranean that it implied. But Douglas, born in 1868, was in
his seventies when David met him. David's cookery writing was as much in
tune with a more contemporary strain of understanding of Britain and
'elsewhere' amongst the conservative literary intelligentsia of the day (of
which, incidentally, her first publisher, John Lehmann, was very much
part). There were many in such circles who poured scorn on the greyness of
Britain in just the way that David is often quoted as doing, and who feared
that all that they held dear in cultural and intellectual terms – civilisation
itself – was under threat in the wake of the war and with the advent of state
intervention in all aspects of national activity (including the high cultural
domain). More particularly, it was far from unusual to find food and the
contrast between British and European cooking used to prove the argument

about a diminution in the richness of British cultural life. Looking at, for example, Cyril Connolly writing for *Horizon* in 1947, we can see how cheerless and squalid eating-places could be used as metaphors for a state of mass cultural dreariness against which those such as himself could scarcely hope to assert 'personality' or 'elegance'. In the following passage, we read of London as if it were itself an unappetising meal revealed beneath a 'metal dish cover':

> Most of us are not men or women but members of a vast seedy, overworked, over-legislated, neuter class, with our drab clothes, our ration books and our murder stories, our envious strict, old-world apathies and resentment – a care-worn people. And the symbol of this mood is London ... with its miles of unpainted half-inhabited houses, its chopless chop-houses, its beerless pubs, its once vivid quarters losing all personality, its squares bereft of elegance ... its crowds mooning round the stained green wicker of the cafeterias in their shabby raincoats, under a sky permanently dull and lowering like a metal dish cover. (151)

Conversely, the idea that experiences of eating out of the city or out of Britain might provide not merely a nostalgic pleasure, but a restorative activity as intellectually satisfying as the reading of canonical fiction and as socially acceptable as, say, genteel horticulture is simply taken for granted in, for example, the comments made by Edward Shills in April 1955 in *Encounter*:

> Continental holidays, the connoisseurship of wine and food, the knowledge of wild flowers and birds, acquaintance with the writings of Jane Austen, a knowing indulgence for the worthies of the English past, an appreciation of 'more leisurely epochs', doing one's job dutifully and reliably, these are the elements in the ethos of the newly emerging British intellectual class. (Wilson, 1980, 125)

This expresses the same bitterness at the degeneration of British cultural life and the same view of the possibilities of cooking as a signifier of cultural health as that which underpins Elizabeth David's early writing. She pits the 'cool, passionless destruction' practised by restaurants and hotels, the 'pillaging horde' of unwelcome visitors, 'the blithe acceptance of travesty ... deep within our national temperament', against the humble, the honest, the simple 'art, or the discipline, of leaving well alone', 'the calm confidence, the certitude that all is as it should be' (David, 1986, 11, 21, 27, 48, 70).

David's writing of the Mediterranean resonated with those strands of literary activity, Edwardian and Modernist, that marked a sense of the diminished possibilities of the urbanised, industrial society in Britain. The habit of cherishing the elaborate rituals of Mediterranean 'peasant' life for their primitivism and authenticity, of celebrating the supposed simplicity of the daily lives of 'peasants', died hard in Anglo-American letters in the first half of the twentieth century. Paul Fussell (1980) describes a 'British literary diaspora' to Europe in the 1920s and 1930s but even after the Second World War an expatriate life in the Mediterranean remained popular amongst writers. The same celebration of the more authentic ways of rural occurs in David's work. Here David describes such an interlude, a 'bucolic feast in the Vosges':

> We were making, rather unusually, a Saturday morning visit to a factory, a frying pan factory as it happened. We were invited to lunch in the village by the two brothers who ran the factory. Rather reluctantly we abandoned our plan to escape into the delicious countryside – it was early spring and the hedgerows were white with hawthorn blossom – and have a picnic lunch. We were introduced to the three ladies who ran the *pension*. Two were thin and spinsterish ... and the third was young and graceful. All were quiet and dignified. First, inevitably in the district, came a *quiche lorraine.* It was about fifteen inches across, served on a handsome flat earthenware platter, the filling risen like a soufflé, supported by only the thinnest of pastry ... With the quiche came a salad of crisp little green leaves. These I have never exactly identified, but in the native habitat of the quiche they are its almost obligatory accompaniment ... After the quiche came a mighty platter of hot coarse country sausage, poached with vegetables. So far, so good, and it *was* good. (69-70)

In this account of a meal, with its rigorous detail evoking the inextricable experience of earthiness (the sign of the continuing presence of an authentic rural world) and fragility (the tenuous hold of that world in the twentieth century), and its three quiet ladies, whose effortless production of five courses sounds an appropriately otherworldly note, David is able to describe the essential experience that she and her contemporaries, travellers and expatriates, pursued. This was 'the composition of a real country lunch as taken for granted by the ladies who ran that *pension de famille* in the 1960s. It was not, I think, anything out of the ordinary in the region ... The food was good honest food, honestly cooked' (David, 1986, 69–70).

Visiting or relocating to the rural Mediterranean offered David and certain of her contemporaries a position from which to write back to a Britain that they found repellently inauthentic and dishonest. To some extent, it seems also to have allowed writers to revisit the power relations of what, during the 1950s, was fast becoming a colonial past. Writing in 1955, in André Simon's exclusive *Wine and Food*, David recalls Kyriakon, her servant during a sojourn in wartime Egypt, only to erase his world: she describes him as a curiosity, 'not entirely of this world', 'Chaplinesque' (David, 2000, 165). Meanwhile, Angela, her sister's cook, is described thus:

> As I have said, she was a born cook, otherwise how could she have known the secret of that dish of Marcel Boulestin's which has poached eggs in the middle of an airy cheese soufflé mixture – she cooked it to perfection, and never were the poached eggs too hard or the soufflé undercooked. (164)

For David, it is not conceivable that Angela's skill could be demonstrative of knowledge acquired in Cyprus. It must therefore be instinctive. Indeed, she points out that Angela cannot learn:

> ... she seldom remembered that the English take it for granted that potatoes are served with every meal and so do not include them in the orders of the day: meal-times were frequently tended by the drama of 'Where are the potatoes, Angela?', 'Oh, Madam, I forgot'. (163)

David, living in the last gasp of British colonialism in the 1950s, does not imagine a rebellious impulse or even an independent point of view. The 'native' remains child-like.

All this, the gastronomy, the high literary aspiration, the rejection of modern Britain, the colonial and post-colonial world-view, seems to add up to a very coherent vision of Britain in which David shows, through the experiences of a privileged traveller in France and the Mediterranean, an order of value lost to Britain. She wrote, she said, in order to retain some sense of the warm humanity of Europe: to 'work out an agonised craving for the sun and a furious revolt against that terrible, cheerless, heartless food' (1986, 21).

It was surely with this sense of David's position that the presenter of a two-part biography of David shown on primetime television at Christmas in 1998, *In the Footsteps of Elizabeth David*, was chosen. At the forefront of the programme, tracing her 'footsteps', was Chris Patten, a Conservative Party ex-minister, the last colonial Governor of Hong-Kong and an apparently highly cultured pro-European.[6] As the viewers followed Patten on his gastronomic travels through France and Italy, they witnessed, interspersed with footage of Mediterranean countryside that seemed to confirm its preservation in a pristine Edenic state, Patten consuming – with wryly greedy relish – various foods associated with or described by David. He reiterated her terms of 'simple and honest' to describe 'peasant' food;

he visited cooks apparently working according to the same timeless, unlettered tradition as the three spinsters in the Vosges and Angela.

Interestingly, however, even as Patten's privileged voyage of consumption in a Mediterranean confected for our enjoyment and according to our desires matched the kinds of positions that I have associated with David, and even as his characterisation of the relationship between a cheerless, narrow-minded Britain and a brighter Europe more accepting of pleasure, seemed to echo the spatial relationships expressed in her work, the quality and mood of his narrative actually had very little in common with that of David's writing. In the gap between Patten's position of privilege, his lofty gaze on national life, his sentimental attachment to a 'simple', 'authentic' world of Mediterranean tradition, and the position adopted by David, lies David's particular sense of the space in which she was operating.

First of all, and this is the most noticeable difference between Patten's narrative and David's outlook, the travels that David describes – in search of food 'correctly' cooked and the means of reproducing it exactly – are characteristically extremely strained. Her travels involve the rushing from place to place or, more precisely, from restaurant to restaurant, to catch the flavour of the authentic. This is no work for the gastronomic dilettante; it is not a retreat into the primitive or the past. And there is no trace of self-mockery, I think, in David's later descriptions of her state as she pursues the dish that she has set herself to record: as 'arriving on a scorching summer day, hot, flustered, extremely late and despairing of lunch after a prolonged tangle with the Lyon motorway' (1986, 71).

It is true that the travel writer often elevates the seriousness of his or her quest by expressing it in terms of travail. Certainly David's patronage of hotels and restaurants in particular is loaded with difficulty in ways that are familiar to us from travel tales. In David, we recognise a patrician suspicion of waiters' lack of interest in the comfort of those who pay them, and a general sense of corrupt relations pervading the scene: of suspicion between potentially grasping proprietors and their customers, and between proprietors and undiscriminating tourists. This is the stuff on which scholars of travel build their arguments about how such writing is structured by a post-colonial mentality.

Cookery writing of all kinds is indeed strongly linked with travelling, but the connection is not always the same. Claudia Roden spoke recently of her work as 'writing and collecting recipes', describing journeys in which she converses with strangers, striving to find their 'secrets' and to penetrate their homes. Roden is unequivocal about the association between writing recipes and finding 'a way into their life and their kitchen'. David, by contrast, proceeds always in anticipation of being shut out of restaurants, of disappointment that a dish is not correctly made, of deterioration in standards. Where Roden strikes out in the spirit of post-colonial exploration, David matches the cheerless spaces of Britain in which, inevitably, dullness and dishonesty must literally be forced down one's throat, with the unpredictable and deteriorating scene greeting the traveller in search of the true food in France: 'It is with some experience that I record the melancholy fact that during those fifteen years I have eaten far worse meals in France, and more expensively – a bad meal is always expensive – than I would have believed possible in any civilised country' (1986, 67).

This is a form of gastronomic travel writing that often rests on the oppositions between home and abroad, false and true, degraded and authentic favoured by some of her contemporaries, but which, in David, becomes instead a breathless, ceaseless movement around spaces that vary only in the level of dissatisfaction and uncertainty that they may provoke. Where some merely return to a past located 'at home' in the kitchens of rural Britain or 'peasant' Europe, David occupies the less defined context of restaurants. Here relationships with strangers are anything but predictable and the visit may proffer relief or despair. The journey to find what is simple and honest is only occasionally rewarded by a sense of satisfaction in finding the form of a food associated with an 'original' national or regional identity and recording its qualities.

It is not difficult to understand David's apparent anomie in biographical terms: she was in many ways insecurely positioned as a divorced woman and in terms of her relationships with men; it is interesting to read of a woman of so privileged a background position herself on racial margins, having (by means of a remote ancestor) inherited, as she put it, 'a touch of the tar brush' (Chaney, 220). Jones and Taylor (2001), in a rare scholarly analysis of David's work, see in her writing the contradictory position of a career woman in flight from domesticity and yet still associated with the post-war fetishisation of the preparation of food in the home.

Whether 1950s exhortations to devoted housewifery meant anything to someone of David's class is, in my view, arguable. A more powerful context through which to understand David's account of rushing around Europe in search of simple, honest food may lie with what historians of the period have described as a moment of profound cultural uncertainty for Britain. How might the nation be formulated at a point at which the empire was draining away, leaving the British with a fast-diminishing power-base on which to rest long-held convictions of superiority? The 'special relationship' with America seemed increasingly to underline the draining away of British power (Porter, 1997, 102–3), and yet it cast a pall on closer ties with European allies. A European community loomed.

Certainly it was not unusual to find writers evoking a state of homelessness in the post-war period. The first volume of the autobiography of John Lehmann, *The Whispering Gallery* (1955), finishes with the following:

> Everyone who has been deeply attached to a home, a local habitation, in his early life, learns, sooner or later, that he has to find another home: not the separate home that he makes for his own family and friends apart from his parents, but a home that is independent of the four walls of a house, the apple-trees in an orchard, a particular river, seascape or woodland scene on which his early affections had fastened.

Continuing, Lehmann concludes that, in the present, this other home remains elusive: 'bricks and stones' are dissolved 'into a puff of dust, obliterating ... long cherished landmarks in a blinding second': the result is 'the pain, the sense of despair caused by ... homelessness' (333–334).

In writing recipes, of course, it would seem possible to preserve the 'bricks and stones' of identity in a form that allows them to be experienced with enjoyment. But recipes occupy an unusual position in David's work. Indeed it is often observed that what she offers in terms of instruction is difficult to follow or somehow incomplete.[7] Certainly we find David's recipes either suggesting the difficulty of reproducing the authentic – perhaps because of the inaccessibility of ingredients, or perhaps because of the crucial importance of context and ambience – or not really offering a recipe at all. This latter mode is common in her work, as in *Summer Cooking*:

A SUMMER HORS D'OEUVRE
A dish of long red radishes, cleaned, but with a little of the green leaves left on, a dish of mixed green and black olives, a plate of raw, round, small whole tomatoes, a dish of hard (not too hard) boiled eggs cut lengthways and garnished with a bunch of parsley. A pepper mill and a salt mill, lemons and olive oil on the table; butter, and fresh bread. Not very original perhaps, but how often does one meet with a really fresh and unmessed hors d'oeuvre? (420)

The identity of this in national terms is vague. To attribute provenance to such a 'recipe' seems superfluous. What distinguishes it is not its origin or its originality, but its insistence on 'unmessed' food.

In David's work, there is a striking intensity of interest given to instructions for and descriptions of meals that involve no work and no cooking at all. This intensity may be traced back to David's admiration for Norman Douglas. Writing about Douglas after his death, she made much of his obsession with the sources of food. She describes his travels each morning to establish the freshness of the food in restaurant kitchens and the provenance of every ingredient: 'Was the mozzarella dripping, positively dripping fresh?'(David, 1986, 124)

Yet David's descriptions of the quest for fresh food are not about checking for the value of what may be consumed later in a restaurant, as is the case in Douglas. They appear rather in the context of the highly serious and dedicated pursuit of small moments of consumption to relieve toil and displeasure. Where in the description of Douglas we seem to hear an echo of his praise of the sensual, his identification of food with sex, and perhaps also the obsession with purity that signals anxieties about the touch of social and racial Others, David's desire always to produce and consume very fresh food is not apparently related to sensual pleasure, an issue surprisingly absent in a writer so lauded for her opposition to English Puritanism. Nor is it a matter of the food being as innocent as possible of human contact: on the contrary, she often writes of feasting on ready-cooked food bought from a delicatessen:

> Pâtés and terrines, large jars of freshly made fish stock, saddle of rabbit rolled and stuffed ready for roasting or baking ... all the good things from the bakery ... all play their part in making every meal a treat as well as extraordinarily simple to prepare (1986, 78).

In fact, the food freshly bought and eaten not in a restaurant nor at home but on a picnic proves to be the epitome of the 'simple honest food' for which she searches. Certainly the search for what can be bought or cooked, and then consumed *as soon as possible afterwards* brings her closest to the achievement of the authentic and traditional: 'the towering heaps of tiny, sweet, briefly cooked mussels', or the peppers dressed with 'the good olive oil we have bought direct from the little oil mill', or the picnic where 'you ... sprinkle your bread with olive oil and salt, and eat it with ripe tomatoes or rough country sausage' and 'feel better off than in even the most perfect restaurant' (1986, 14, 78, 74).

The moment of triumphant discovery and unity with this 'true' food is not only unpredictable in the sense of being contingent on ceaseless searching; it involves food, a frail and changeable thing that, even as it is found must hastily be ingested before it spoils. Simple, honest, 'unmessed' food is rarely accessible to her readers, but even David, the scholarly connoisseur, experiences satisfaction only in snatched moments and in transitory situations, and can preserve that sense of access to a true experience only partially in recipes that can offer only the most prosaic details of the experience.

To conclude, then, it is ironic that Elizabeth David's work should be lauded for its triumph over the mean-spiritedness of the post-war era and that David herself should appear as the harbinger of a brighter national scene. In whatever ways David and her work may have been drawn into such changes, her writing itself takes a very different approach to the possibilities of national life, British or otherwise. The comparison of David's work with the writing of those whom she admired and with whom she associated gives us surer directions towards grasping David's construction of place. Certainly it draws to our attention the strong echoes in her writing of the view, prevalent amongst the privileged, that Britain was in cultural decline. But, while others of her generation seem to have found or at least imagined a retreat from this decline into the rural, David, searching for the same authenticity and tradition and pursuing its culinary traces with utter concentration, writes with a far less confident sense of the availability of escape routes. On the contrary, David's work does not so much organise an original space against which to measure national decline as extend the influence of that decline into all but the briefest moments of satisfying individual experience. David's Mediterranean is only ever an Other space in the sense of being the focus of memories of happier times. The Europe of the present, by contrast, is merely an arena in which she works tirelessly and with little success to taste the last traces of an authenticity already utterly lost to Britain.

The way in which cookery writing fixes certain national dishes draws it into the discourse of nation and national identity. Of course, the claims of authenticity that are made in cookery books are flimsy in the sense that all such claims are: they construct an understanding of what is true by forming a boundary that excludes other understandings. In some ways, they are flimsier still: the very appearance in print of 'authentic' recipes traditionally copied by example and explained in speech compromises them. And, as Appadurai points out, those who write cookery books are characteristically outsiders who tend to include 'the easy to grasp and more portable examples from alien ethnic or regional cuisines, partly because their own tastes for the exotic are first nurtured in restaurants or other public eating contexts, where the subtleties of that cuisine (which are often domestic) have already been pared down' (17).

Susan Leonardi (1989) has done much to convince us that recipe writing is about the creation of community and that communities may be made to cohere, however synthetically, in the writing of these instructions.

But, of course, communities, including nations, cannot truly be summarised into coherence. Food also appears to hold the possibility for defining ourselves culturally. The idea that we are what we eat has endless possibilities for self-congratulation, blame and exclusion. But food, often elusive and always in a state of deterioration, imperfectly fulfils the role we wish to give it. In Elizabeth David's work, we find a writer trying, literally, to place an experience in which truth and authenticity prevail, in which she can recognize something that is essential and original. But this is also a writer who evokes the complexity of a world that makes the achievement of such ideals impossible.

Notes

1   Claudia Roden interviewed in *Desert Island Discs*, 3 August 2001.
2   For discussions of the links between recipe writing and migration see Goldman, '"I Yam What I Yam": Cooking, Culture and Colonialism', 1992; Fordyce, 'Cookbooks of the 1800s', 1987; and Floyd, *Writing the Pioneer Woman*, 2002, Chapter 3.
3   The friendship is evoked most powerfully by David herself in an article published in *The Spectator* in 1963 and reprinted in David's anthology of her journalism, *An Omelette and a Glass of Wine*, 1986, pp. 120–133.
4   Levy's and Norman's conversation took place at the Royal Festival Hall in London on 27 February 2002. For two lively discussions of British post-war eating that take in a wider range of national culinary experience, see Hardyment, *A Slice of Life: The British Way of Eating since 1945*, 1995, and Driver, *The British at* Table, 1985.
5   The identification of David's work as gastronomy is also made in Jones and Taylor, 'Food Writing and Food Cultures: The Case of Elizabeth David and Jane Grigson', 2001, though they take that identification in a different direction in their analysis of David.
6   *In the Footsteps of Elizabeth David*, Channel 4, 1998.
7   This is the subject of a recent essay about David by the novelist Julian Barnes, 'The Land Without Brussels Sprouts', in *Something to Declare*, 2002.

CONTEMPORARY CONTEXTS

Chapter 9

Liberating the Recipe:
A Study of the Relationship between
Food and Feminism
in the early 1970s

Laurel Forster

We know that food communicates: it speaks of culture and class, of social custom and of familial habits; equally importantly it converses on a more intimate level, and relates in manifold ways to our emotions and moods, and even to our sexuality. This article seeks to question whether food might also illuminate the exigencies of a political movement. Indeed, if food, cookery and eating habits can be seen as an 'effective prism through which to illuminate human life' (Counihan, 1998, 1), then how might food and cookery illuminate the new way of life for women, suggested, campaigned for and dreamt about by the Women's Liberation Movement of the early 1970s in Britain? This article discusses the representation of food in recipes and articles appearing in the magazines and newsletters of the 'Feminist Seventies', and suggests that in this context too, food issues might be seen as a barometer of a changing feminism. By examining the range of ways in which food and cookery were utilised in feminist writings and publications, I argue that differing modes of food representation raised different issues, spoke to different political agendas and reflected the complexities of feminism at the time.

The relationship between women, food and power has been both enduring and complex within feminist study. At various times it has been seen as both an empowering and a disempowering aspect of women's lives. The women–food–power triangle continues to be seen as an oppressive force: from prescriptive nineteenth-century ideas of *kinder kirche küche* to contemporary culturally induced conditions such as anorexia and the obsession with dieting, the issues are wide-ranging and culturally embedded.[1] Alternatively, though, it has been argued that food offers a creative medium for women: cooking has been seen as an activity that can compensate for other, duller aspects of life (Giard, 1998); it has also been argued that female sexuality has found positive expression through the literary metaphor of food (Sceats, 2000). Moreover food has long been seen as a means of empowerment for women: as early as 1943 Kurt Lewin described women as 'gatekeepers' for the flow of food through various 'channels' into the home (McIntosh and Zey, 1998, 128), and over half a century later, it has been argued that 'Men's and women's ability to produce, provide, distribute and consume food is a key measure of their power' (Counihan, 1998, 2). Women, food and power remain of interest in general culture too, witnessed by the opening exhibition of the new Women's Library in London in 2002: 'Cooks and Campaigners'.

My concern here is with the diverse appearances of food and food issues within the magazine culture of the early British Women's Liberation Movement. I want to investigate whether food and gender politics within the movement can tell us anything about the broader feminist scene. In overarching terms, food can be seen as a site of discussion within 1970s feminism in a number of ways. Most obviously, food as a basic need came to the fore at times as the site of political activism in opposition to the capitalist system, such as when the miners' wives of the 1972 strike forced food prices down by collective purchasing, and when East London women formed their own low-priced food cooperative, also in 1972. But, at another level, through recipes and articles in women's liberation magazines, and in many ironic or self-deprecating food jokes, food played its part in raising awareness within the movement. Lastly, food and its associated chores (shopping, cooking, clearing away and so on) formed part of the 'Wages for Housework' debate which sought wider recognition of women's domestic labour in social and financial terms. The present discussion will concentrate on the latter two modes, where food was the subject of written communication between feminists and society at large: firstly questioning how the recipe itself, as a means of communication, played a part in the movement, and then discussing how food became assimilated into wider discussions of women's oppression.

The Women's Liberation Movement (WLM) might be described as a grassroots, consciousness-raising exercise which was both political and personal in its motivations and activities. It brought together women from a range of backgrounds and interests to demand social change. Besides consciousness-raising meetings, women organised marches and demonstrations, held conferences and supported picket lines. Women wanted financial independence, sexual liberty and freedom from oppression for themselves and other minority groups. Many feminists – intellectuals and agitators – campaigned for specific socialist issues and causes (Rowbotham, Segal and Wainwright, 1979). But the WLM also had a more general and diverse project within the social and cultural system: to bring patriarchal dominance to public attention. Women's double workload – in the traditional domestic sphere and in the workplace – was made evident, as were many other inequalities. Gradually, some women, often as part of a local, informal, consciousness-raising group, shared their experiences and began to find a voice. This voice spoke politically or personally of their subjugation and oppression as women, wives and mothers in a society where male social and economic dominance was the norm. Some of these individual expressions have been recorded in the form of testimonial in books such as Elsie Adams and Mary Louise Briscoe's *Up Against the Wall Mother* (1971) and Michelene Wandor's *The Body Politic* (1972). Such self-appraisal and personal statement by women at the time illustrates one of the prominent slogans of the movement: 'making the personal political'. Making previously personal and private aspects of their lives part of a public political movement was a radical step for women. As Sheila Rowbotham (1999) has more recently suggested: 'The collective culture of the new movement was springing from individual desires for a personal transformation which went deeper than any ideology. It involved a psychological break with all that had gone before' (398).

Rowbotham, involved in the feminist movement of the 1970s and still a feminist writer thirty years later, has an interesting retrospective position.[2] She argues that there were tensions in women's liberation ideals from the beginning. One irresolvable issue was the 'distance between the discontents of daily life and images of alternative Utopian possibilities'; and another was the problem of 'oscillating between making a separate culture and demanding access to the mainstream' (399). These two issues then, reality versus utopia, and separatism versus empowerment within the status quo, remained problematics for feminism in the 1970s, and for feminist discussion thereafter. The turbulence caused by these dual positions fighting for prominence is perhaps one of the reasons the Women's Liberation Movement became inward-looking and academically oriented, rather than expansive and practical. These and other dichotomies permeate much of the women's liberation writing, even sometimes to disastrous effect![3] Indeed, J. M. Bardwick (1980) argues that the feminist movement was clearest about what it rejected rather than what might replace the social norms it was rejecting (21).

None the less, one of the successes of the WLM was to bring feminism to mainstream attention. Mainstream media took notice of woman's changed role and represented it in various ways: for example, Marguerite Patten's *500 Recipes for Working Wives* (1970) and *Busy Cook's Book* (1973) were just two of the many books which appeared, adapting cooking methods and expectations in order to accommodate the busy working wife and mother. Also some mainstream commercial magazines for women, such as *Cosmopolitan, Options* and *Woman's Own*, were editorially aware of the changing nature of the family and of women's roles, indicating this through articles about domestic life, and about cookery. Some saw this new role of 'working wife or mother as an acceptable – desirable, even – member of society' (Ferguson, 1985, 110). Mainstream magazines are significant in the way they simultaneously represent the realities of women's lives and their fantasy or aspirational lives too. It is argued that mainstream magazines send out mixed messages to women surrounding the myth of femininity, regarding what they are and what they 'ought' to be (Ballaster et al., 1991, 124–125). One of the reasons for the great appeal of women's magazines is that this duality of female existence echoes the contradictions inherent in many women's actual lives. This indicates a mainstream acceptance of, even play on, female reality and utopia, as well as a feminist one. Thus, this contradiction was also reflected, in various guises, in the feminist, non-commercial magazines.

The mainstream attention to the evolving role of woman has significance for the women's movement, not least because it highlights the unsure relationship of the new movement to mainstream culture: the WLM seemed to both emerge out of the changing social and cultural scene, and to become a counter-culture of its own, separate from other counter-cultures. Moreover, as Elizabeth Nelson (1989) argues, the feminist movement suffered, like other counter-cultures, from the fundamental problem of the difficulty of creating a new social order while trying to argue with the existing one (4–8). This awkward position of owing something to the mainstream and trying to create a new social order is a duality which I would like to apply to the discussion of food at the time. Indeed, the varied deployment of food discussions and recipes in the feminist newsletters and magazines of the 1970s closely echoes some of the wider issues and tensions within the movement itself, as well as, in format and contents, borrowing from both mainstream and alternative culinary cultures.

Food was also a strong presence in the counter-cultural scene. As early as the 1960s, alternative foods and modes of food consumption became, and stood for, a new way of life. For instance there was a newly resurrected interest in vegetarianism and a concomitant focus on new health foods and ingredients, often only available in new and quirky health food shops. These new foods made their way into communes and to events such as rock concerts which typified the hoped-for new social order. Similarly the 'Mother Earth' figure became a trope of feminism, often symbolised, caricatured even, by the home baking of bread: a virtually forgotten phenomenon at the time. The macrobiotic diet came to the fore as a means of controlling the body–food relationship, and the epitome of alternative eating, the veggiburger, was patented at this time too. Such a positive, self-empowering decision to consume differently by selecting different foods and different modes of eating came to symbolise, at least for a while, the choice of a new way of life for the individual: an alternative culture.

This aspiration towards a new way of life through the consumption of everyday food, again a mixture of fantasy and reality, explains much about the occurrence of the feminist recipe in WLM newsletters and magazines. Just as Ellen McCracken (1993) has argued that women's magazine covers offer women the attractive prospect of a 'future self' (13), so I want to suggest that there is a link through a recipe which subtly communicates with a future self. Recipes themselves can be seen not only as 'embedded discourses' (Leonardi, 1989), but also as fluid narratives which operate in different ways: they have a structure to them which constructs us as reader or as participant. They also have a varying language in their introduction, ingredients and instructions. This language may reflect the style of the cookery writer, the mode of the publication or even the community of the anticipated audience. A recipe may be precise and authoritative with a list of ingredients followed by instructions of varying difficulty and detail, or it may be merely a casual food suggestion. Furthermore these recipes, once read, may or may not ever be actually cooked. They may address, in a *lisible* or *scriptible* manner, a number of other issues such as tourism, regionality and identity, where the reader learns much more than a new recipe. So, when a recipe is read without much intention of following it through to the end product, it performs a different function. The reader might, pragmatically, mentally file it away for future reference or inspiration when she next has the main ingredient to hand. Or, she might, more romantically, imagine a version of herself where time and opportunity permit her to enter into this dialogue concerning lifestyle; where this interesting recipe becomes part of a more interesting, more sharply defined, unburdened life where cooking perfection might be achieved. Combining the practical with the phantasmogorical, recipes are often aspirational narratives as well as instructive ones: they are an indicator of what we might cook (or even be) if our lives were different.

It is this same distance between a utopian impulse and a stark examination of the everyday that Rowbotham identifies as one of the major problems within the feminist movement of the seventies. And, interestingly, critics of women's mainstream magazines, such as Cynthia White (1970), have also identified the dual impulse of fantasy and the everyday, or the aspirational and instructive aspects of many women's magazines (298–299). This is one aspect of women's lives which carried over from the mainstream to the feminist magazines, as both forms of feminist appraisal and appeal – utopian and quotidian – can be found in the many newsletters and magazines of the movement. Understanding this duality seems central to understanding the feminist cause of the early 1970s, and the various feminist food writings provide good illustrations of the problematic as they often simultaneously offered down-to-earth practical advice and invoked ideas of utopian lifestyle aspirations.

One of the most important and enduring modes of communication for the WLM was the range of non-commercial magazines and newsletters which proliferated at the time, such as *Spare Rib*, *Red Rag* and *Shrew*. Some newsletters were produced nationally and others more locally. The local newsletters might be hand-written and home-typed news sheets, photocopied and stapled together, such as *Bread and Roses* produced by a Leeds women's collective, or they might have a more professional look, like *Brass Tacks*, a 'newspaper for women that men read', similar in appearance to a thin free local paper, and produced on a printing press in Manchester. The national magazines like *Red Rag*, *Shrew* and *Spare Rib* also have a home-spun, anti-commercial look to them, and even the Married Women's Association, which sounds much more official, produced only a flimsy booklet. However what the majority of dedicated women's liberation newsletters had in common was a desire to 'communicate with other women'.[4] Generally they lack the commercialism of glossy pictures to attract the eye or the bombardment of advertisements and hence big influxes of manufacturers' money; they carried low-key adverts mostly for products typical of cottage industry. So not only were liberation magazines not glossy; the contents were more hard-hitting too, often not written by professional journalists, but by housewives, mothers, activists and academics, all interested in pursuing the cause of sexual equality and in promoting issues which concern and interest women.

Recipes appeared in a number of these newsletters and, before moving on to a detailed discussion of the appearance of food-related items in *Spare Rib*, it is useful to briefly discuss a small sample of the range of recipes in other WLM low-key publications. The recipe features in a number of 1970s feminist publications often tried to reflect the objectives of the movement as a whole by raising women's awareness and consciousness through collective communication and education, just like other forms of WLM activity such as the local women's groups of the time. From the examples below we can see how different magazines tried to make connections with political issues, or at least gesture towards a feminist voice. They resonate with feminist agendas of sexual preference, sexual oppression and the trap of the domestic. Using humour, an important aspect of the WLM, some treatments of food issues managed to say more than one thing, whilst others dissipated any feminist message they might have had.

One such example appears in the June 1976 edition of *Brass Tacks*, where, in a home economy page spread, Val Tebbutt encourages us to 'Use rice instead of the expensive spud'. This article is 'feminist' only in its title. An explicitly anti-male banner heading reads: 'Just before the sports section we offer a page covering another sport women excel at ... feeding the brute, and the kids too!' This feminist, or rather anti-male, slant of a jibe at the male obsession with sport is in truth merely a superficial nod towards feminism, a reactionary feminism which dissipates any true commitment to radical feminism with knowing, accepting humour. The article is really a home economics lesson in substituting one staple foodstuff for another. The 'feminist' heading earns the article a place in the newspaper. So this article exemplifies the mode of maintaining status quo of the domestic sphere as female domain, while acknowledging the feminist politics of the time.

Closer commitment to women's liberation can be seen in a recipe feature called 'Jane's Journal', which appears in several issues of *Femme*. In one edition, 'Jane' discloses her sexual orientation within her introduction to her 'Arabic recipes':

Well, I managed to get myself invited to dinner with the Arab family just around the corner – actually, between you and me, there's a rather luscious-looking daughter, so if I serve up more than your fair share of Arabic recipes in the next few months, you'll know why! (June 1977, 4)

Sexual experimentation was of course one of the defining aspects of the hippie movement and the right to self-determine sexuality continued into the WLM. Such a gleeful announcement of non-heterosexual orientation was all part of sexual liberation for women, and here 'Jane', the recipe writer, is able to both 'come out' in the context of her food writing, adding her voice to the lesbian number, and yet retain her anonymity by withholding her full name. She thus uses the introduction to a recipe feature as a moment for self-declaration. It becomes a personal narrative, integrating different aspects of her life through her cookery writing.

Another more overtly feminist occurrence of recipes is in *Bread and Roses* magazine, which intersperses its recipes amongst its other articles. A hand-written 'Recipe for Brown Bread' appears after an overtly ironic invective about women's supposed victim-like behaviour and hence responsibility for male sex crimes (9). This typed piece ends with the word 'RAPE' in large bold letters, hand styled in an oriental script. Immediately below this comes our recipe for home-made bread. The arrangement on the page may be an accident of space shortage and a roughly fashioned page layout, as *Bread and Roses* is a newsletter of the most home-produced kind. None the less, this juxtaposition is starkly arresting; the layout on the page says much about the disparate and positive attitude to feminism in the 1970s: it mixes harsh reality with idealised womanhood. Women were considered simultaneously sufficiently worldly to fight against the sexually offensive remarks and gestures of the 'omniscient male population', and also sufficiently domestically skilled to bake bread. Similarly, in the spring 1975 edition, a 'Recipe for Delicious Macaroni Cheese' appears underneath an article on battered women and next to a sardonic fantasy column on male–female role reversal (10). To the community of women who read the newsletter, the juxtaposition of these ideas of womanhood would have spoken to the cohesion and the disparity which structured the WLM.

Ironic humour was a persistent and effective mode for the WLM, and food, with its polysemic implications for the gender struggle, was frequently at the heart of the joke. *Shrew's Own* (later *Shrew*), for instance, makes a sarcastic pun through a photograph of a pie crust with the words 'Humble Pie' imposed on top. The recipe title, 'This week's recipe for keeping a man ...', is followed by the instruction, 'First catch your man ...'. This uses the conventions of a recipe, well understood by women, to make a self-deprecating joke about love, domestication and docility expected within marriage (August 1971). Complex issues about male and female behaviour and potential behavioural changes are addressed through a combination of humour, knowingness and hard-hitting irony. These examples serve to demonstrate how various feminist agendas were approached through food in a number of different modes. The connection with feminism might be slight and occasional, through a title, an introductory remark, the position on the page or an ironic joke, but the intention to connect with the movement through the representation of food, and extend different feminist agendas to the recipe context, is apparent.

Different feminist agendas were perhaps nowhere more prominently discussed than in one of the best-known women's liberation magazines, *Spare Rib*, which arguably 'spoke to and for the Women's Liberation Movement' (Ballaster et al., 112). Started in 1972, *Spare Rib* certainly played an important part in the consciousness-raising programme of the WLM, as Janice Winship (1987) suggests: 'Editorial production, design and administration of the magazine, what appears and how it is represented, and *Spare Rib's* relation to its readers are all informed by a sense of responsibility to women in the women's movement' (123). Using more direct terms, Braithwaite (1995) has described *Spare Rib* as a magazine which 'knew its market and enjoyed the iconoclastic, left-wing Greenham Common reputation. The life span of twenty years was a tribute to its uncompromising and honest commitment to the feminist cause' (102). However this was not as straightforward a mission as it might appear. *Spare Rib* struggled with the same dichotomies as the movement generally. For instance, Marsha Rowe, editor of *Spare Rib*, explained that the magazine was 'a product of the counter-culture and a reaction against it' (Nelson, 1989, 140). And, as Winship has argued, '*Spare Rib* could hardly straightforwardly adopt a "feminist approach" when it wasn't wholly certain what that involved politically, or journalistically' (133).

These tensions and difficulties of expression can be detected in *Spare Rib's* changing and developing attention to issues of food. Through the following detailed discussion of the recipe features I will argue that this shifting approach to food consumption in the magazine can be seen to echo wider feminist political shifts, and reveal the tensions and dichotomies of the feminist movement as discussed above. The recipe features in *Spare Rib* were in early editions, mostly in 1972. Some of these early features borrow their formats from the layout style of mainstream women's magazines, but most attempt a different ideological outlook. One early article in the August 1972 edition, entitled 'Natural Earth Drinks', bemoans the 'Summer-time blues' suffered by women (25). Through this shared experience, the recipe introduction assumes a sense of community in the readership. The article offers advice about the benefits of vitamins and gives suggestions for vitamin-packed drinks. Recipes with 'natural earth' names like 'Sunset Reverie', 'Yoghourt Yin' and 'Scorpio Rising' use a variety of ingredients. Some ingredients are everyday, but others, such as wheatgerm and sesame seeds, are a bit funkier, echoing the new mood of alternative, anti-commercialist lifestyles grounded in self-determined food choices. The mixed genres of the page – recipes, explanatory and informative text, line sketches and poetry – all serve to portray educational messages about the benefits of vitamins to women's health and the food sources of each vitamin. The recipes themselves offer information and encourage women to be healthy and feel better through their intake of such foods. However, this article communicates more than just recipes or indeed relatively new information about vitamins: it assumes that women will need to increase their vitamin intake in summer due to the common experience of feeling run down and 'having the blues'. The opening paragraph structures this shared understanding between author and reader thus:

> To be down in the Summer seems much worse when you contrast your mood to this season's growth and vitality. [...] To help you 'break on through to the other side,' here are 5 special summer drinks, each containing a powerful dose of natural vitamins.

The recipes which follow provide the cure. This recipe feature then functions as a medical consultation, where treatments are offered for a given ailment. Here, the patients – all women who read *Spare Rib* – do not need to be individually consulted. Rather it is accepted through mutual understanding that women's lot is overly demanding and that these recipes, if not the full answer to the women's cause, may at least help her to cope in some measure. This article speaks to the community of women and feminists, addressing silent but understood assumptions that women are overworked. It foregrounds a basic feminist premise of the 1970s that women were unrecognised, unpaid labourers of the most hard-working kind. This food article, then, is concerned to offer a healthier, happier summer for women through new foodstuffs and new information about traditional foods. It recognises the general problems of depression and lethargy suffered by many women and tries to educate them out of this debilitating state through better food knowledge.

Not all the food features in *Spare Rib* were as clear in their feminist message. In the following month the September edition of *Spare Rib* had a feature called 'Munchy Business': largely a collection of recipes suitable for a fairly elaborate picnic (31–33). However there is a self-consciousness about this article, as if the author really knows that the content does not fit well with the tone of the rest of the magazine: 'It's no use trying to oust me from this issue with plans for expert information on nutrition. I have got some even more expert information of the serious business of greedy picnics', writes Fran Fogarty, humorously justifying her article's inclusion. The introduction and contents of this article send out mixed messages. The introduction tries to position the recipes as part of the new alternative lifestyle, the author sounding at times like a trendy rock chick, but at others like a cheery middle-class mother trying to make sure that the children have a nutritious diet:

> Seriously, picnics are a true hit, not to mention noshing at all the disaster-ridden festivals some of us feel bound to endure in order to take in some funky sounds. Just because you may look like a drug-crazed hippie, there's no reason why you should live off congealed brown rice or up-against-the-

Walls undesirable Wimpy creations. All you need is a box of goodies to keep your pecker up, be you at Bickershaw or an Atom Heart Mother meadow in wildest Wales.

Tensions can be detected here between 'feminism' and 'food'. Lip service is paid to the new supposed freedoms in lifestyle experienced by a 'drug-crazed hippie' attending open-air rock concerts, but no mention is made about the gender/family politics behind the responsibility for providing the meal, or about the time invested in the healthy-eating plan for the family. The language is similarly contradictory: 'up against the wall' is a borrowed phrase, presumably added to lend a feminist dimension, but 'keep your pecker up' echoes tired oppressive platitudes. In this heavy-handed introduction, there is little space for the reader to position herself or engage with the fantasy picnic offered. 'Doreen's Kipper Paté' and 'Serena's Biscuit Cake' may not be complex recipes, but they are surrounded by a complex of unacknowledged language and gender politics. The tone of the article rings untrue, as if Fogarty were forcing her recipes into the cultural and ideological frame of 1970s liberated woman. She does this by drawing upon current linguistic and cultural tropes of the alternative lifestyle but falls short of addressing, indeed deliberately ignores, the feminist outlooks on freedom and education expected of *Spare Rib*. As in the article which promotes 'rice instead of spuds', the feminism here is superficial.

This is revealed in other ways in the writing of the recipes too. Some of the recipes are formally structured and others add a throwaway line, while the recipe for home made bread is there in the abstract only:

> I just can't face sounding off about how easy it is to bake your own bread, there's a bit too much of that sort of thing going round at the moment [...] If you want to know [the recipe] write to me at *Spare Rib*, adding much praise for the brilliance of my writings to ensure a quick reply.

Food is the purveyor of these mixed messages of unconvincing feminism. The carnivalesque tone of this feature is enhanced by the accompanying photographs by Sue Wilkes. The photographs, on sepia film and hand tinted, add to the sense of artificiality and psychedelia of the article, showing an incohesive family group, dressed and made up like clown-figures, rather surreally and awkwardly staged in a picnic scene. This recipe feature strains towards a feminist approach but reveals an unclear feminist focus. The article relies on an imagined lifestyle for its relevance, and depicts a halcyon setting of leisure, countryside and good food, not gender power struggle and quotidian reality. Because of this utopian outlook it feels out of kilter with the feminist perspectives of the other articles on, for example, science education for girls (30), or the often female illness of agoraphobia (5–7). There are important implications here for the relationship between food and 1970s feminism. Perhaps the tone which portrays food as an enjoyable leisure activity was incompatible with a political struggle. Although there was always a utopian element to early 1970s feminism, perhaps this article fails to convince because of its imbalance: the feminist fantasy utopia of rock concerts and picnics, far removed from the daily existence of many oppressed or minority groups of women, outweighs any feminist content such as education or the gender struggle. The narrative of the recipe feature speaks to a particular image of 1970s feminism; the awkward tone of the introduction – 'It's no good trying to oust me' – signals an unspoken recognition that the community of editors and readers had changed.

In a similar vein, in another article published in December in the same year, 'The Edible Present', Patricia White extols the pleasures and virtues to be gained from home-made Christmas presents. Recipes such as 'Sugared Nuts', 'Cheese in Pots', 'Bread and Butter Pickle' and 'Orange Pomanders' follow the tradition of Christmas fare (32–33). The accompanying photograph by Valerie Santagto is a close-up of a wicker basket full of preserving jars of the Christmas goodies, decorated with bows and ribbons. A housewifely arm in a flowery smock holds an admirable basket of wares to which the reader may aspire. This article is hugely sentimental, appealing to that strong emotional link women feel between giving food and giving affection, which, it could be argued, serves only to reinforce the nineteenth-century chains of the domestic angel. A feminist reading might declare the partial anti-commercialism of the article; in the introduction, the giving of such presents is considered to be beyond the 'measure of money'. However in a broader feminist sense there is little consciousness of the oppression and sense of duty many women suffer in order to provide the perfect 'home-made' Christmas, this being the most obvious cultural construct of the domestic calendar in which a simple tradition has become a materialist nightmare. Furthermore, there is no acknowledgement of the limited time working mothers have to engage in this sort of activity. Instead, this kind of recipe article could appear in almost any kind of middlebrow women's magazine. And like many articles in mainstream women's magazines, it appeals to a 'mythical *individual* woman' outside feminist politics (Storey, 2001, 134). Indeed, in stark contrast, a later article in a mainstream woman's magazine, *Woman's Own*, urges women to earn an independent income from this sort of work (18 July 1981). Here the mainstream press has picked up on the demands of 1970s feminism: money of one's own, to release women from the nuclear family trap of an unquantifiable emotional exchange, was one of the main demands of the WLM. Ironically 'The Edible Present' offers no such suggestion for independent earnings. In feminist terms it is full of contradictions: it tries to be alternative in the sense of avoiding the commercialism of bought presents but, in truth, in its middle-class orientation, it only adds to the trap of the domestic. Unspoken is the assumption that a good wage (a man's wage?) has afforded the expensive ingredients and that a woman's time (unpaid and unacknowledged) has daintily prepared all these confections, proving her worth through the cultural statement of domestic ability and bestowal of affection through food.

Thus the recipe features in early editions of *Spare Rib* engage with many of the issues of the feminism of the time: there are elements of education and collective understanding of woman's burden in society; but there are also mixed messages in articles which try to combine a fantasy image of womanhood with an actual domestic chore, cooking. The recipe stands for a constant reminder of the daily reality of woman's work (shopping, cooking, setting the table, washing up) and the early feminist magazines made some attempt to use the recipe as a vehicle through which to integrate feminist ideologies and daily life. That these recipe features may now seem naïve serves to highlight our disbelief in a life which could encompass both an idealistic fantasy and an everyday reality. The utopian ideals of early second-wave feminism faded, as women began to find it difficult to reconcile an idealised world with day-to-day reality. The two recipe articles, 'Munchy Business' and 'The Edible Present', epitomise this: fine ideals of healthy open-air picnics and home-made consumable Christmas presents are anti-commercialist and would indeed add to the quality of life, but the very idealised nature of the articles conceals the domestic labour involved, and so in reality contrives to support the status quo.

Food issues from about 1974 onwards in *Spare Rib* became subsumed into wider sociological contexts of women, domestic work (of which cooking is a major part) and the necessity for a social wage. The intense focus on domestic issues meant that recipes mostly gave way to political discussion. The sociological neglect of women and their domestic labour was made clear in Ann Oakley's *The Sociology of Housework* (1974). And as the utopian inclinations of the early WLM declined, so a stronger theoretical position took hold: Marxist feminism. The feminist call for 'Wages for Housework' was highly significant to the movement and was largely promoted and discussed by the increasing number of intellectual and Marxist feminists. The long-running Marxist debate about female contributions to the economy through domestic labour emerged in direct opposition to the constraints the capitalist system imposed on women. An important initiating document was Selma James and Mariarosa Dalla Costa's *The Power of Women and the Subversion of the Community* (1972), which discussed housework and women's roles and argued for the rejection of the role of housewife. Selma James argued radically that, as women's unpaid domestic labour is crucial to the functioning of the capitalist system, it should be recognised as part of the base chain of productivity, and receive monetary reward.

In 'When is a Wage not a Wage?' published in *Red Rag* in August 1973, Caroline Freeman takes issue with some of Selma James's claims and offers a different solution (16–18). Wages for housework, Freeman argues, do not constitute a total solution: they 'could not undo the identification between housework and being available twenty four hours a day by virtue of being a woman'. Wages for housework might even, through increased state regulation, restrict women's freedoms further. Freeman, by contrast, suggests that if the physical labour of housework could be removed from the home, this would permit technological efficiency to perform some of the basic domestic chores like laundry and cooking. This would provide jobs (for women and men) and demystify this so-called women's work. For Freeman, the wages for housework debate in itself does not solve the issues and social preconceptions which women face, nor is it a broad enough debate to 'fill the strategic and theoretical vacuum in the women's movement'.

Marxist history was an important discourse for feminism in the 1970s as it demonstrates that women were not always so far removed from the nexus of productive and valued work in the home/workplace. Roberta Hamilton in *The Liberation of Women* (1978) points out the advantages of the older feudal system, where home and work were not defined by being different places; and domestic duties and other forms of labour were not separated. Hence women's place in society was determined as a result of their important contribution to their family's livelihood (23–39). In a similar vein Evelyn Reed (1971) reminds us of the earlier anthropologist Briffaut, who concluded that women had a leading role in primitive societies because they produced the necessities of life (19). Kate Marshall (1982) points to women's oppression under a capitalist system and argues that with more working women the only way to free women was to make domestic work into a public industry (18–24).

Such studies of Marxism and women's history were taken up by many feminist writers of the 1970s and reworked into women's contemporary political situation. In this vein, Freeman's *Red Rag* article discussed above tries to close the gap between domestic and other forms of work by arguing that those forms of domestic labour which can be mechanised, such as laundry, day childcare and communal cookery, should be taken out of the home and effectively into the workplace. By suggesting that men or women perform domestic tasks in a technologically efficient way, in return for an appropriate wage, Freeman is adopting the feudal idea of domestic work being of equal status with other work, and forcing this to operate in a capitalist framework. Here the idea is adapted so that all forms of work take place in the same location, the workplace, thus diminishing the difference in status and cultural recognition, and refusing the spatial separation and differentiation of domestic and other work.

The thorny issue of domestic work is approached in a different way by Jenefer Coates (1974), in an article called 'Shared Housework' (*Spare Rib*, 25, 28–29). This article is particularly important to the present discussion because it combines the wider context of cookery in the housework debate with actual recipes reinforcing the author's political message. Here Coates challenges women to remember: 'When was the last time you came home from work and found a meal waiting on the table?' She goes on to discuss how we must arrive at a 'new concept of domestic duty' if we are not to either overwork ourselves (as already working women) or to end up paying someone else to do it. Both solutions are unacceptable, Coates claims, and create problems elsewhere. She argues that we each rely on domestic functions for our well-being, and so we should each be responsible for those functions. It is patriarchal attitudes that have subordinated women into accepting those chores as 'women's work'. Whilst men and boys must learn to take responsibility for themselves on the domestic front, women must also learn a new modus operandi: 'The only way to avoid being cast in the traditional role of household drudge is to refuse to play the part: women must withdraw, Lysistrata-style, their domestic favours.' With reference to Le Corbusier's idea of home as a 'machine for living'. Coates claims women must demystify domestic tasks and educate men into completing them, 'The kitchen must become [...] neutral territory'. This will take planning, a carefully conceived routine and will probably mean a drop in standards. Moreover women must be prepared to articulate what has been intuitively learnt by them over years. With regard to cleaning, 'Anyone tall enough to grasp a Hoover handle or a broom is old enough to work it'; and as for laundry, 'Any casualties or damaged clothes must be regarded as a cheap price for freedom.' Coates suggests a period of training or skills development before a more feudal system of shared labour (in the home and elsewhere) might be reinstated.

Coates then moves on to the introduction of her recipe section, with an extensive series of lifestyle suggestions for gender and family equality in the home. She offers practical solutions, such as shopping once a week, making use of late night openings and shopping to a menu plan. On the cooking front she suggests cooking double quantities of a basic dish and serving it differently on consecutive days; similarly 'Many vegetables may be eaten hot one day and cold with salad dressing the next'. Coates suggests we rethink our approach to the evening meal, either preparing it the day before or using recipes that can be prepared rapidly. The recipes are entitled: 'What, after all, is cooking other than fuelling?' Next she offers a few recipe ideas to support her argument. The scientised tone of this piece, and the excruciating level of detail imply that this is a recipe even a man could follow. Thus the language of the recipe acts as a means of achieving gender equality with regard to family cooking, trying to redress the imbalance of kitchen work. Spaghetti Bolognaise and Shepherd's Pie are shown to have roughly the same ingredients and cooking methods, and differ from each other only in the final stages. In the Bolognaise recipe there is a sense of conveying superior home economics knowledge to those just learning: 'Add the very finely chopped garlic, the basil, the wine and thinly sliced chicken livers (these are worth the extra 10p or so).' And a seemingly male-oriented precision dominates the style of the very lengthy and detailed instructions:

> For the spaghetti itself: heat up a large pan of salted water (1 teaspoon salt). When boiling, turn down to simmer and begin to ease the spaghetti into it, holding the stiff ends until the part in the water has softened and you can slowly submerge the entire length of spaghetti strands. Do not overcook spaghetti: 10 minutes is a maximum. You can test it after 9 minutes by hooking out one strand on a fork and biting through it. It should be firm and when you drain it off in a colander or sieve, it will be rather slippery (it is overcooked when gluey). Serve immediately.

This level of detail is surely for someone who has barely seen spaghetti in the packet, let alone ever cooked it before. Similarly for the potatoes to top the Shepherd's Pie there is mind-numbing level of detail given: 'When the potatoes are ready (twist with a fork to make sure they are not hard at the centre) drain them well and mash them. For best results the potatoes should be forced through a sieve. The addition of a knob of butter and a tablespoon or two of milk will make them creamier.' And so on, salt, pepper and nutmeg notwithstanding. For such standard family recipes, such basic cooking techniques, and given the audience of adults, the recipes have the tone of a school domestic science lesson, with little left to imagination or creativity and the sole emphasis on quantitative success.

For this writer, then, cookery is not a creative act but a scientific experiment in which the instructions must leave nothing to chance and assume no prior knowledge. These recipes do not offer escapism or an aspirational narrative for the reader; they make only practical, direct demands of their reader in order for the household to function efficiently. More specifically, they show men how to survive and achieve in women's culture of everyday cookery. Basic home economics in this case becomes a technological process where economies of scale, time and duplication may be revealed and therefore the process simplified. The tone of this piece implies that in the pursuit of equality, women must sacrifice the essentially female secrets of the kitchen. Here is a mode of communicating all those assumed knowledges supposedly passed on in the kitchen through maternal generations. As Bardwick (1980) has argued, a dual-career marriage requires a degree of self-confidence in the husband (115). Through entering into this female confidance, male confidence may now be achieved. Coates's article implied that men may, indeed must, now share this female knowledge, written for them in their own scientific and logical lexicon and, like so many mothers on a daily basis, must make the Shepherd's Pie! This article calls for a practical attitude towards radical feminism, and interestingly is one of the last occurrences of the recipe in *Spare Rib*. There were no more time-saving recipes for women in *Spare Rib* or instructional recipes for men. However mainstream magazines such as *Cosmopolitan* and *Family Circle* continued to produce features such as 'Cosmo's Cook-Ahead Dinner'.[5] Conversely *Spare Rib* provided plenty of articles to enable women to carry out traditionally male tasks such as 'How to Mend a Toilet' (July 1977, 20). And herein lies one of the difficult paradoxes of the women's movement: whilst women were arguing against the oppressing and unpaid labour of housework, children still had to be brought up, clothes had to be washed and food still had to be cooked. Collectives, communes and shared housework may have provided solutions for a minority, and presumably many traditional heterosexual relationships deteriorated or even collapsed as female consciousness was raised, but someone still shopped, prepared and cooked for whatever remained of the family. In the end, perhaps, the social stronghold of the nuclear family was too powerful to be disbanded or denied completely. And the recipe, as both domestic instruction and a site of female aspirations, instead of being explored further as a means of gender communication, seemed to encompass and express the incompatibilities of reality and utopia. This was the paradox at the heart of the WLM.

Coates's 'Shared Housework' is an article which tries to offer political argument combined with practical advice. In 'Foodmaking as a Thoughtful Practice', Lisa M. Heldke (1992) discusses how 'headwork' and 'handwork' have been formed into a dichotomy of activity: philosophy is linked conceptually to ideas of eternity, and everyday activity to the temporality of the physical world. Following John Dewey, Heldke finds another way of thinking about these two forms of practice:

> Dewey describes the distinction between theory and practice as a difference in degree between two modes of practice. Contrary to the philosophical tradition, he suggests that there is no sharp distinction in kind between the two. Rather they may most usefully be regarded as two forms of practice, one of which might be called 'thoughtful practice' rather than 'theory.' (214)

Heldke suggests that this concept provides insight into the significance of foodmaking. Almost all the food articles discussed in the present essay try to offer some sort of 'feminist' flavour in the commentary which accompanies the recipes. Some use humour to varying levels of pithiness; others promote specific aspects of female liberation. Some recipe features seem naïve in their unsophisticated utopian visions; others have a sharper, more hard-hitting feminist agenda. However 'Shared Housework' offers both a philosophy of the domestic routine and how that might change, and actual recipes that are made simple in order to enable a transference of skills from women (traditionally the unskilled workers) to men (perceived as the thinkers and therefore superior earners). Using a particular mode of discourse, the scientised overly explanatory recipes enable a transfer of knowledge from one culturally assumed mind-set to another. Food writing for women often makes assumptions about a well-kept larder for store cupboard ingredients, and takes for granted a good deal of basic knowledge and competence around home foodways. But these recipes, in their precision and laborious detail regarding basic cooking tasks (such as mashing potatoes), assume little or no prior knowledge. Even down to minute details, such as the appropriate pan size for boiling potatoes, these recipes pass on knowledge that would be assumed in most female home cooks. But the recipes do not sacrifice taste in the cause of simplification. They expect men to be just as capable as women of making on-the-spot autonomous decisions about their cookery: 'You may prefer more tomatoes, in which case another tin may be added now'. And they aim to allow men insight into the way women think when performing the ongoing task of family catering, such as making enough for two meals in one go. In this article, then, the recipe is liberated from being a female-only mode of communication and speaks as much of gender differences as it does of

Spaghetti Bolognaise. The recipe is freed from the limitations of a form of communication which plays to a patriarchal hierarchy or is limited by an exclusively female medium. Thus the combined attempt to deliver the recipe in logical 'masculine' style, and the insight into the mental gymnastics performed by working women everywhere in order just to keep the family going, results in an optimistic expectation, if not of a Shepherd's Pie utopia, then at least the reality of a shared domesticity. Set in an article which discusses the philosophical framework for such a shift in consciousness about the domestic arena, this is an example of practical and philosophical feminism which might truly be considered as 'thoughtful practice'.

Regrettably perhaps, this mode of inter-gender communication was not sustained in *Spare Rib* and, by 1973, the recipe features had more or less disappeared and food discussions became more overtly politicised. Another simultaneously emerging feminism and food discourse saw food and its media representation in our culture as a major form of oppression. This changing mode of food discussion within *Spare Rib* illustrates the developing militancy and direction of the movement. In May 1973, in 'How Vital are your Statistics', an extract from Dr Hilda Bruch's book *Eating Disorders*, the question is raised as to 'why food has come to play such a distorted role in women's lives' (31–33, 38). The article investigates the psychological effects of food-related issues in childhood and adulthood, and considers the impact of family life, emotions and advertising on the female psyche. Bruch discusses the social pressures on women to be thin, and, paradoxically, the constant media representation of food with women and sex: 'She may be hooked on sweets and wooed with wafer thin mints, but to be socially acceptable, she must be sylph-like.' Nor does dieting, which causes self-disgust and unhappiness, provide an answer. Bruch advocates that women must rethink their relationship with food, and liberate themselves from 'artificial rules and regulations' so that they can recognise their 'genuine nutritional needs' rather than using food to respond to emotional needs. This article, littered with simple drawings of 'forbidden' foods like chocolate, ice cream and cake, makes food a political issue; it brings to light what until recently was kept hidden: women's secret relationship with food. No longer will the idealised version of woman as provider of food suffice to explain this complex relationship. This article contains no recipes; it seeks to problematise the cultural pressures concerning women and food, exposing media manipulation of women and consequent problems that women have in their relationship with food.

These ideas were taken further by Susie Orbach, whose best-selling *Fat is a Feminist Issue* first appeared in *Spare Rib* in November and December

1976 as a two-part article. In this she discusses women, food and psychology, and brings to light the issues of compulsive eating, fatness and reveals the emotional pain that eating excessively and bingeing can conceal. Food, then, according to Orbach, has become a depository for confused emotions (guilt, anger, sexual concern and so on). Orbach's project was to help women unpack other emotional baggage from their comfort eating. This mode of food discussion implies that food, and its associated emotional and cultural meanings, has become for feminists the enemy, to be exposed, deconstructed and conquered.

This strident approach shows the rapid development in feminist thought and the momentum of the movement. Almost unbelievably, only a year before, in articles like 'Munchy Business' and 'The Edible Present', this ideological hegemony remained unexplored. By 1973, reflecting a more radical feminist mode, the mood with respect to food in *Spare Rib* had changed from one of self-expression and education (for both sexes) to one of revelation and sociocultural political criticism. This changed tone reflected the changing direction of the WLM and, concomitantly, the changed steering of the editorial board of *Spare Rib* concerning the direction of the magazine (Winship, 140–143). It would seem, then, that the issue of women's love/hate relationship with food, anorexia and mental health suits the mould of liberation and the exploding of female myths, whereas ideas about food in relation to health, education and entertainment communicated through the medium of the recipe may have been seen to be less radical by the *Spare Rib* team of editors. This raises a series of questions about the mode of the recipe: whether it is indeed the recipe or its context which provides true meaning for the reader. If, as Joke Hermes (1995) has argued, meaning in magazines is only produced through reader appropriation and engagement (12–28), then as the community of *Spare Rib* readers started to reject roles of 'Mother Earth' and 'housewife', so the fantasy suggested by recipes for the self-improved, healthier, better educated, more organised woman and homemaker proved inadequate. The recipes aimed at non-cooks (men), which combined ideological and quotidian instruction, and offered the fantasy of true equality in the home, were not continued: they did not fit the radical mode.

By 1977, the relationship between feminism and food had changed again. The July edition of *Spare Rib* shows how food had reached an aestheticised status in two different artistic forms. Fay Weldon's short story 'Pearly Oats' uses porridge oats, an old-fashioned food, as a metonym for the old-fashioned female role (54–57). Following two women's life decisions, one to follow a career, one to stay at home, the story shows how neither provides the perfect solution. Weldon combines the superficiality of the advertising drive for an old product with the realities of the nuclear family meltdown. The fact that neither the path of career woman nor self-sacrificing housewife leads to happiness serves as a barely concealed warning of the downside of female consciousness-raising. The article has a depressing air of decline and despair; based in a relentless realism, it shows none of the optimism of the early stages of the movement. Another article by Rozsika Parker, 'Portrait of the Artist as Housewife', features works signifying the trap of the domestic for 'Feministo', the woman's postal art event, held in London that month (5–8). For example, a crocheted breakfast, featuring egg, bacon, sausage, and boxes of chocolates as lips or fetishised body parts, expresses their protests and statements. These artefacts capture strong feminist sentiments, they point to the domestic trap of women, and they tell of female objectification and consumption as bodies. Thus food, by the mid-1970s, whilst it had become appropriated as a cultural phenomenon and was used to express a political message, was no longer politicised in itself.

Recipes and food writing, then, in the WLM magazines and newsletters of 1970s second-wave feminism, chart an interesting trajectory through a period of significant change for women. Early recipes and food articles in magazines such as *Spare Rib* owe much to conventional women's magazines in terms of format and layout. These recipes, however, show adaptation as well as imitation, and most attempted to engage the reader in some aspect of feminist thought, be it self-awareness, ironic reflection, education about new foods or more general consciousness-raising. I have argued that these recipes are 'aspirational narratives', which suggest a new mode of living. That many of these early features are flawed in their feminism reflects one of the major dichotomies of the feminist movement at the time: the attempt to articulate a utopian fantasy of true equality whilst still dealing with the day-to-day realities of a patriarchal system.

As the decade progressed, and arguably as the WLM matured, issues of food and cookery became part of the wider debate about housework, which invoked more academic arguments concerning Marxism and women's history. Attempts to bring together philosophical approaches to shared housework with practical solutions and advice about cooking and other domestic chores, although valiant, thoughtful and helpful, were too few to provide a viable alternative for the direction of feminism.

The focus of feminism's discussion of food quickly became more culturally centred, with women's psychological and social relationship with food discussed and debated in terms of feminist consciousness and women's entrapment. A few well-known publications dominated the discussion and provided a more political and less practical framework for food.

Towards the end of the decade, food was still a political issue in the Women's Liberation Movement magazines, but aestheticised more than anything, as artistic subject-matter for feminist expression. Recipes themselves had disappeared, along with a practical approach to feminism. One of the main sites of gender inequality, the home, had long been identified and yet the challenge, for feminists, of providing their own quotidian solutions to the distribution of labour in the home proved inappropriate to the national debate. Furthermore, perhaps women felt that there was too much at stake in the complex nature of the exchange between recipe and reader to make this personal narrative into a public and political statement.

Notes

1   For further discussion of various aspects of food and women's oppression see for example: Beardsmore and Keil, *Sociology on the Menu*, 1997, pp. 173–190; Counihan, *The Anthropology of Food and Body*, 1999; and Williamson., *Decoding Advertisements*, 1978.

2   Rowbotham has also recently given her own story of the 1960s, in *Promise of a Dream: Remembering the 60s*, 2000.

3   For instance see the discussion in Winship of the tensions which beset the editorial board of *Spare Rib*, 1987, pp. 140–147.

4   The *Bread and Roses* newsletter was named after a strike song of the 1912 Lawrence Textile Strike.

5   This was a fairly regular feature in *Cosmopolitan* at this time. See, for example, 'Cosmo's cook-ahead dinner' by Margo Rieman in the April 1972 edition.

Chapter 10

Regulation and Creativity: The Use of Recipes in Contemporary Fiction

Sarah Sceats

In its essence a recipe is a blueprint and an inspiration, a contradictory mixture of given rules and creative possibility. The root of the word in the Latin verb *recipere*, to take or to receive, suggests something of its complex potential. It is no wonder that cookbooks provide favourite bedtime reading, when they provide such an opportunity for imaginative creation of aesthetic visual, oral and alimentary satisfactions. Written recipes have the peculiar metaliterary status of anticipating the creation of material entities and events beyond the text. But as Susan Leonardi points out in her witty and perceptive 1989 article, 'Recipes for Reading', a recipe is generally an embedded discourse; it gives and is given life and meaning by its context. Whatever a recipe's provenance, it is the context – be it cookbook, letter, food programme or magazine – that provides anecdotes, illustrative tales of particular meals or mouth-watering accounts of tastes, smells and ingredients.[1]

The context of fiction is rather different however. To begin with, recipes themselves are rarely the point of the narrative. They may be crucially implicated in plot; they may reveal character, comment on the action or provide oblique commentary; their function may be literal or suggest more abstract meanings. The same may of course be said of food itself, for the literal and metaphorical functions of food and eating are manifold, and the intricacies of human behaviour are played through in a whole variety of food situations and eating occasions. It is through food that we are first socialised and that behaviour is regulated. It is in relation to food that women are seen as nurturing, trapped in servitude or immeasurably powerful. And it is food, as much as sex, that gratifies our primal appetites. Since fiction concerns itself with all aspects of life it is hardly surprising that appetites, food and eating should figure largely.[2]

How then do recipes feature distinctively in fiction and what, if anything, might be their significance? This essay sets out to consider some of the implications of the use of recipes in late twentieth-century fiction by exploring ways in which they are perceived and incorporated in a range of contemporary texts. This exploration is pursued through close consideration of the fictional texts, from – as will become apparent – an approximately feminist perspective.

It is worth pausing initially to consider what exactly constitutes a recipe in a fictional context. Are there, for example, significant differences between recipes that are formally set out according to the conventions of a modern cookbook, with a list of ingredients followed by instructions, and those that are more loosely conveyed, vague or allusive? In other words, is there a significant relationship between form and function? Patrick Suppes (1992), measuring recipes against Aristotelian and Euclidean models, points out that explanatory passages constitute illuminating justification for the procedures recipes express.   Susan Leonardi goes much further, stressing a necessity for context and suggesting that bare lists of ingredients and directions are 'surprisingly useless, even for a fairly experienced cook, and surprisingly seldom encountered' (340). For the purpose of cooking she is probably right, if only because of the prior skills that such recipes assume and the intuitive knowledge they ignore.[3] But no such test of utility applies where fiction is concerned, and characters certainly make use of all kinds of recipe.   For the most part it is true that novelists do not tend to reproduce lists of ingredients and 'method'. There are exceptions, however, perhaps the most notable in recent years being Laura Esquivel's *Like Water for Chocolate* (1993).

Traditional recipes are essential to Esquivel's novel, structurally, thematically and metaphorically.   The book's subtitle is 'A Novel in Monthly Instalments with Recipes, Romances and Home Remedies' and each chapter has a title-page giving month and recipe title, followed by a page with a list of ingredients for the recipe, or, in a few cases, for part of the recipe. Each chapter begins with the subtitle 'Preparatio', followed by a colon and some initial instructions: 'Heat the vinegar and add the chillies after removing the seeds' (79). There are twelve major structuring recipes, each of which is followed through as its chapter proceeds. The dish or formula is developed literally (method, further ingredients and descriptions are given in some detail) as the meals (or in one case matches) are produced and the narrative progressed. The recipes are also put to use as metaphor. In most cases the metaphorical resonances are fairly obvious, as with swelling bread and pregnancy, matches and passion, or in incidents such as the making of chorizo sausages, which are prepared and stuffed under the authoritarian supervision of Mama Elena but – subverting and commenting on her cruel domination – turn out to be full of worms. There is also some witty suggestion: Christmas rolls with their odd combination of sausage and sardines parallel Pedro's peculiar solution to the embargo on his marriage to Tita (he marries her sister to achieve proximity to his beloved). The incremental cajoling of turkeys to eat walnuts, in preparation for a *mole* made to celebrate the christening of Pedro's son, strangely echoes the coaxing of the baby to the breast, the slaughter of the birds inverting his unwilling entry into the world in the first place.

These small details are no less important to a consideration of the use of recipes than the big set piece scenes, but it is the latter that clearly stand out. The baking (and eating) of the wedding cake for the marriage of Tita's sweetheart Pedro to her sister Rosaura and the inflammatory quail in rose petal sauce that communicates Tita's feelings to Pedro are the most memorable and significant recipe-related scenes. The recipe for the wedding cake – ingredients and method – is divided into three sections, two supplementary lists of ingredients and instructions (for the apricot filling and fondant icing) appearing during the course of the chapter. This division of the recipe breaks up the chapter and slows its pace, the effect of which is to emphasise what a burden it is for Tita to cook and decorate a wedding cake for her usurping sister, and to reflect the length and arduousness of the task. Sorrow leaches from Tita into the cake as she works. The preparation of this cake is the last episode of an ordeal that brings her to the point of collapse. Sending her to bed, Nacha the Indian cook is moved to lick some of the icing just to see if Tita's tears have spoiled the flavour. Although the flavour is unaffected, Nacha finds herself overcome with longing. This small scene prefigures the emetic and cathartic effect of the cake at the wedding reception itself, when all the guests fall under a spell of longing and vomiting, expressing the grief Tita has inadvertently cooked into the cake.

Esquivel's culinary magic realism is even more dramatically realised in the cooking of quail in rose petal sauce. At this point in the narrative, Tita has become the ranch cook, following the death of her beloved substitute mother, Nacha. Tita is so cast down by this event that Pedro (now married to Rosaura) is moved to give her a bouquet of roses. The sisters' domineering mother, Mama Elena, always alert to the possibility of connection between the erstwhile lovers, orders Tita to destroy the roses, though not before Tita's clasping them to her breast has turned them from pink to red. Tita, who cannot bear to discard the flowers, hears the ghostly voice of Nacha seeming to dictate a recipe, and Nacha goes on to 'oversee' the killing, dry-plucking and frying of the birds and preparation of the sauce. The recipe for the sauce is narrated in detail, from the removal of the petals from the roses and their grinding with anise in a mortar, through skinning chestnuts, to the explanation of why no more than two drops of attar of roses might be added, and the instructions for steeping the birds in the sauce. What is not part of the recipe but nevertheless enters the food is Pedro's passion encoded in the gift of roses and Tita's hot blood staining the petals. The meal is transformed by these 'unofficial' ingredients:

> It was as if a strange alchemical process had dissolved [Tita's] entire being in the rose petal sauce, in the tender flesh of the quails, in the wine, in every one of the meal's aromas. That was the way she entered Pedro's body, hot, voluptuous, totally sensuous. (49)

Thus the lovers communicate. But Esquivel does not leave it here. The amorous fire she has incorporated into the recipe finds its physical expression through Tita's other sister Gertrudis, who is so overwhelmed that she rushes to take a shower. Not only does her heat set the wooden walls of the shower cubicle aflame, but the rose aroma of her sweat draws from the distant battle a rebel soldier, who sweeps the naked woman onto his horse, and the two ride off into the sunset, making love at the gallop. As though to assuage her sorrow at not so escaping, Tita begins to write a cookbook that very night, so as in some way to capture experiences that may then be repeated, relived or vicariously shared through food. At the same time she ensures her own small immortality.

These justly celebrated episodes suggest an escape through the medium of food from all kinds of tyranny and oppression (it is no accident that the novel is set during the Mexican revolution, nor that the rose petal sauce is a pre-Hispanic recipe), and offer means of expression in a context of repressive social expectation. The fact that Tita does not escape but remains and continues to cook, collect and write her recipes illustrates not rebellion or transformation but a subversive endurance. Thrilling though Esquivel's culinary magic realism is, it gains power and gravitas by being embedded in a mundane, prosaic world involving chores and recipes, including some for non-edibles, such as ink and toothpaste. The 'home remedies' of the title are also included in the form of recipes, with instructions on how to castrate chickens, use leeches, treat burns, eradicate bedbugs, embroider sheets, prevent conception or entertain appropriately:

> Before putting down the table-cloth, it's necessary to protect the table with a table cover, so that the glasses and dishes don't make any noise when they strike it. It should be a white baize one, so the whiteness of the cloth is intensified. ... Bordeaux wines should be taken from the wine cellar several

hours in advance and put in a warm spot so the gentle warming develops the flavour. ... at a social gathering one does not bring up the subject of personalities, sad topics or unfortunate facts, religion or politics. (141–142)

The 'method' is almost invariably written in imperative mood as a set of instructions. This both emphasises the compelling nature of Tita's duty (and how well her superego has ingested the 'script' her mother intended for her) and suggests to the reader that she is dealing with a matter-of-fact set of rules for an ordered life. It is a bit like reading an old-fashioned cookbook illustrated with anecdotes, the recipes offering a blueprint for a simple yet sensuously poetic mode of living. They are also clearly Tita's recipes, extracted from the cookbook she writes, and thus are not simply regulations that control her, but part of her life narrative, part of her identity.

The recipes as given are generally complete, if interspersed with narrative. They appeal to the reader of 'exotic' cookbooks, with descriptive detail and localised contexts. They are not, however, for novices. When Tita makes a dish it sounds delicious, hard work certainly, but almost invariably successful. But when her culinarily ignorant sister Gertrudis tries to follow Tita's written recipe for fritters with syrup she feels as though she is reading hieroglyphics; the rules appear baffling, complicated, almost impossible to follow. She has to enlist her devoted but barely literate sergeant's assistance and seek elucidation of the terminology in a large reference cookbook from the storeroom. The result is ultimately a triumph for the inexperienced cooks and is all the more delicious for their efforts. It is hard to avoid the conclusion that, far from intolerable, rules and order are in fact absolutely necessary and that their scrupulous interpretation yields greatest satisfaction.

There is no doubt that a recipe involves discipline and submission of the will to the facts of the material world: eggs curdle, liquids boil over, bacteria multiply. (The subversion of control and power – whether colonial or familial – in this novel is not only enacted through cooking, eating and sexual passion but is also reflected in the magic realist challenge to these material, physical facts.) There are recipes that go wrong precisely because of failures of attention to the external world: Tita cuts her finger through haste, and runs up and down stairs so often, dancing attendance on her niece, that she drops the pot of *mole* for the *champandongo* and has to begin all over again. The discipline involved in successful cooking – the need to follow instructions, give undivided attention, observe closely, exercise judgement – is echoed in the formal layout of the recipes in this novel. Mama Elena's insistence on protocol reinforces the sense of regulation; she is a perfectionist where food is concerned and can cut a watermelon with elegant, mathematical precision. Unfortunately, her skills lie principally in one direction: 'when it came to dividing, dismantling, dismembering, desolating, detaching, dispossessing, destroying or dominating, Mama Elena was a pro' (87). She is, in short, a tyrant. Rules, discipline and control, Esquivel implies, are *both* indispensable *and* oppressive.

The linking of food with oppression is a recurrent trope, especially in women's writing, both in relation to the kind of servitude exemplified and exaggerated in Tita's case and as manifested in the control of eating. Restriction or prescription of food is obvious enough, as in Margaret Atwood's *The Handmaid's Tale* (1985) for example, where 'breeding' women are limited to an enforced diet. Where the enforcer is oneself, the situation is more complicated and the source of oppression less obvious. There are numerous late twentieth-century texts that focus explicitly on eating disorders, and most of these make use of recipes in relation to issues of power, control and anxiety about boundaries. The implication of self-regulation is echoed in cooking instructions, though where actual recipes are included they are not necessarily whole or formally constituted. In Margaret Atwood's *The Edible Woman* (1969), the 'planned cow' that protagonist Marian calls to mind is sufficient to suggest a prescriptive recipe making. Hardly much of a cook herself, Marian is drawn to identify with the cow, which she remembers from one of her cookbooks, its body marked off into discrete and clearly labelled parts. The point is that Marian feels as helpless and about-to-be-consumed by her fiancé as is the food she becomes progressively unable to eat. Her life up to this point has been lived according to a socially constructed recipe, as predictable as the cuts of meat from the planned cow: university, job, marriage. As the novel's title suggests, Marian is more cooked against than cooking, until the end of the novel, when she bakes a symbolic cake, suddenly becoming proficient, working as though by instinct, without following a cookbook. She effectively abandons pre-existing patterns and creates her recipe, her cake and her future from a newly self-conscious and empowered position.

Marian suffers through much of the novel from a symbolic anorexia. It is real inasmuch as she cannot eat but symbolic because it represents her refusal of the life set out before her, and because she suffers no physical ill effects, not even weight loss. In novels featuring literal eating disorders, by contrast, both recipes themselves and food may seem to be oppressive. Jenefer Shute's *Life-Size* (1993) and Lucy Ellmann's *Sweet Desserts* (1988) use recipes of a kind to indicate a feeling of being controlled. Both novelists give their narrators a flippant, sarcastic voice, and use pastiche magazine extracts. In Shute's portrait of an anorexic/bulimic, most of the extracts concern dieting, with bossy advice on counting calories, avoiding eating or how to slice a cake so that boys will take big slices and girls 'slim' ones. A recipe for 'his and hers' packed lunches is given, noting calories for each item: 'his' totals 1010, 'hers' 301. One recipe in the book comes from an anthropological text, indicating how best to butcher humans to avoid waste, a more sinister echo perhaps of Atwood's symbolic cannibalism. What all this adds up to – despite the protagonist Josie's rigorous self-control and exercise regime – is an overwhelming impression of disempowerment. In a book centrally concerned with eating, there is no food creation: Josie reads sensuous descriptions on the food pages, and desires to be a food technologist, but the processes she imagines are nailing and blow-torching food for the photographer rather than producing something to eat.

Ellmann's novel covers something of the same territory, juxtaposing different kinds of text (Shakespeare, women's magazines, government forms, letters, jokes, advertisements, diet sheets and so on) with narrative passages. There are recipe-like instructions, such as a series of numbered tips for eating and living, as well as actual recipes for food, mostly featuring sweet or decorative items. None of the recipes is given in full. Sometimes there is an extract from the method, or there may be a list of ingredients or even simply an allusion to a recipe, as with cooking pancakes when they 'followed Irma Rombauer's instructions' (5). The narrative is generally less claustrophobic and the construction looser than that of *Life-Size*. In addition to the plethora of textual fragments, the focus shifts between the sister protagonists and the narrative voice moves from first to third person, the result of which is that much of the burden of meaning-making is placed with the reader. The third chapter begins thus: 'Bone two large eels, fill them with diced truffles. Wrap in a piece of muslin and tie with string. Cook in wine and well-flavoured fish stock. Drain, unwrap, and cool under a press' (9). An interesting recipe, if imprecise. But what is it *for* in the text? Does it signal eating disorders (feeling fat, stuffed?). Elsewhere there is a similarly marooned and unexplained extract from a recipe for a salad in aspic. Another chapter ends with remedies for constipation. The instructions for making marzipan flowers make them sound analogous to genitalia: why?

One thing all these extracts have in common is a bodily focus, which connects with the preoccupations of the two young women. There are also other indications: portions of fussy recipes for decorative foods, for example, serve to puncture discussions of Art. The diversity of textual fragments suggests the multiplicity of discourses, not to say instructions, that may be said to influence our lives, but it also conveys distress, suggesting – to this reader at any rate – a young woman or women unable to focus. Some of the juxtapositions are more obviously symbolic. A sexual conquest overtaking a champagne supper under the shadow of the girls' father's illness is interrupted with the instruction: 'Hull, pod, shell, bone, fillet' (124), followed a few sentences later with a portion of an operation report, without commentary, like a memento mori. A marbled angel-food cake 'like a foretaste of heaven' ironically prefigures the bitterness of Daddy's demise (136). Overall the multiple juxtapositions may offer a kaleidoscope of meanings to different readers: Ellmann's refusal to elaborate, to give, as it were, the whole recipe, suggests some such intention.

Like Tita and Marian, both Shute's and Ellmann's protagonists struggle with questions of control and empowerment. Even seduction meals (in Josie's case a seduction cup of tea) are fraught with anxieties: 'Looking at the spread I've laid out on the table, I begin to feel wary of the competition' worries Ellmann's Suzy self-deprecatingly (124). Gender seems to be crucial here; male characters who cite recipes – especially where seduction is in prospect – display no such trepidation. The egregious, cynical narrator of Helen Simpson's short story 'Sugar and Spice' (1992) is so confident of his recipes and seductive culinary skills (and so contemptuous of his prospective conquest) that he is genuinely surprised by the girl's revulsion. Preoccupied as he is with self-congratulation, he does not even notice her recoil as he recites the ingredients of *saltimbocca*, altogether misinterpreting her gaze and her silence as he manifests the 'erotic spectacle' of concocting *îles flottantes* (30). The story as a whole represents a failed recipe for seduction, enacted and articulated through the implied recipes for the food described and produced by the narrator during his attempted conquest of the young girl. Its failure, in his eyes, lies neither in the recipes nor his intent, but in the small-mindedness of the unappreciative girl.

John Lanchester takes a similar idea much further in his novel *The Debt to Pleasure* (1997), creating a veritable monster in the erudite psychopathic gourmet Tarquin Winot. Here we see a complex mixture of power and powerlessness, order and chaos, regulation and creativity. Tarquin Winot, the first-person narrator, demonstrates a similar degree of misguided self-display to that of Simpson's roué, but his exhibitionism is complicated by a simultaneous need for concealment. The novel plays on this contradiction in both action and narrative strategy, as one death after another is slyly revealed and progressively acknowledged – if only by implication – as murder. Winot sails closer and closer to the wind both verbally (hinting to prospective victims of mushroom poisoning that his brother died of mushroom poisoning) and sartorially, pursuing his prey while dressed in a green and ochre checked suit with a pink shirt and yellow and blue spotted tie. The possibility of exposure, the plight of his victims and the multifariousness of food arouse in him an equal response: restrained excitement coupled with intellectual curiosity. Winot's nerve holds even when confronted by the forces of law; indeed his *chutzpah* is reminiscent of the apocryphal parricide who threw himself on the mercy of the court on the grounds of being an orphan.

Parading itself initially as Winot's disquisition on food (the opening lines state, 'This is not a conventional cookbook'), the novel contains a discursive mixture of recipes, anecdotes and allusive, knowledgeable discussion of food and history. These speculations are combined with a pursuit narrative and an oblique, self-justifying confessional. Here, recipes are concerned overwhelmingly with the exercise of power, through snobbery, exclusiveness, ruthlessness and ultimately by poisoning. Winot frequently approvingly cites his Provençale neighbours, two old peasant brothers whose lack of sentimentality about the animal world – verging on cruelty, such as drowning guinea fowl in brandy – he conflates with his own amorality concerning the human. The narrative ingredients are smoothly blended; neither food writing nor thriller aspect dominates, while Winot's voice parodies and exaggerates a style of gourmet writing that is intolerantly arrogant.

The recipes in the book vary from the lengthy and detailed (blinis, with eight precisely delineated ingredients and several stages of preparation culminating in the use of a special pan), to briskly minimal ('put two egg yolks in a blender with four cloves of garlic and slowly whizz in a pint of olive oil… and the juice of a lemon' (179)), to the frankly dismissive: 'As to the mango sorbet, you should: 1. buy a sorbetière; 2. buy some mangoes; 3. follow the instructions. The curry recipes you can look up in a book' (114). The occasionally contemptuous tone, deliberately outrageous, is undoubtedly comic – appallingly so: 'Serve the pancakes with sour cream and caviare. Sour cream is completely straightforward, and if you need any advice or guidance about it then, for you, I feel only pity' (15). The tone does much to highlight Winot's culinary elitism. It also, of course, plays to that of the reader. As with all erudite or allusive novels, there is a satisfaction to be gained by being on the inside, part of the club that does not need to have advice or guidance. Generally in such cases the implied knowledge is intellectual or literary; here it is practical and experiential.[4]

All the recipes are embedded in layers of text and context. On one level, like some loquacious old raconteur, Winot is portrayed as unable to resist a digression. The recipe for *bouillabaisse* – heralded by several pages of personal reminiscence, metaphysical speculation about its nature and ingredients, evocation of myth and anthropology and discussion of the effects of geography – wanders immediately from the 'two pounds of assorted rockfish' to a sketch of how the fish might be bought and from whom before coming back to instructions for cleaning, chopping and assembling the rest of the ingredients (50). Even these are punctuated with comments about the benefits of modern life and the poor quality of English tap water. The instructions for fast boiling are brisk, but at this point Winot loses interest, says he can't be bothered with giving the recipe for *rouille*, and goes on instead to elucidate 'non-canonical' versions of *bouillabaisse* and a raft of regional and national variations (including the surprising observation that there is no equivalent English recipe). The calculated impression, here and elsewhere, is that the provision of a full recipe with detailed instructions is somehow mundane and hence beneath the dignity of a person of fine sensibilities.[5]

But there is more than simply self-display going on. Many of the anecdotes and digressions around and within the recipes concern episodes from Winot's past, which both suggest how recipes may be enriched by personal experience (as in Tita's cookbook in *Like Water for Chocolate*) and provide revelations of various sorts. The encomium on *bouillabaisse*, for example, traces Winot's love of fish soups and stews back to an apparently formative meal at a Paris restaurant with his mother. More subtly, we are treated to a slow revelation that Winot's 'art' is not the gastronomic one at first supposed, but the art of 'absence'. From the first anecdote of nauseating ingestion of boarding school cottage pie, 'the mince grey, the potato beige' (11), Winot begins to articulate an 'erotics of dislike', a perverse and life-denying self-separation from the world. 'Any dislike', he says, 'is in some measure a triumph of definition, distinction, and discrimination – a triumph of life' (12), an inversion of the libidinous surrender seen as life-giving in *Like Water for Chocolate*. His 'erotics' are not those of Eros but of Thanatos. Later (after roast lamb with garlic and haricots) he recalls the gestation of his idea for a lifetime project centred on the 'aesthetics of absence' (69). The absence left by a murderer is more perfect than the 'timid megalomania' of an artist's work, he argues, being both more natural than 'artificial' art and more characteristic of the age we live in. This argument is a complicated rationalisation, for Tarquin Winot's brother Bartholomew, of whom Tarquin slowly reveals himself to be pathologically jealous, creates tangible sculptures for which he is celebrated. Tarquin Winot, overshadowed, perversely opts to exacerbate his own lack of endorsement through an 'art' (murder) that can give him none, for it cannot be acknowledged.[6] His perversity is echoed in relation to food, for example when he claims that the smelliness of *andouillette*, his favourite form of offal, provides a 'thrilling sense of taint', for it reminds him he is eating a 'dead fellow-animal' (157).

The emphasis on variety and complexity, on taste and discrimination, revelation, absence and completion suggests that food constitutes this narrator's entire perspective. Recipes (of whatever sort) provide his means of engagement with the world and the theory of cooking parallels his (re)arrangement of knowledge and truth. There are a few quasi-philosophical observations sprinkled amongst the discussions.[7] Cooking, claims Winot, manifests a Cartesian hedonism, the mind being exercised to the full for the benefit of the body. There is certainly widespread evidence in this novel of the exercise of mind, sometimes in support of creativity or in anticipation of physical pleasure (almost the definition of a recipe) and more often in the pursuit of power. There are Cartesian resonances in character too, for Winot seems to be essentially divided: his mind functions in a vacuum, his physical manifestations curiously disconnected.[8] Mind is predominant, not to say ingenious, and there is some apposite linguistic musing about the possessive formulation in French. Citing as example '*ris de veau et sa petite salade de lentilles de Puy*' (177), Winot plausibly claims that such use of the possessive '*sa*' on a menu implies that the subsidiary ingredients outshine the main element. In such a way, he suggests, aioli becomes the main feature of a meal in which it is 'supported' by fish and vegetables. Epistemological speculation, aesthetic appreciation and Winot's self-display are all present here, as well as an indication that some ingredients are *essential* to a recipe, as anyone who has ever forgotten to put the eggs in a flan will know. But the inversion is equally significant in its thematic connection with a sculptor whose little brother longs to outshine him. This is just one of many examples in the text where Winot embarks on a long and aesthetic rationalisation for what turns out to be personal malevolence. Most of Winot's speculations function thematically, in progressively revealing his megalomania, as well as providing an entertaining surface to the novel. But occasionally something radical is sneaked into the discourse. In the process of holding forth on the dry martini, for example, Winot asserts a law that grants recipes and their realization the status of art: 'there is [a] law of proportion and rhythm that underlies all of the plastic arts, from cocktail-making and cooking to architecture, sculpture, pottery and dressmaking' (96)

Winot's 'law' brings us back to the emphasis on rule and order. As suggested earlier, the very act of cooking (whether following or creating a recipe) enacts a creative ordering within specific physical laws, the transformation of certain edible entities into a consumable whole. Each time a recipe is recreated into that consumable whole, the ordering process recurs, with variations perhaps, but still within the rules. Tarquin Winot is shown to be fully aware of the appeal of imposing order on chaos, which he characterises in terms of the menu, something that 'lies close to the heart of the human impulse to order, to beauty, to pattern' (4). Indeed, he goes so far as to claim that nothing can be achieved without planning, that there is 'no such thing as a pleasant surprise' (145). He even disputes Freud's emphasis on the role of randomness and accident in life. Together with the arrogance of tone, dismissal of others' tastes and opinions, emphatic pronouncements on food and drink (his suggestions for apéritifs consist largely of injunctions and prohibitions), the preoccupation with order indicates an obsessive need to control. Add in murder, the ultimate act of domination, and the desire for planning, order, rules – even recipes – begins to appear distinctly sinister, and Bartholomew's spontaneous and undisciplined life encapsulated in the 'fry up' seems more desirable than the finest *bourride*.

Like Esquivel's novel, *The Debt to Pleasure* provides more than recipes for food. In this case what is offered is blueprints for lighting fires, conducting break-ins, stalking, poisoning and similar nefarious practices. If it is 'not a conventional cookbook' (1), the novel certainly offers a series of recipes for murder: poisoning, explosion, electrocution, arson, pushing someone in front of a train. The emphasis on control – both in terms of the ultimate control over life and in the intolerance of the gastronome – does seem to suggest a gendered relationship to recipes. It is difficult to imagine Winot as female, though the homicidal methods employed (poisoning as opposed to stabbing, the transfer of agency to a hunter or train driver) and the 'domestic' situation of almost all of the murders are factors traditionally associated with women.[9] Indeed, if we compare Winot to Mama Elena (ignoring, for a moment, the cultural, literary and linguistic gulfs), he seems distinctly feeble. But that, perhaps, is the point: unable to prevail in the world, he takes refuge in his philosophy of separation, his erotics of dislike and his perverted valuing of death over life. The fastidiousness of his taste – unlike Tita's ebullient meticulousness – merely reinforces his lack of human pleasure.

It does seem then that the ordering, controlling, rule-imposing aspect of recipes, when it is not associated with eating disorders, is overwhelmingly used to reflect abusive power relations. The matriarch Mama Elena, in many ways a 'masculine' character, exerts a tyrannical rule.[10] Elsewhere, abuses of power or position are associated with male cooks, wholeheartedly in *The Debt to Pleasure* and in the more limited arena of seduction in Simpson's story. Even in the tales of eating disorders, young women's pathology is more or less attributed to the ills of living in a patriarchal system. But perhaps I overstate the emphasis on control and oppression. There is more to recipes than sets of rules and women writers in particular are inclined to focus on creativity and the sensuousness of food and cooking. Not surprisingly, perhaps, quantities and procedures are often less strictly observed where the major emphasis is on tactile, visual or oral pleasures – or, indeed, on eating. Underpinning these undisciplined pleasures and mitigating apparent self-indulgence, however, sensuous creativity may itself be seen as a source of power.

Michèle Roberts is perhaps the pre-eminent British writer on women and food and there are numerous scenes of food preparation, cooking and eating in her novels. *In the Red Kitchen* (1990) even features a writer of cookbooks as one of its four female protagonists. Hattie, as a young woman on a trip to France, enters an empty confessional where she hears a voice reciting recipes. Cooking subsequently becomes her vocation and she makes a modest living writing recipe books and cooking part-time. It is through learning to cook, she later says, that she becomes real: 'I discovered that flour and butter working between my fingers, carrots falling apart under my quick knife, egg whites rising in the bowl as I beat them, all began to give me a sense of my adequate power, my reality.' Through inventing recipes Hattie reconstructs the world, learns to discriminate 'how to select and to classify ... when to separate and when to merge' (87). It is perhaps surprising that no actual recipes are given in the novel but the emphasis is rather on Hattie's appetite and satisfaction in eating, which are seen as positive and energised, and on pleasure in the assembling of ingredients and the anticipation of cooking.

A similar pattern occurs in other Roberts novels. In *Daughters of the House* (1992), for example, the two adolescent girls frequently help the cook, Victorine, to weigh ingredients for *gougère* or *gâteau à la peau de lait* or to prepare vegetables for cooking. A powerfully female world is conjured up, of capable, strong and nurturing women. We are told of the existence of the recipe book ('stiff blue cardboard covers, battered and cracked, pages of coarse paper yellow at the edges' (46)) but the recipes themselves are implied rather than specified. The effect is to intensify the mystery and sensuousness of the experience. The sound of the bean pods cracking, the smell, colour and appearance of the beans and the feeling of them trickling through the fingers are all evoked before the taste is mentioned. Description of the cooking method is equally calculated to appeal to the senses: 'they might be mixed with onion and garlic softened in butter then stewed with carrots and rosemary to go with roast lamb for lunch' (70). Fragmentation and omission of parts of a recipe, on the other hand, are used to generate emotional force, such as when the bereaved daughter Thérèse prepares a sauce for her father's homecoming lunch. Her distraction is enacted through the interrupted recipe, which Roberts emphasises by transferrring the epithet 'curdled' from the sauce to the phrases jostling in Thérèse's head.

Recipes and their realization have a strong thematic import in Roberts's fiction. The ability to cook, to find pleasure, which is inextricably linked with transformation and even salvation, through food is almost a *sine qua non* of her female characters. In the short story 'The Bishop's Lunch' (1993), Roberts blasphemously reverses the notion of salvation, as novitiate Sister Josephine discovers a profane deliverance through recipes secreted in her notebook by her rejected mother. She uses the recipes to prepare a triumphant Easter meal, thereby kindling her interest in cooking, and the story ends with her contemplation of a new life, as a chef. As with *In the Red Kitchen*, recipes are seen here to be instrumental in self-discovery and empowerment. Informed by feminist ideas though Roberts's writing undoubtedly is, this empowerment is not simply shown as a question of prevailing in the world; sensuous creativity, she suggests, is a vital ingredient of femaleness. The appeal of food to the senses, foregrounded in much of Roberts's fiction and delineated through her manipulation of partial and implied recipes, is essential to her picture of active, fulfilled, life-loving women.

That there are strong connections between food and sex hardly needs to be spelled out here and, for mostly very obvious reasons, the two are frequently combined. Indeed over the last twenty years or so it has become almost obligatory to include food in any erotic film or fiction.[11] What is curious is that recipes find their way in even here. In Linda Jaivin's popular Australian novel *Eat Me* (1996), amongst the descriptions of food-assisted sex (and vice versa), titillating female confessions and confidences, the four women around whom the various sexual exploits are woven meet for a dinner party. Philippa, the writer, prepares soup:

> She first took the crushed almonds and poured them into the blender. Then she picked up the bread she had soaking in milk and pinched it between her fingers, letting the milk run over her hands as, mashing the soft pulp, she squeezed out the last drops of liquid. She dropped the bread pulp onto the almonds. Extracting four large cloves of garlic from the head, she lay them on the cutting board and crushed them under the flat end of a large carving knife.... Separating the lacerated and juicy flesh from the skin, she dropped them on top of the bread pulp and almonds.... She turned on the blender until all the ingredients turned to paste. She added the olive oil, a few drops at a time, then in a flow. Finally, she added water that she'd been cooling with ice,

a touch of salt and white vinegar, and poured the creamy thick mixture into bright green bowls. She tore the skin off several fat and juicy green grapes, cut them in half, scooped out the seeds and floated them in the white liquid. (133)

The description is garnished with the voluptuous evocation of Philippa's tactile and olfactory pleasure, but the list of ingredients given as part of the narrative, and the excess of detail in description of the method nevertheless indicate a recipe; it is in fact 'ajo blanco, an Andalusian white soup' (132). The question is, what purpose does it serve here (apart from providing an opportunity for yet more sensual indulgence)? As with Lucy Ellmann's novel there is plenty of scope for speculation. Perhaps Linda Jaivin wanted to cover all aspects of food and eating in relation to sex (the soup is not part of a sex act here, but the grapes recall one, and the appearance of the soup prompts discussion of oral sex). Or, since the soup is prepared by the 'writer' among the friends – there is some postmodern trickery in the narrative – perhaps the recipe is a metaphor for the fictionalising process. There is an implication that the creation of soup, of fiction and of sexual excitement have something in common; all require ingredients and some kind of ritual, and there is pleasure in the process as well as the result.

Pleasure, be it intellectual, creative or sensuous, should, one would hope, be of the essence in a recipe, even if only in anticipation. That it is by no means the whole story – in fiction as in life – is what I have tried to suggest in my focus on aspects of power and control and their abuses. With something so fundamental to life as food the situation is bound to be complex, even contradictory and, as suggested earlier, regulation is not of itself undesirable: discipline is necessary. A good cook is most certainly in control. Inherent in the recipe are rules and prescription, without which any amount of sensuous creativity will fail to transform ingredients into an edible whole, to create order out of chaos.

But there is another other important feature of recipes that I have not so far considered explicitly, which is that almost without exception they are designed to be shared – indeed published recipes are so by definition. Susan Leonardi (1989) makes much of this in 'Recipes for Reading'; she even capitalises Irma S. Rombauer's (1931) original cookbook selection principle as a 'Grand Tradition of recipe sharing' (342), and her reading of Nora Ephron's *Heartburn* (1983) draws attention to the exchange of recipes as 'an act of trust between women' (346), a trust capable of grand betrayal. The recipe in this situation may be seen as a transactional vehicle, a medium of communication and connection. Alice Hoffman places a trope of this kind at the heart of her novel *Seventh Heaven* (1990). The story centres on newly separated Nora Silk, who moves into a more or less derelict house in a sedate suburb on Long Island in 1959 with her small child and baby. In attempting to put their lives back together, her plan, as newcomer and housemaker, is to buy cookbooks and 'ask her neighbours for their favorite recipes' (36).

Nora is not what the neighbourhood would call a Good Mother. She wears high heels and nail varnish, gives her children inappropriate food and lets them get dirty; she listens to Elvis, is candid instead of pretending that everything is hunky dory and – worst of all – she has no husband. In short, she is an object of suspicion, threatening the bland, unquestioning lives of her neighbours. Hoffman does not steep her protagonist in luscious ingredients and implied recipes as Michèle Roberts does, but every reference to recipes or cooking is telling. Nora's struggle to be positive in the face of neighbourhood hostility and her little boy Billy's misery, for example, is reflected in her cooking:

> Nora went inside to fix macaroni and cheese; she always had trouble with casseroles: they came out too watery – you had to eat the noodles with a spoon – and sometimes she just threw the whole thing out and served Frosted Flakes or beef jerky on white bread. (66)

She is constantly on the lookout for the right recipe, literally and metaphorically, but frequently gets it wrong, seeking guidance from inappropriate sources. She consults recipes on the back of cereal boxes in the supermarket, not noticing that her son is meanwhile stealing sweets. She cooks meatloaf from a recipe on a tin of tomato sauce. She finds a recipe in *Good Housekeeping* for an apple pie that requires freshly picked apples, which she and the baby stop off and gather on the way to collect Billy from school. Dressed in black, with a basket of apples on her arm, she is immediately dubbed a witch by the school bully.

The problem is exacerbated because Nora tries too hard, looking to the consumer world for role models when her own strengths are instinctive. When they first move in, while the moving men bring in bed frames and couch, she tears open packets from her bag of groceries and bakes cookies before even unpacking: 'Nora never measured ingredients, and she wasn't much of a cook; she might even have been considered awful. But she was always lucky with her baking' (32). She is also tenacious. Eventually, by dint of Tupperware parties, manicures and a covert sexual relationship with Ace, the misfit son of one of the neighbouring families (who befriends and champions the unhappy Billy), a kind of integration is achieved.

The uneven progress is mirrored in the evolution of Nora's macaroni and cheese, the dish she always has trouble with. Her first real encounter with one of the wives is with Donna Durgin at the supermarket checkout, when, to hold her attention, she rather desperately tells Donna that she needs a 'decent recipe' for macaroni and cheese and asks whether she should use Cheddar. This time it is Donna whose children are taking sweets; she answers Nora vaguely and begins to cry. Nora has finally made a connection, but it is with someone who is about to walk out of her own life. Macaroni and cheese resurface again near the end of the novel, when Ace skips his graduation dinner in favour of a visit to Nora and the children where, though he claims he is not hungry, he eats 'two servings of the macaroni and cheese Nora had made' (244). That Nora finally belongs is reflected in the fact that she gently sends Ace home to his parents, telling him that his mother has made him a vanilla fudge cake. The friendship between the two women has been forged over a recipe:

> Marie took the pie out of the oven and the crust was so perfect that Nora got to her feet. She stood next to Marie at the stove and watched the steam rise from the golden pastry.
> "How do you do that?" Nora said, awed.
> "The secret of a pie is in the crust," Marie confided. ...
> "I can bake everything except pie crust," Nora said. "Mine are always white. They look like glue."
> "You use butter," Marie guessed.
> "Butter and sugar," Nora said.
> "Never," Marie told her. "Use Crisco instead."
> "Ah." Nora nodded.
> Nora and Marie looked at each other and smiled.
> "Prick the top with a fork seven times after you flute the edges," Marie said.
> Nora put her arms around Marie and thanked her. (236)

Recipes, for women, provide a creative context for interaction, support, conversation, friendship. Many women writers, at least, seem to think so. The trading of domestic and culinary favours (as exemplified in *Seventh Heaven*) suggests an interconnecting communality that foregrounds the importance of nurturing and highlights women's historical pre-eminence in the field. From a feminist point of view this may seem a limiting conclusion, entrapping women in a retrograde domesticity. On the other hand, the combination of networking, mutual support, shared knowledge, creative experiment and the creation of a specific discourse may be viewed by anyone as an empowerment greatly to be desired.

Notes

1 See LeCroy, 'Cookery Literature or Literary Cookery', 1989, for a survey of different kinds of cookbook.

2 Food and eating in fiction are explored at length in my book *Food, Consumption and the Body in Contemporary Women's Fiction*, 2000.

3 See Heldke, 'Recipes for Theory Making', 1992, for some interesting reflections on what constitutes a recipe, and whether it is absolute or relative.

4 Indeed, the cover of the 1996 Picador paperback edition cites part of a review by John Walsh of *The Independent* that demonstrates the practical impact of the text itself: 'several pages of my copy are flecked with stains of *ragu* and *ratatouille* to mark the moments when I could stand temptation no more'.

5 Perhaps, too, Lanchester, erstwhile restaurant critic of *The Observer*, takes some delight in displaying his own undoubted culinary (and historical) erudition, taking the opportunity to air a few prejudices along the way, on 'curry-house' food, for example: 'standard glop + vindaloo gunk = finished dish', p. 112.

6 In a similarly perverse way, he manipulates the riddance of the servant Mary Theresa, the one person in the novel he describes as having been kind to him.

7 These references serve to strengthen the interweaving of the various elements of the text, rather as certain binding agents do in cooking. Winot enumerates some of them: 'cream, butter, flour, arrowroot, *beurre manié*, blood, ground almonds ... dissolvable ... potato', pp. 22–23.

8 The novel itself of course caters to the mind while appealing to or evoking sensations of the body. In microcosm this process is surely echoed and realized in the recipe.

9 See Visser, *The Rituals of Dinner*, 1991, 277–278. For comparison with Winot, see Angela Carter's *Wise Children*, 1991, where the sexy television cook (Saskia) makes classic 'female' use of poison for both deathly and erotic ends.

10 She shoots chickens out of the hand of a looting revolutionary; she has a daunting gaze nobody can meet; she breaks her adult daughter's nose with a blow to the face; she is furiously humiliated by her own physical debility and so on.

11 See films such as *The Empire of the Senses*, 1976, *Three Weeks*, 1977, *Tampopo*, 1987, even *Eat, Drink, Man, Woman*, 1995, as well as countless erotic and borderline pornographic fictions.

Chapter 11

Nigella Bites the Naked Chef:
The Sexual and the Sensual
in Television Cookery Programmes

Maggie Andrews

The last fifteen years have seen an unprecedented rise in the popularity of cookery programmes on television, not merely in the marginalised slots of daytime television with distracted and transitory viewers, but in the more popular primetime evening slots where a more dedicated evening audience watches for leisure and relaxation. Perhaps the strongest evidence of the popularity and multiplicity of styles of such programmes lies in the introduction of cookery-only channels such as 'Carlton Food' and 'Taste' on digital, cable and satellite television. Although 'Taste' was short lived, its demise was followed by the introduction of 'UK Food', which now relies on the premiere league of audience-pulling television cooks and chefs, both past and present, including Fanny Craddock, Delia Smith, Jamie Oliver, Anthony Worrall Thompson, Ainsley Harriott and Nigella Lawson. 'UK Food' is following the now proven formula of promoting cookery programmes in terms of the personality of the presenter. This focus on television cooks' personalities is echoed in this essay's discussion of Nigella Lawson's *Nigella Bites* (1999) and Jamie Oliver's *The Naked Chef* (1999) primetime series shown on Channel 4 and BBC2 respectively. Both were regularly watched by audiences of around two million, placing their programmes amongst their channels' most popular viewing. Recognising the intertextuality that lies at the heart of the production, programming and viewing of television, I will also refer to other television cooks such as Delia Smith, who since her first appearance in 1973 has had a pivotal role in the development of the cookery programme in Britain.

Broadcast media personalities, as Brand and Scannell's (1991) utilisation of Erving Goffman points out, can be seen as 'presentations' or 'performances' of self within their broadcast programmes. These carefully constructed performances do not finish at the 'studio' door, but involve, in the case of Jamie Oliver for example, websites, regular columns in *GQ,*

Marie Claire and the *Sunday Times Magazine*. The cook or chef, furthermore, is also consumed by the viewer in the light of celebrity gossip and interviews and photographs in magazines and newspapers, all of which serve to construct their status as television personalities. Indeed the numerous spin-offs from television cookery programmes operate, as Strange (1998) suggests, as 'textual meteorites' and include videos, books, magazine features and exhibitions such as the BBC's *Good Food Show* (311). Thus, Jamie Oliver's recent *Happy Days with the Naked Chef* (2001), for example, reached the number two slot in the best-selling non-fiction list. Although, interestingly, the response in the USA to *Nigella Bites* has been mixed, television cookery programmes are sold successfully abroad. All this serves to make television cookery programmes a very important commercial area of the broadcasting and media industries.

The BBC now produces *Good Food* magazine, which provides advertising and publishes recipes from cookery programmes in the corresponding month. This, alongside the widespread provision of teletext and internet sites, has freed the television cooks and chefs from even the semblance of conveying recipes to the viewer. In recent years, with the growing significance of food within consumer culture, cookery programmes have shifted away from a generic instructional mode (with a format akin to a visual recipe book), such as that used by Delia Smith whose cookery style, from the 1970s, is encapsulated in a steady plodding attention to detail appropriate to a skilled domestic craft for which the correct tools are required. Contemporary cookery programmes, however, offer not merely instruction on cooking but recipes for a whole lifestyle. *The River Café Book* (1995) is perhaps the supreme example of this. Simultaneously cookery programmes have stretched to incorporate different genres; mixing cookery with game shows and even dating programmes has allowed these programmes to become a central feature within lifestyle programming.

The rising popularity of the cookery genre is not without its critics. It has been blamed for Kitchen Performance Anxiety Syndrome (KPA), which newspapers have described as a debilitating domestic insecurity restricting women's ability to cook. Identified by a Reading University psychologist, Professor David Warburton, KPA has apparently been found to be so incapacitating that it is leading to the death of the middle-class institution of holding dinner parties (Mulkerrins, 2001). This is not perhaps hugely significant, although it highlights the target audience for these programmes: the middle classes, the primary watchers of Channel 4 and BBC2. Arguably a more useful line of enquiry is to explore the cultural and individual anxieties that lie behind the rising popularity of cookery programmes. As Nigella Lawson (1998a) herself has suggested, given the centrality of cooking, 'it is impossible to write about food, without writing about life'. Thus, the pleasures provided by the consumption of television cookery require a plethora of explanations grounded in both cultural specificity and the specificity of the medium of television.

Within this essay, I shall suggest a number of contributory factors in the rising popularity of television cookery programmes, focusing on how such texts speak to a range of anxieties and insecurities in relation to the pleasures of eating, gendered identity formation, domesticity and the place of television within the 'family'. Such explanations are not exhaustive. This popularity may also be linked to what Claude Fischler (1998) describes as 'a period of gastro-anomy', where uncertainty exists over what we should eat and, given the centrality of food and consumption to identity, over who we are as socially positioned but insecurely gendered individuals (291). The multi-faceted nature of this growing phenomenon of television cookery programmes is, however, too varied and complex to be explored in detail within the limited space this essay allows, and consequently my primary focus will be upon one particular aspect: the sexualised cookery programmes that Jamie Oliver and Nigella Lawson's first series epitomise. The potential readings of these two very different versions of sexuality are not straightforward. I want to argue that this new strand of sensual and sexualised cookery programmes is symptomatic of both an anxiety and a reworking of domesticity and the boundaries between public and private spaces. This is suggestive of some of the wider cultural and economic changes taking place in society that have been linked to postmodern culture.

Firstly I want to suggest that the development of the more overt sexualisation of television cookery programmes in recent years has rested upon the inclusion of eating into such programmes. Historically cookery operates on a continuum between the twin pulls of domesticity, chores and the mundane, and pleasure, sexuality and leisure. Cooking without eating is not necessarily sexy; on the contrary it may threaten to remain in the seemingly unsexy area of domesticity. Yet nowadays images of eating pervade the finale of cookery programmes. The BBC's *Ready Steady Cook*, first broadcast in 1996, would not work without the contestants' public consumption of the food accompanied by sexually suggestive noises and responses. Similarly in programmes featuring the 'Two Fat Ladies', Nigella Lawson or Jamie Oliver, the focus and the point of closure is on a display of carnivalesque feasting.[1] This sexually linked consumption of food enables the cooking prior to it to connote for the viewer something of sexual foreplay. This must be contrasted with previous television cooks such as Delia Smith who, as Stuart Jeffries (2001) points out, avoids eating (329). Consequently Delia's *How to Cook* (2000) programmes tend to remain predominantly although not exclusively in the sphere of the domestic. Such is Delia Smith's respectability that the widespread appeal of her books has enabled her to become not only the first television cookery millionaire, but part of British establishment culture, to the point that her first name is now included in the *Collins Dictionary*. 'Doing a Delia' is understood to mean the down-to-earth performance of domestic cookery.

It is to the domestic that I now want to turn with an awareness that the very term 'cooking' carries associations of the domestic and the private sphere of the 'home', and that television is itself a domestic medium (Ellis, 1982; Silverstone, 1990). Thus an explanation of the centrality of eating to cookery programmes lies in part in the very medium of television itself and thus perhaps needs a little more analysis. Corner (1995) has pointed out that criticism of the detrimental cultural consequences of television falls broadly into five popular discourses which articulate concerns about time wasting, cultural invasion, taste debasement and attitudinal influence. Moores's (2000) ethnographic research has identified families for whom the shared watching of television is seen as an indication of their family cohesion, arguably a role which the shared family meal was once expected to fulfil. Indeed I want suggest that this implied replacement of the family meal by television evokes an anxiety upon which popular discourses critical of television are predicated. (It is interesting to note that the use of the colloquial term 'couch potatoes' for those who over-indulge in television watching connects ideas of laziness and the activity of eating with becoming a foodstuff to be eaten.) The replaced image of family eating together serves as a structuring absence to such discourses, an anxiety-provoking structuring absence which can be temporarily banished in watching television cookery programmes.

The specifically domestic style that television cookery programmes have developed over recent years also needs consideration. Arguably watching television has become a central activity in discourses of home and the domestic, part of the familiar, mundane minutiae of everyday life. However, as Moores suggests, 'television makes available to its viewers a specific sort of "look" at various happenings which take place in the world beyond the living room, but its modes of address and presentation are once again shaped by the profoundly domestic character or "feel" of broadcasting' (216). Thus television cookery programmes are both a mediation and mediator of the changing styles and focus of the cultural understanding of domesticity as well as the economic changes within which it has operated in recent years. The very nature of broadcasting means that the consumption of a text is more than a matter of a viewer watching within their own domestic setting; hence cookery programmes transfer cooking, an activity which usually takes place within the private sphere, into a very public display articulating a public concern for nutrition and hygiene as part of British culture throughout the twentieth century. This public education in the private sphere of the home is consistent with British broadcasting and television's public service tradition (albeit a fading one) of educating and informing as well as entertaining, exemplified in the title of Delia Smith's last three series, *How to Cook*. The television cookery of Marguerite Patten in the 1950s, Zena Skinner in the 1960s and, since the 1970s, Delia Smith has operated predominantly through discourses of health education and straightforward instruction in domestic skills. Their presentation, somewhat akin to that of a domestic science teacher, developed, through the language of television, the stylistic associations and the authority of news-based programming. Cooks tended to speak directly to the camera in the factual, unemotional style of a newscaster. The predominance of the medium shot of the upper body only, the minimal camera movement utilised and limited background music, conveyed that cooking was a serious business of public social significance and worthy of the space that it took up in the programming schedules. Significantly Delia Smith's programmes, set within her own home rather than a television studio, adopted a particularly domestic 'presentation of self', softening the distance between the viewer and the presenter. As Strange suggests: 'the specificities of this *mise-en-scène* – domestic, private, enclosed, secure – serve as an extension of Smith's personality, reinforcing her solid, rooted and reliable presence' (305).

Arguably the popularity of no-nonsense style epitomised by Delia Smith lies in a nostalgic recompense for a version of domesticity that no longer exists, rural or at least suburban in setting and incorporating a desexualised version of motherhood. Such a version of domesticity or motherhood may have little relationship to the lived experience of women, except perhaps in the images they consumed in early television advertisements in the 1950s and 1960s.

The relationship between motherhood, television and the domestic is however a complex one, and significant for the analysis of cooking on television. Silverstone (2000), drawing upon object relations theory, suggests that television may provide ontological security, operating as a transitional object in a child's entry into culture (similar to the bits of blanket and stuffed toys that children carry around with them). Indeed television's capacity always to be there, potentially available even when switched off, complete with the routines of regular programmes such as soaps, news and talk shows, enables it to operate as a idealised form of mother figure. Analysts of television have noticed the common practice of turning the television on when entering the house and keeping it on, even in vacated rooms, as evidence of how television operates as a transitional object. Indeed the vast majority of cookery on television in the past and on digital channels now operates, I would suggest, only as a reassuring background for viewers.   The idealised and nostalgic versions of domesticity and motherhood conveyed by cooks such as Zena Skinner and Delia Smith have this kind of audience appeal. What could be more reassuring and comforting than a cook such as Delia Smith issuing instructions on how to make toast, fruit salads or purchase saucepans? Only perhaps images of fireplaces popular on American chat shows in the late eighties (Tichi, 1991). I would therefore suggest that the almost universal placement of cookery programmes in the perceived, if not actual, kitchen of the presenter in recent years can be seen in relation to the security it offers the viewer while simultaneously facilitating an increasing emphasis on lifestyle.

Although at one level *Nigella Bites* can also be seen as invoking a reassuring version of domesticity and motherhood, at another level, alongside the *Naked Chef*, it is a noticeable example of the significant shift in the cookery genre in recent years towards a more overtly sexualised style. This should come as no surprise. Food and sex, as Phillippa Pullar's history of English appetite and food, *Consuming Passions* (1970), argues, have long been intimately linked, and a variety of analytical approaches can be utilised to shed light upon an understanding of this inter-relationship.

A Bakhtinian approach suggests that both food and sex bring into focus the fluidity and temporality of the boundaries of the body. At time of carnival, an excess of eating and sexual activity serve to highlight the base physicality and degradation of all social groups and the potential uncontrollability of both lusts. Feasts of eating draw attention to the fluidity between what is inside and outside the body, a fluidity, which as Bakhtin (1984) has pointed out, is linked to the sexual in the carnivalesque. He suggests that 'To degrade also means to concern oneself with the lower stratum of the body, the life of the belly and the reproductive organs; it therefore relates to acts of defecation and copulation, conception, pregnancy and birth' (21). Away from the licensed discursive space that carnival provides, eating is the only one of these functions that is commonly undertaken in public and thus may serve as a public reminder of the others. Thus the sexual connotations of eating, now included in many cookery programmes, enable eating to serve as a substitute for sex. An acknowledgement of the bodily pleasures that food offers carries with it an implication of the bodily pleasures of sexuality. This style was successfully articulated in the carnivalesque qualities of *Two Fat Ladies* (1996) cookery series popular in the 1990s.

Meanwhile, psychoanalysis emphasises the oral phase as fundamental to the development of sexual subjectivity. Indeed Freud, in *On Sexuality* (1905), suggested that in childhood 'sexual activity has not yet been separated from the ingestion of food; nor are opposite currents within the activity differentiated' (117). Thus 'a child's sucking at his mother's breast has become the prototype of every relation of love' and the mouth becomes an erotogenic zone for the child, although he argued that sexuality is fundamentally latent during childhood (145). Bedell (2001) presents such arguments in a popular form for the chattering classes in an article on food and sex in the *Observer*, pointing out that:

> One of the first lessons a baby learns about is the bond between food and sensual pleasure. In her book about food and eroticism, *Aphrodite*, Isabel Allende points out 'the sensation of the baby clamped to the maternal teat, immersed in a mother's warmth and smell, is purely erotic and leaves an ineradicable mark on that individual's life. From nursing to death food and sex go hand in hand'.

The mouth remains an erotogenic zone in later life, and thus the giving and consuming of food remain a significant element of sexual and romantic routines in many Western societies.

Lacan's (1982) more recent development of Freudian analysis suggests that both the oral and the sexual phase of development and their inter-relationship can be seen to operate at, or at the very least through, symbolic codes and realms. Cadbury's successful advertising campaign for chocolate 'Flakes' in the 1980s, in which chocolate and oral sex were explicitly linked, suggests that such an analysis may have something to contribute to the understanding of the representational paradigms of food and sexuality at play in the media. Similarly the images on the front of Lawson's recent book *Nigella Bites* (2001), and utilised in media promotions for the *Nigella Bites* series, operate at the symbolic level as *fellatio*. She is frequently presented suggestively placing food between her parted lips.

Finally it is important to be aware of the fundamental role that prohibition, regulation and taboos with respect to food and sex play in structuring and controlling societies, communities and groups. The cultural prohibition on the consumption of certain forms of meat by various religious groups or national communities provides numerous examples of this, as do the taboos and codes of conduct surrounding what can be eaten with what and in what order in many societies (Beardsmore and Keil,

1997). Michel Foucault (1980a) suggests that societies' control of sexuality is fundamental to the exercise of power, historically shifting from external control to internalised self-regulation. Similar paradigm shifts can be seen to have operated in relation to food. The rise in variety in supermarkets in Western societies, including a more multicultural choice of foods in recent years, is more than matched by increasingly frequent voices in political, scientific and popular discourses which articulate the self-regulation of eating. Thus both food and sex are policed biological desires, which function within a framework of the forbidden and consequently the desired. This is a theme explored by Ros Coward (1984), who, in discussing the popular female pastime of reading cookery books and recipes in magazines in the 1970s (an activity which she argues was predicated upon women's problematic relationship with both food and their bodies), describes such images in terms of food pornography (99–106). In the context of the 1970s, Coward was arguing that oral gratification for women themselves was tabooed and hence all the more desired. The fulfilling of the oral desires of others was at the time perceived to be a primarily female responsibility.

Cultural shifts since Coward's analysis mean that a more complex approach to the recent phenomenon of sexualised cookery programmes on television is required, and one that treats these programmes as symptomatic of specifically postmodern anxieties. The postmodern culture of the turn of the millennium, with its ending of certainties and emphasis on the temporal and the contingent, has contributed to a number of once culturally understood boundaries and identity positions becoming blurred, especially those for example between masculinity and femininity or between private and public. A range of media from pop videos to comedy programmes celebrates and plays with the fluidity of such boundaries and the multiplicity of identity positions on offer. Whatever the lived experience of individual men and women, the representational paradigms through which an individual's relationship to food and cooking are articulated are now more fluid than Coward suggested. It would seem that both men and women have some responsibility for the provision of food and that their relationship with cooking and the oral gratification that food offers are problematised; neither is able to avoid a plethora of discourses of both prohibition and desire in relation to food. In such a cultural context the television focus on food and cookery programmes offers the viewer the space to desire food, which the presenter may display without any physical consumption necessarily taking place. Beardsmore and Keil have pointed out that food, because it meets physical needs as well as symbolic ones, is the one area that compromises Jean Baudrillard's notion of wants being unlimited (69). The food focus of much of the media allows unlimited wants and desires to operate without biological constraints.

It is not merely desire for food that produces anxiety in a postmodern culture of uncertainty and fluidity. Domesticity, in particular the domestic kitchen, has traditionally been seen as a private and a female sphere. The gendered delineation of private and public spheres was particularly marked in the nineteenth century through discourses of sexuality, as Jeffrey Weekes (1989) points out. This delineation has since been utilised to express anxiety about the boundaries of private and public in contemporary Western culture. As Harding (1998) suggests:

> Sexuality in turn helps to demarcate the 'private' and the 'public' as discrete and separate domains, through various instances in which it crosses over ceasing to be merely a private act and becoming a matter of public concern. (23)

So the sexualisation of television cookery can be seen as a development of the private act of cooking having become a public concern about nutrition and hygiene. However I want to suggest that, in *Nigella Bites* and *The Naked Chef*, this is interwoven with anxieties about gender and domesticity themselves.

In recent postmodern culture, boundaries of both domestic spaces, such as the kitchen, and of gender have become more fluid. The perceived increases in women's economic activity outside the home and in commercial food preparation have contributed to women and men's relationship to domesticity and to the kitchen becoming areas of uncertainty and anxiety. Another strain of Foucault's work suggests that sexuality has become one way of articulating anxieties and concerns within culture (1980b). I am suggesting that, in programmes such as *The Naked Chef* and *Nigella Bites*, anxieties over boundaries of both masculinity and femininity, and the private and the public (which domestic cooking brings into relief) are displaced onto, or at least articulated through, sexuality. Thus these programmes do not merely explore cookery within a continuum between domesticity and sexual eating; they present a sexualised version of cookery. This is done in a number of ways: through the inclusion of carnivalesque feasting, tasting and nibbling of food, sexual *double entendre* in the titles, a sensual visual style and sexual verbal references. These are all more usually associated with sexualised entertainment programming rather than educational genres with which cookery programmes were once associated.

The connections and contradictions around socially constructed boundaries of public and private, feminine and masculine, are an important element structuring cooking within the televisual. Predominantly female television cooks' authority has been legitimated by reference to their domestic setting or a knowledge that has been culturally constructed as innate. In the 1980s and 1990s Delia Smith's programmes provided an image of the domestic, filming her in a kitchen or indeed in a converted conservatory with her garden visible through the windows behind her, rather than merely in a studio. This serves to merge the public significance of cooking with its private domestic setting. Arguably such cookery programmes blur public and private boundaries while also endorsing and offering status to cookery and the 'feminine' domestic sphere. Alternatively the male sphere of cooking is culturally constructed as the restaurant kitchen, a public space of hierarchical relations, business and professional performance as well as skill. In the 'presentation of self' and the construction of their television personalities, many male television chefs foreground their work in or ownership of restaurants. In the sphere of television cookery programmes the distinction between chef and cook is almost exclusively predicated upon gender. Jamie Oliver for example was 'discovered' during a documentary on the River Café.[2] In the introductory voice-over for *The Naked Chef* he presents himself as a professional chef who has reworked his cookery and his recipes for the domestic sphere. He maintains that 'What I cook at the restaurant isn't what I cook at home', claiming that, for the domestic context, he 'strips recipes down ... to the bare essentials'. The synopsis of his life inside the cover of his books presents a narrative of his development from 'cooking in his parents' pub at eight' to 'working with some of the biggest names in British cooking'. In the first episode of *The Naked Chef*, Oliver establishes his credibility by cooking for 'chef' and his mates from the restaurant where he is at one point shown working. In the following programmes he frequently refers to his experience in the commercial world of restaurant cookery.

By contrast, Nigella Lawson invokes an authority based upon a tradition of femininity with references to her mother's, aunt's and grandmother's cooking, as well as to other female cookery writers such as Jane Grigson. Indeed she expressly positions herself in opposition to the public world of restaurant cooking when, in the little chat she gives the viewer from her armchair at the beginning of the first episode of *Nigella Bites*, she suggests that 'chefs have to innovate to impress' because they are being paid. She goes on to explain that 'home cooked food should be relaxed and casual', about giving 'herself and her guests pleasure' and that it 'doesn't matter what you buy and what you make'. Hence, the first episode of *Nigella Bites* establishes her approach to cooking for her viewers. She constructs a 'feast' for friends including: shop-bought hummus perked up with olive oil, chilli and pomegranate, alongside home-constructed *guacamole* with what look suspiciously like Dorritos, a huge hunk of oozing Brie. A veritable postmodern shopping trolley dash through what is presented as her milieu: the London of the chattering classes.

It is a long way from the rural nostalgia previously invoked by the use of pine kitchens in cookery programmes, on television channels such as Carlton Food. *Nigella Bites* offers not the nostalgia of an imaginary world when women's place was in the domestic private sphere of the kitchen, but an image of a post-feminist world where women can have it all: the public spheres of work and the private spheres of children and partner. Significantly the construction of the television personality 'Nigella Lawson' has rested from the start upon an already existing set of signifiers. The name Lawson carries connotations of the public sphere of power and politics not just from her father, the Conservative Chancellor of the Exchequer in the 1980s, but also from her brother, the editor of the *Telegraph* newspaper. Furthermore when *Nigella Bites* was first shown in 1999, Lawson herself already had an established name as a journalist for *The Observer*, a food writer for *Vogue*, a Booker Prize judge and author of *How to Eat* (1998b). Thus she already had a publicly constructed persona, which the programme gave the illusion of circumventing by taking the viewer into the private sphere of her kitchen.

Lawson's style of cooking merges an established public persona with a feminine tradition of cookery. It is relaxed, involving stirring, pouring and food left unattended simmering on the stove or cooking in the oven in an unhurried way. Her recipe for shoulder of pork, for example, takes twenty-four hours. She emphasises the preparing of food in a style to suit individual tastes or lifestyles. In 'Weekends', while adding oregano to a lamb stew she explains:

> With stews you really don't have to be too hung up on
> is it a teaspoon or half a teaspoon
> one bay leaf or two
> two or three carrots
> none of it makes any difference and you'll feel so much more liberated if you just bung things in
> you know, within reason .[3]

She then proceeds to empty into the stew a can of tomatoes and a bottle of white wine. Her approach, she claims, is based upon building up the viewers' confidence and 'liberating' them. This is emphasised by a presentational style which is conversational, involving chatting to the viewer using a linguistic framework familiar on radio. The camera moves around the kitchen with her, invoking the hand-held home video style often used now to bring into play notions of authenticity and realism. The camera's relaxed style underlines her spoken dialogue, which is only occasionally directed to the camera. Thus the camera positions the viewer as a friend, not as pupil in educational situation.

This is reminiscent of Jamie Oliver's avoidance of the instructional approach. While cooking he carries on a dialogue with the never-viewed producer of the programmes. Her voice ringing with the middle-class tones of Southern England acts as a mediator for the audience who are watching a 'man at work' rather than a man being taught by a woman how to cook. Furthermore this style of presentation provides accessibility in allowing different points of identification in the text for both female and male viewer.

The private domestic and public restaurant styles of cooking articulated by Lawson and Oliver respectively are fundamental to the structure and format of both programmes. In *Nigella Bites*, Lawson is presented as inhabiting her kitchen in a relaxed and languorous fashion, shifting between cooking and looking after children, kissing them goodnight, laying tables in a dining room, driving her car, putting on make-up or chatting with friends, wineglass in hand. Cooking is constructed as part of a domestic lifestyle, often shot in soft focus, connoting a soft comforting aura to the construction of her domestic world. In one episode she makes French toast for her daughter while still in her dressing gown. On another occasion she is shown similarly attired, taking a clementine cake out of the oven and explaining it can cool in the tin overnight. Extolling the virtues of this particular cake she points out how simple it was to prepare and then goes on:

> you can make it say
> at the weekend when you've got the time
> and then in the middle of the miserable week
> when you're feeling deprived and exhausted
> you can come home from work and eat it ... ('Weekends')

The assumption is that, in an alien, stressful, insecure and post-Fordian working world, food, the kitchen and cooking may be a comfortable retreat. Cookery in *Nigella Bites* is presented as sensual leisure activity, the foreplay to eating, perhaps a specifically feminine pleasure. Although it may be that the implied reader of her books or viewer of her programmes is not necessarily female, by implication the reader or viewer is at least prepared to engage with and value traditionally feminine spheres of activity. In the introduction to *How to Be a Domestic Goddess* (2000), Lawson elaborates:

But I do think many of us have become alienated from the domestic sphere, and that it can actually make us feel better to claim back some of that space, make it comforting rather than frightening. In a way, baking stands both as a useful metaphor for the familial warmth of the kitchen we fondly imagine used to exist, and as a way of reclaiming our lost Eden. (vii)

Her focus is on the comfort of food, a quality that is often reflected in her cooking: cakes and meringues, roasts and stews, 'pigs in blankets', feasting food and a significant representation of mood-enhancing carbohydrate. She offers a reworking of the comfort and reassurance factors of both television and cooking with a style which is overtly sexual and sensual. The feel, texture and aroma of food are dwelt upon while the spoken dialogue emphasises indulgence and doing what feels 'right for you'. When folding egg whites into a chocolate cake she explains:

if you're scared I think it somehow does sometimes
permeate into the cooking
you just have to relax and it'll get better. ('Weekends')

In an almost deliberate flaunting of the anxieties that Coward argues women have about the consumption of food, *Nigella Bites* features an episode entitled 'Home Alone' on cooking for one or two. The title is of significance, referencing in the series of 'family' films where a young child turns a potentially frightening and threatening situation – being left alone by his family in a large house – into one of indulgence and carnivalesque fun. The opening shots show Lawson sitting down, talking with hands gesticulating in a conversational rather than instructional mode, and explaining the pleasures of solitary eating. The stolen (and usually very private) pleasures of eating left-overs are highlighted at the end of another episode when she helps herself to a spoonful of trifle straight from the bowl still in the fridge ('Leftovers'). Her consumption of the trifle is accompanied by leafing through a holiday brochure of sandy beaches underlining the sense of relaxed indulgence that food can offer. Her reclamation of the pleasures of eating for women has all the zeal and some of the linguistic turn of phrase of the reclamation of female masturbation in the feminist writing of the 1970s, such as in the magazine *Spare Rib*. At other times, Lawson emphasises the importance of 'cook's treats', pointing out the necessity of leaving a good dollop of cake mixture in the bowl for a 'cook's treat' which she refers to as a 'must have' in cooking. There is an implication that one of the key pleasures of cooking lies in the access to eating food in various states of preparation and condition before the pressures of timing and synchronisation have deprived them of their edge, an implication many cooks I suspect would not deny. The sexualisation of solitary food consumption reaches its pinnacle in her enjoyment of Yorkshire puddings with cream and syrup over them in order to demonstrate a variation on the traditional Sunday Roast. Having first remarked on the magnificent size to which this pudding has risen, Lawson goes on to explain:

> I just love this so much ...
> Must have some not least to show you how gorgeous it is. ('Weekends').

Having suggestively poured cream and syrup over the pudding, she places a large forkful in her mouth, turning slightly away from the camera, her mouth overflowing with white cream. Within moments the setting has shifted to her taking her children for a picnic in the park.

Within a postmodern world of numerous fleeting identity positions, Nigella Lawson's books and television programmes, with more than a touch of the tongue-in-cheek about them, offer women the identity of 'domestic goddess' rooted within the physical space of a kitchen simmering with sexuality. This is not something that has been met with unparalleled enthusiasm. Journalist Julie Burchill (2000), writing in *The Guardian*, was quick to condemn what she sees as a perverse mixing up of nesting and sexual emotions, arguing that: 'The New Domesticity is the buzz of glamorous denial that desire is dead.' Probyn (2000) also criticises Lawson's style: 'Beyond the now tattered dream of liberation in the bedroom, and freed from the obligations of cooking, the kitchen is now sold to women as the new sphere of sensual liberation' (4–5). Probyn's criticisms are facile and carry the air of condemnation or at least condescension towards the many viewers and followers of Nigella Lawson's style of cookery who have taken her books into the bestseller lists in 2001. Arguably both domestic skills (including cookery) and sexuality are, and have been for some considerable period of time, areas of power for women. These are not the only sources of power available to women or even necessarily the sources of power women would choose. However given that, as Marxists used to point out, individuals make their own history within circumstances not of their own choosing, domestic skills and sexuality are sources of power women frequently utilise. Taking this into account, it could be argued that, amongst the multiplicity of readings that a viewer can draw from *Nigella Bites*, one interpretation of Lawson's ironic and excessive performance rests on seeing women's relationship with domesticity and sexuality as itself a tongue-in-cheek performance.

If women's relationship with domesticity and sexuality is often seen problematically, so is their relationship with consumption and consumer culture, which is an underlying theme in all cookery programmes. Both journalists and viewers were quick to point out that *Nigella Bites Christmas Special* (2001) was more concerned with the lifestyle of 'Nigella Lawson' than cooking style. Shane Watson (2001) suggested in *The Guardian* that '*Nigella's Christmas Special* has nothing to do with cookery. It was about how great she is compared to us.' Significant for both *Nigella Bites* and *The Naked Chef* is the array of ingredients and implements, including Kenwood Chefs,⁴ griddle pans, food processors and pasta makers that may be said to belong to a class-specific consumer culture or lifestyle, and which serve as a reminder that television chefs are not merely salespeople for the broadcasting and media industries but also, directly or indirectly, for the manufacturers of significant number of household consumer durables. The use of equipment defines the different styles of cooking: Jamie Oliver whips with a metal balloon whisk, defining him as professionally trained while Nigella Lawson resorts to the Kenwood Chef to save effort and time; Jamie Oliver chops onions quickly and professionally with a professional-style knife while Nigella Lawson throws them in the food processor. The equipment with which Jamie Oliver cooks in the first series of *The Naked Chef* is industrial: stainless steel bowls and cooking trays, large wooden chopping boards. The front of his first book *The Naked Chef* further contributes to this construction: he is placed in front of a cold, bare, blue wall on one side leaning on a wooden workshop with an array of knives on the wall behind him to his left. The whole serves to connote the public world of the restaurant kitchen brought into domestic kitchen, and the fluidity of work and home.

Arguably the restaurant style of Jamie Oliver's cooking is that of an urban-based restaurant with a European influence, where the food is never prissy or over-decorated. For all his 'Essex lad' television persona, Jamie Oliver's restaurant food has an emphasis on look, image, texture and colour closer to 'nouvelle cuisine' than comfort food. It implies a clientele of businessmen, professionals, the chattering classes and New Labour, those Beardsmore and Keil describe as middle-class groups 'rich in what Bourdieu terms "cultural capital" if not economic capital ... maintaining distinctiveness by cultivating tastes for exotic and foreign foods' (88). The ingredients Oliver uses often require purchasing from small shops such as cheese shops, delicatessens, specialised butchers, bakeries or fishmongers found only in the urban milieu in which he is presented as living. Location shots of his shopping are interspersed throughout the programmes but are never of supermarkets, which could be anywhere in the country. Images of

London taxicabs and the Post Office Tower emphasise the London base of his restaurant associations and by implication their expense and quality.

Within *The Naked Chef*, Jamie Oliver's cooking is constructed as an extension of his working life in a number of ways. It involves earnest chopping, pounding, kneading and mixing, whipping, all overtly utilising physical prowess. The performance of masculine strength that this involves is most easily demonstrated with reference to his regular use of the pestle and mortar. He relies upon the movement of his shoulders and a shifting of his body to ensure that his weight is, so to speak, applied to the garlic or herbs being crushed. (When Delia Smith uses a pestle and mortar she invokes a stirring action with no more than the lower part of her hand or arm involved; Nigella Lawson rarely bothers with one at all.) His cookery requires a great deal of attention, necessitating the hierarchy of the restaurant kitchen, a hierarchy that is sometimes recreated with assistance provided by friends or family, to prepare various meals. It is significant that whilst Nigella Lawson covers two Jamie Oliver focuses on only one. Leisure time 'earned' during the programme is taken at the end of his programmes, in the form of consumption of food with family and friends. The programmes are structured around the visits of, for example, 'the band', and 'the girlfriend'.

The pleasure offered by the *Naked Chef* is also linked to the consumption of a display which is in content and style overtly sensuous and sexual. Such themes are exaggerated by the particular televisual style utilised, involving close-ups, a range of camera angles, fast movement editing and lighting more familiar in pop videos, while the cookery demonstrated employs much physical contact with the food: kneading, stirring, stuffing, tossing and rubbing food by hand. As I have suggested above, a sensual and sexual connotation to the programmes has already been privileged in the *double entendre* of the title, despite Jamie Oliver's determined negation of this implication in the initial voice-over at the beginning of each programme. When he retorts 'No way, it's the food that's naked not me', this serves not to negate such potential readings but to place them firmly in the viewer's mind. Thus viewers are tantalised with what is then denied, as the sight of the food tantalises them with what cannot be tasted or consumed. Jamie Oliver minus clothes serves as an ever-present structuring absence in the text and is potentially interwoven with the viewers' readings of his very physical style of cooking.

The construction of the television personality of Jamie Oliver in terms of his sexuality is further emphasised in the second episode of the first series, 'The Hen Night'. This episode's narrative is of Jamie Oliver cooking a meal for his sister and approximately ten young women (who uniformly conform to media discourses of attractiveness) as they set off on a hen night. Such a narrative allows for a significant number of laddish exchanges with other young males as he undertakes the preparation and shopping. Arguably this may be seen as a response to the tensions around gender evoked in relation to cooking in what has a cultural history of being seen as a female domestic space, the home as opposed to the restaurant kitchen.   At the beginning of the hen night episode this tension is articulated as he explains how he likes to make bread whereas some boys of his age like to play around with Escort S3Ls. The dialogue while he cooks bread for 'lairy ladies, city girls and students' includes the throwaway remark: 'Rough and ready, that's how I like my women.' He goes on to explain how 'this Italian guy' taught him to make bread which was supposed to be 'like making love to a beautiful woman': 'you have to treat it gently and be vigorous at all the right points and all that sort of stuff'.   The ending of the episode, however, ensures an anchoring and fixing of Jamie's sexual and gender alignment (and by implication that of any of his male viewers) as he stands by his front door to embrace, in turn, the women as they leave.

Moseley (2000) argues that Jamie Oliver's appeal may be an articulation of cultural shifts in masculinities coupled with an aesthetic style, which can appeal to a new male audience. She suggests he 'uses pop video aesthetics, pop slang ("pukka" "peaches" "mate") and above all demonstrates that "real lads" do cook' (27). Whilst shifts in the social constructions of femininity and a rise in the overt participation of women in the labour market in recent years have apparently led producers of cookery programmes to attempt to broaden their intended audiences across genders and ages, Oliver's appeal is perhaps rather more complex. His dress and physical movements, boyish jumps, including the characteristic laddish sliding down the banisters in the first two series, portray a version of youthfulness further evidenced by scenes of him playing table football with 'mates' and his performing in a band. His scruffiness in clothing and hairstyle – at the end of 'The Girlfriend', an episode in the first series, he pulls on a jumper with a hole in it – arguably implicating the middle-aged female viewer in the twin modes of viewing as mother and as lover with all the complexities of their interweaving and inter-relationship. Whilst much media and scholarly attention has been paid to the 'Lolita syndrome', rather less attention has been focused on the fluidity of the boundaries between maternal and sexual feeling that middle-aged women have for younger men. The constructed 'presentation of self' that makes up Jamie Oliver's broadcast personality is both child and sexual icon. Thus an analysis of middle-aged women buying his books for themselves and their sons might provide an example of the popularity of some cookery programmes on television being partially attributable to a blurring, challenging and playing with a range of cultural boundaries.

Indeed this essay has attempted to argue that an understanding of cookery programmes must rest upon an exploration of a range of perceived cultural boundaries brought into play by the topic of cooking and the medium of television, in particular the boundaries and categories of areas such as 'public' and 'private', 'male' and 'female' and the significance of the domestic to them. I have suggested that within a postmodern culture the boundaries and meanings of such categories have become more fluid, giving rise to anxiety, an anxiety that is expressed through discourses of sexuality in both *Nigella Bites* and *The Naked Chef*. Within this framework I would suggest that boundaries between sexual and maternal feelings are but one more inevitable twist. The medium of television, however, is a live and changing one. The constructed personas of Jamie Oliver and Nigella Lawson, here explored primarily in relation to their first series, are constantly being reworked. They and the television cookery genre remain a rich and under-worked minefield for analysis.

Notes

1   *Two Fat Ladies*, first broadcast on BBC2, October 1996.
2   The documentary in which Jamie Oliver first appeared was *Italian Christmas at the River Café* broadcast on BBC2, 14 December 1996.
3   All references are to Nigella Lawson's first series.
4   In fact, Nigella Lawson makes specific and effusive reference to a KithenAid mixer, 2000, p.viii.

Chapter 12

Adapting and Adopting: The Migrating Recipe

Marina de Camargo Heck

This last essay demonstrates the relevance of the cultural context of the recipe to those wider fields of study that consider human experience: anthropology, the study of migration, contemporary sociology and oral history. The results of a sociological survey and oral history project conducted in 1997–1998 have raised complex questions about the social and psychological significance of recipes and meals in the collective consciousness and memory of the immigrant populations of São Paulo. The 'Food and Memory' research project took as its underlying premise the suggestion that amongst different forms of collective memories, one of the most persistent is culinary memory. The research which I discuss here involved a social group where food and culinary habits could be seen as a distinctive category: immigrants and their families settled in the city of São Paulo from the turn of the nineteenth century to the 1950s.[1]

Discourses about food are present in almost all memory work.   The reminiscences of culinary experiences are rich in aromas, colours and tastes that resist not only the impact of time and technology but also cultural and geographical change. This research has already resulted in the production of a cookery book which describes the adaptation and retrieval, through memory, of particular recipes and meals that evoke memories of personal, familial and social significance (Heck and Belluzzo, 1998).

   This essay will discuss how cultural values can be transmitted through food memories, focusing on how immigrants have preserved their food repertoire and adapted their recipes to the new ingredients found in the host country. My research raises the general question of how immigrants have experienced the acculturation process. This is not to say that looking at acculturation in and through food habits has precluded looking at changes that have occurred inside the host nation. The host nation does not so much prompt or enforce a change in immigrant habits as itself adopt new habits brought in the country by the immigrants. This adaptation/adoption of eating habits has consequences for the food of the immigrant families but, at the same time, it intervenes in the host community, mixing and modifying both culinary cultures.

Food is absolutely central to our sense of identity as we are constructed biologically, psychologically and socially by the food we incorporate into our bodies (Fischler, 1988). Much research has been done showing how food exchanges develop sociability and express bonds of solidarity within communities. Throughout history, cookery has always had an eminently ritual character, following the cycle of seasons and the religious calendar. Very often the history of popular diet is linked in profoundly important ways with the history of folklore (Camporesi, 1998). And, indeed, a sense of the symbolic significance of food and how it is used to express ties of kinship, solidarity and difference has underpinned and informed this study.

In terms of the transmission of culture from generation to generation, culinary habits are crucial to the process of understanding and perpetuating national mythologies. Roland Barthes (1972) has explored ways in which food is able to transmit so much about culture and daily life. He shows how strongly rooted the consumption of wine is in French society and how shocked the French were when President Coty, 'allowed himself to be photographed ... sitting at home before a table on which a bottle of beer seemed to replace the familiar litre of red wine' (60). Wine here becomes an issue of national identity and cohesion, a *raison d'État.*

At the same time, tastes and feelings, rules and recipes have reflected not only social changes but also technological developments such as the introduction of new forms of energy. The evolution of manners at the table and forms of manipulating food are as important as the development of human knowledge and hierarchy systems in society (Elias, 1994).

Equally we may observe that sex and food have always been linked together in our everyday language. In particular the discourse of love cleverly conceals a good deal of reference to food vocabulary in almost every language: 'honey', *'mon chou'*, *'mon poulet'*, *'il a devoré avec les yeux'*. Love is full of eating fantasies, of cannibal desire (Zeldin, 1994; De Certeau et al., 1998). We may consider people's expectations at the table or in bed as part of a same process of imagination that prepares the way to the satisfaction of unrealised personal appetites. At the same time, Elias's study suggests that the 'civilising process' begins with the individual's talent for concealment, for being able to control emotions and to disguise the spontaneous and unruly. Food thus becomes a 'civilised' and accepted way of satiating desire.

Essential to the promotion and control of desire is the visual presentation of food. Food photography has created a culinary practice based on glazed surfaces, coatings, trimmings and ornaments which disguise the nature of dishes that have not been made to be eaten but rather to nourish dreams and alibis (Barthes, 1972). Recipe books, meanwhile, have left the kitchen shelves to compete with art books and landscape photography for a place on the coffee table of trendy sitting rooms.

However if food has played a part in strengthening ties of solidarity and arousing desires and dreams, it is also true that choices of food, etiquette at the table and the whole *savoir-faire* of gastronomy have throughout history served to intensify social segregation. This is an issue that has preoccupied the contemporary social sciences. Elias evokes that segregation in a 'conversation' between the poet Delille and the Abbot Cosson: the poet questions the Abbot on his behaviour during a dinner at the court in Versailles: how he ate the bread, what he did with his napkin, how he drank coffee, and so on. After listening to all the answers, he concludes: 'everyone must have noticed that the Abbot came from the provinces'. The Abbot's response is to proclaim that he had only done exactly what was 'normal' (84).

Food also speaks to class difference. Pierre Bourdieu (1984), with his sociology of social distinction, assigns '*goûts de necessité*' to the working classes and '*goûts de luxe*' to the bourgeoisie. In essence he argues that social classes face their socio-economic reality at mealtimes. The working-class meal is characterised by foodstuffs that include soups and sauces, pasta and potatoes in almost every meal. These are usually dishes that are served with large spoons or ladles avoiding too much measuring, and, for Bourdieu, such practices express the rebelliousness within differentiated social groups.

> The art of eating and drinking remains one of the few areas in which the working class explicitly challenges the legitimate art of living. In the face of the new ethic of sobriety for the sake of slimness, which is most recognized at the highest levels of the social hierarchy, peasants and especially industrial workers maintain an ethic of convivial indulgence. (179)

A strong allegiance to foodways is, of course, very marked amongst immigrant populations. The customs and practices that immigrants bring with them from their native land are habits, however, which soon have to change in the host country. While they may often hold very strongly to their food culture, they are forced to adapt to new forms of culinary culture. Yet culinary habits mark a strong resistance to a complete acculturation, so that old and new culinary habits are mixed and modified in ways that affect the cuisines of both immigrant families and indigenous groups. The adaptation of their native culinary habits, as well as the adoption of new eating habits, has consequences regarding the food of the immigrant families but, at the same time, it intervenes in the host community, mixing and modifying both culinary cultures. The intervention of ethnic cuisine, particularly for example in America, whereby foreign foods have been domesticated and incorporated, is becoming more and more evident. The present discussion aims to observe that process, especially the changes and resistances that have transformed these habits and consequently the recipes.

The immigrant has, in his or her ethnic food, the symbolic larder that guarantees the autonomy of his identity and subjectivity. Culinary practices represent an intricate system of identities which do not break down in contact with other cultures, but rather maintain the alterative tension of multicultural cohabitation, a tension that resists the pasteurising effects of globalisation. I am not suggesting that traditional ethnic food can be safeguarded from industrial 'fast food' and the effects of a so-called 'postmodern global gastronomy' characteristic of the globalisation of diversity (Hall, 1991, 31–33). Nevertheless the desire to preserve tradition and to protect ancestral feelings through tastes and odours belongs to a group of sentiments which find their best expression in countries where immigration played an important role. Ethnic food which was 'regional' back home comes to represent an ethnic national cuisine in the new country. The need to maintain a traditional identity within a foreign country is so strong that food may develop a mythical status, a 'more authentic' flavour, than actually found in the country of origin.

The immigrants selected for this study came to Brazil for different reasons and at different periods of time. Some intended to stay; others thought they would go back to their home country one day. Some fled from wars, others from famine; they were seeking a better life in America. Once they arrived they had to re-adapt their social relations and work out a means of participation in the new society. Very often they had to adapt their skills and work, but they were also obliged to adapt their cultural and religious habits and, above all, their foodways.

The history of immigration into Brazil in the nineteenth century is a complex one: a process of attraction of and resistance to migrant populations. After Brazilian independence from Portugal and even before slave abolition, landowners were anxious to replace the slaves in their farms and great efforts were made to stimulate immigration. Between 1881 and 1915, around 31 million immigrants arrived in the Americas. The United States received around 70 per cent; in second place came Argentina, which received 4.2 million, followed by Brazil with 2.9 million immigrants.

The incorporation of free immigrant workers in the Brazilian coffee farms was complicated in the beginning. The food habits of the Europeans were not consistent with what was on offer in Brazil. The immigrants were seen as ravenous and wasteful for expecting to eat delicate dishes and to drink alcoholic beverages. The 'delicacies' to which they referred were cheese and bread, and the beverages were wines and ales.

The range of ethnicities was considerable. According to Immigration Census, between 1819 and 1939, almost 5 million immigrants came to Brazil. Amongst them 1.5 million were Italian and 1.4 million were Portuguese; these were followed by almost six hundred thousand Spanish and almost two hundred thousand Japanese and Germans; after this came Jews, Turks and Syrians (Alvim, 1998). Immigrants mainly from Christian communities in Syria and the Lebanon arrived more or less together from the Ottoman Empire mostly with Turkish papers, some with Greek passports. In actual fact this demographic research was undertaken exclusively in the region of São Paulo; therefore it was very influenced by the immigrant groups present in the Southeast region of Brazil, particularly in the city of São Paulo. The immigrants represented in this study are mainly those who came to work in the coffee plantations. It is important to bear in mind that São Paulo is, above all else, a city of immigrants. The history and memory of immigration has served to define and construct the identity of the inhabitants of São Paulo. Old traditional families, descendants of the coffee-farm owners, are the ones who have today to distinguish themselves from the immigrant descendants, calling themselves 'paulistas' of 400 years' standing, meaning they have been there since São Paulo was founded by the Jesuits in 1554. Immigrant-related families constitute a large majority of the population of São Paulo, and since the 1950s there has also been a large population of internal migrants from the Northeast of Brazil. The attraction of studying immigrant food habits in São Paulo is enhanced further by the fact that gastronomy in the city has, in the last twenty years, generated considerable economic activity and a large range of restaurants of different cuisines.

The immigrants interviewed for this project were picked from the files of the São Paulo Immigrant Hostel archives to reflect both the range and size of different immigrant communities. In selecting testimonial data we also looked to represent the range of class origin and work, a balance of gender, and different kinds of interaction with the mainstream of Brazilian society. We worked with the life stories of immigrants told either by themselves or sometimes through relatives: sons, daughters, or grandchildren. Tape recordings of unstructured interviews were made with 35 immigrants and their kin. The life stories were put together in national groups: Italian, Japanese, Armenian, Syrian, Lebanese, Spanish and German, and a composition of national groups united by their Jewish identity. The Portuguese were also considered immigrants since so many arrived within the timespan selected (while Portuguese who came during the colonial period were excluded). Other references were also used in the choice of testimonial data, such as class origins, profession and work skills, gender and actual insertion in the Brazilian society.

By drawing primarily upon life stories as a testimony, taped interviews were analysed and transcribed. Testimonial material was written down exactly as it was collected in conversation with the subject. Incorporated within it were the interventions and the prompts, and thus the subjectivities and imagination of the interviewers. In such a situation the researcher is, in any case, entirely involved. His or her values and world-view should not be seen as obstacles, but rather as the condition for understanding differences and apprehending the essence of what is expressed by the subject of the interview. Unlike some oral histories analysed by conversation analysts and ethnographers, which focus on the exotic aspects of their subjects' lives, our attention was mainly oriented to the everyday routine of the immigrant families. It is true that qualitative interview must first of all be regarded as a situation in which all the parties to the conversation use their 'sociological imagination'. They all become active producers of the research material. In-depth interview can be compared to many other forms of data collection; however the actual analysis of the material remains the job of the researcher who is no longer just one party in the conversation but becomes the interpreter of the meanings expressed.

The interviews were first edited in the narrative style of a personal memoir, having in mind the editorial project of a recipe book. We tried to preserve not only the quality of conversation and narrative, but above all the 'colours' and 'atmosphere' present during the interview. The interviews were conducted in a very open way in order to allow each life story to flow freely and randomly. Despite this, interviewees remained conscious that my preoccupation was food and culinary habits, and they were happy to talk about their childhood memories, ancestors and country of origin. It would be overly simplistic to suggest that interviewees use only one narrative frame within which to portray their life story. Certainly these interviews were very heterogeneous in form.[2]

Two main themes shaped the interviews: adaptation and preservation of culinary habits. Life stories evoked reminiscences that were explored in the sense of how these memories had contributed to build a new 'way of eating'. Food reminiscences form a patchwork of memories. Once assembled they may be harmonious or traumatic, depending on how people preserve them in their minds as well as how they transmit them through the preparation of food. Thus we often found a strong presence in the interviews of a Manichean response of attraction and repulsion towards food tastes. Food memories can bring back dreams of pleasurable tastes. Alternatively traumatic culinary experiences may lead to a violent disgust for certain foodstuffs and thus be fixed in eating behaviour for the rest of one's life. Food memories are always about love and hate, pleasure and disgust.

In the case of Maria, for example, who emigrated from Greece in the early 1950s, recently married and not intending to stay longer than a few years: she and her husband went directly from the ship to the Immigrant Hostel in São Paulo, where she was separated from her husband and given black beans to eat. 'They tasted awful ... I had never eaten anything like it before. Still today I cannot eat them. And to think that I live in a country where rice and beans is the main dish. My children are Brazilian and they love it.' Another example is Yvonne, born in Yugoslavia in a Jewish family, who came to Brazil in 1951, having spent part of the war in Switzerland: ' My first contact with America was in Trinidad when the ship stopped and the only thing I can remember was that I was fascinated by the enormous bananas I saw. No one told me they were cooking or frying bananas and I ate them raw. I almost died.' Marisa, however, had fond memories of certain foods. She was born in São Paulo but her mother was Italian from Piemonte: 'My grandmother did most of the cooking at home but she was very strict, even in her cooking. My mother was the one who did the lovely things. I still remember how much I liked to be ill, with the flu, because I would stay in bed and she would bring me a sabayon with little almond biscuits. I loved to get the flu.' Memories of food can recover all these moments; they are privileged moments that are remembered either as a punishment or as the ultimate reward.

In several interviews the immigrants talked nostalgically of certain ingredients that they missed and found essential to maintain their culinary habits. Many of them hesitated to use substitutes and went to great efforts to get the authentic ingredient. Diva, for example, was born in Brazil but her very large and extended family had always lived in a Syrian community in a rural area of São Paulo. Showing us the garden where her grandparents planted most of the foodstuffs for the preparation of Syrian food, she pointed out a particular plant: 'Look ... this leaf. It is called *ramaida*. The first seedling came from Syria. We use it a lot; in soups, in the *tabbouleh* and in all sorts of fillings.' She went on to explain that: 'My grandfather came first with my uncles. When he sent for my grandmother and my mother and her sister, he wrote saying that this vegetable didn't exist here. So when my grandmother came, in the ship, she brought a seedling of it in a little box with earth and she watered it during the trip until they could plant it here. It is similar to the Egyptian *mulokhiya*.'

Other interviewees had found it easy to adapt lentils for beans, beef in place of lamb and would rewrite their recipes according to the new ingredients they found. Fatala was seven years old when he arrived in 1929 from Antioquia: 'My mother tried to carry on cooking her kind of food, but it all tasted different. We never ate beef, only lamb or mutton, and here we could only buy beef. This was the only difference. I also quickly replaced the lentils for black beans, but I wasn't used to eat so much rice as they did here, we used to eat rice only on Sundays. The rest was just the same.'

Tastes, liked or disliked by different members of the family, are not the only memory that stays present in people's minds. Strong odours and the aspect of certain foods are also recollected. As mentioned before, the perception of tastes and smells may not have the same cultural value in different contexts, and different contexts and specific sensations remain attached to life experiences. Acculturation may reverse tastes: what was acceptable in childhood becomes unacceptable when new criteria are brought into play. Mary, a young woman born in Brazil, lived with her grandparents as a child, speaking only Japanese until she was seven years old. She recalled her Japanese grandmother staying long hours in a dark room preparing *miso* (a paste made with fermented beans):

> My grandmother would go into the room, she would stir something in there, would cover it and would tell us not to go inside. No one should go inside or touch anything. I didn't know what it was, but the room was dark and had to remain dark and there was an awful smell. (…) There was also something called *natto*, I think it is soy beans… you leave it in fermentation wrapped in the straw of the corn, for days, the colour is horrible and it gets gooey. A little like okra, but drier. I used to eat it when I was a child but I don't think I would any more.

Even though Mary spent her childhood eating and observing the preparation of very traditional foodstuffs, she confesses that she has 'Brazilianised' her cuisine. 'My mother-in-law says that in Japan they don't have to use detergent to wash up their pans and dishes because they cook with no fat at all. But now I sautéed everything before I add water … I think our generation needs to fry the onions a little bit. I also don't think we like to make fish like the Japanese and I tend to eat more meat than fish.' Significantly, Mary mentions that it is not only a question of keeping the national tradition but that changes occur from one generation to another, implying that such acculturalisation and adaptation happens in a range of ways.

For Taeko, whose mother married in Japan and came to Brazil in 1932, the adaptation of her mother's food habits was not a question of age and generation, as Mary suggested above. What pushed her to adopt Brazilian foodstuffs was the belief in a necessity for feeding calories to the men of the family.

> Basically my mother cooked in Japanese style, however many dishes depended on certain foodstuffs that she could not find here. We had lots of fish and at night usually fish soup; everything was seasoned with *shoyo* and sometimes some ginger. But when my brothers started to grow up ... you know ... Japanese cuisine is not very strong on calories, and my brothers needed to be well fed, because they worked all day. So then she started to introduce Brazilian foodstuffs: rice and beans and meat. She would even cook meat barbecue style!

For most of us the first images through which family is first remembered are those of the kitchen and the table at which the daily meals were consumed. It is around this table that one recalls the unity of the family. The food and the ritual of the meal are alive in the memory of every individual (Muxel, 1996). Often the narratives we recorded started with a description of this ritual and how it was organised: hierarchy, respect and routine are the main characteristics of this ritual. For Natale, son of Italian immigrants:

> We had an absolutely religious schedule in my grandfather's house. There was a kind of liturgy proper of lunchtime. My grandfather had lunch at midday. He wanted to listen, by the radio, the bell toll at São Bento church when he sat down for lunch. And all the family should follow the same schedule ... nobody would answer the telephone if it rang. I remember it irritated me to hear it ringing but my grandfather would say that the mealtime was sacred. We were twelve, sometimes fourteen at the table and the Italian homemade bread had to cut by my grandfather. That was his function at the table; he said there was a way of cutting bread, one should know it in order to do it.

The dishes and recipes also followed a pre-established order and routine:

> For dinner we always had soup, the weather could be hot or cold we would invariably have soup for dinner. Soup was absolutely essential and my

memory of these soups is very vivid, even being Italian, pasta is not so important as soup for me. We would eat pasta every Thursdays and Sundays, the other days it varied, but soup we had every single night.

Food memories do not only bring back recollections of the ordinary daily meal, the everyday routine, but also the pleasures and the constraints of the family relations. Memory retains a strong and vivid picture of everyday life but it also can recall the exception (Muxel, 1996). Interviewees always brought up memories of exceptional meals; the food prepared for celebrations, annual parties and family gatherings. Food is an important issue in religious celebrations such as Christmas, Easter and Pessach. Sundays are also special in the regular weekly routine. For example, Melanie's parents came from Bessarabia. They are Jewish with an extended multi-ethnic family. Many of them have married non-Jews and the family is not particularly observant of religious ritual. Thus Melanie's food habits are very eclectic:

> My family is completely integrated culturally in Brazil, my sister is married to a non-Jew and her sons too; my brother is married to a Jewish woman, their daughter married a Jew but separated and now is married to a non-Jew. My sons, only two of them are married to Jewish girls and they never had a Bar Mitzvah. But they all love Jewish food and the religious parties. For Pessach I prepare exactly the same traditional food every year. The Seder ceremony is performed with all the symbolic foods that celebrate Moses' crossing of the desert. We don't eat bread nor anything prepared with wheat, but a lot of horseradish with beetroot sauce. ... When I was a little girl I remember my mother and her friends preparing the food for the neighbour's Bar Mitzvah. We were a community, we had somewhat of a ghetto relationship where neighbourhood was important and strengthened the links between people.

Christmas is of course the apotheosis of celebratory food festivals and certain Christmas delicacies are eagerly anticipated and then recalled over the rest of the year. Christmas food, characteristically prepared several days or weeks in advance, must be abundant and different from the ordinary. Edith came from Romania to Brazil in the early 1950s and for her the culinary memories are an experience of parties and abundance:

> In my father's farm, not far from Bucharest, they would bake a sweet bread (kind of a *panettone*) made with 200 eggs. It took hours of preparation, a lot of work. For each child there was a baking tray with their name engraved on, and in it the dough would be put and baked in an enormous oven. In the morning when we woke up and there was the bread beside the bed; the bread

of each one of us. Here, I have simplified this tradition, I make a bread that is called *cozonac trandfir.*

In a similar way, Maria Jose remembered Christmas in her village in Portugal. They were poor but the simple delicacies prepared for Christmas were thought of as very special: 'At Christmas Eve we would go to Mass at midnight and when we came back home we would have rice pudding and *rabanadas* (a kind of French toast) and *filhós* (a wafer-thin pancake). The *rabanadas* could be made either with milk or with a mixture of water, sugar and wine.'

There are many traditions that have imprinted a particular message in the memory of all of us. These memories often are linked to a certain smell, taste or eventually, as Diva recalled, by the delivery of a case of Port wine and a sack of walnuts. Her Syrian grandfather would have walnuts and Port wine sent to her house when her mother was pregnant. The wine was for the mother's diet and the nuts were for the tea that would be served to visitors. It was a very fragrant repast, with fennel, star anise and cinnamon sprinkled with chopped nuts. When the children saw their mother in the kitchen breaking the nutshells, they would whisper among them: 'It's time for the baby to come.'

The transformation and adaptation of recipes follow strange trajectories and the origins of certain foods become, at times, difficult to pinpoint. The style of cuisine fixed in the recollections of some of the interviewees has been difficult to reproduce. New ingredients, the daily contact with another food culture, the evolution of the family embracing other ethnic groups creates a peculiar style of cuisine. Traditional recipes and food habits are often modified through this process of negotiation and incorporation. Often the legacy of an immigrant cuisine is a *pot-pourri* of cuisines encountered by the family during their collective history and their recollection of the trajectory of their experience in settling down in a new country.

Maria Jose was nine years old when she arrived from the Portuguese countryside in 1927. Her family's cooking habits were rustic. They lived on a small farm and her mother would slaughter a pig every year, prepare sausages and smoke and dry meat for the winter. In São Paulo all this was finished and the family bought food in the market like everyone else. Consequently her food habits today are very eclectic:

I am married to a Spaniard, for the last 62 years, so now I cook either Spanish or Portuguese food and even Brazilian. My mother-in-law was from Granada and she taught me a lot of things. Today I can cook both kinds of food very well. I open my fridge and I look inside and depending on what I find there I decide the kind of food I will cook. They come from the Mediterranean and they eat a lot of fish, but in my village there was no fish to buy except for sardines.

Other Portuguese interviewees told us that they kept quite a few rural habits even in the urban landscape of São Paulo. Portuguese communities in Brazil and elsewhere are well known for keeping chickens, ducks and rabbits in their backyard and cultivating green kale in any tiny patch of land they find.

However culinary habits do not only change because they have to adapt to a new geographical situation. Food may be made more elaborate when adapted at the hands of an upwardly mobile immigrant community. In this way, when a particular ethnic community settles down and ascends socially and economically, it will promote its own gastronomic background to a gourmet status. In this upgrade process expensive foodstuffs are added to the basic recipe. This has happened with the Italian *polenta*, with the Portuguese *acorda*, with the Jewish *knishes* and so many other dishes that remind the immigrants of their poor background. Thus *funghi porcini* or white truffles are added to *polenta*, shrimps and mussels to *acorda*, smoked salmon to *knishes* and so on.

Alongside this sociological survey, a parallel research project was conducted to produce accurate, usable recipes for these 'memory foods'. Bearing in mind the project of a recipe book that would combine testimonies with recipes, we picked out particular dishes that were mentioned in the interviews. From this starting point, we conducted a bibliographical search as well as a practical cooking workshop on the recipe itself. It was rarely possible to use exactly the same recipe as given to us by the interviewees. In order to make the final recipe practical and operational it was necessary to adapt the measurements and timings of the original instructions. None the less, even with such adaptations to the method, it was a strict criterion that the final dish should look and taste precisely as the one evoked during the interview. There were cases where the dish named and remembered by the interviewee was quite different from the one stipulated by the recipe books that we consulted. The process of transferring a dish or 'memory food' from recollection to a usable recipe was an intricate one. Realising smells, tastes and appearances that had been stored in memories into actual dishes involved much trial and experimentation. At a different level, relating much-reinterpreted 'standard' dishes back to their original recipe book forms revealed how far new methods and ingredients had in fact changed dishes still perceived to be authentic.

Esparregados of Portuguese cookbooks (and often on the menu of Portuguese restaurants) is a case in point. This is a dish of finely chopped cooked spinach which is sautéed until the greens hold together and pull away from the pan as an omelette (Ortins, 2000); this liaison is sometimes achieved by the addition of a creamy ingredient to act as a thickening agent. However, for Alzira, who came from Portugal in the 1940s, *esparregados* is something quite different:

> My mother called it 'esparregadas' and she would start as if she was doing *polenta*, with corn flour and water, but a very smooth and thin *polenta*. Then she would chop finely some green kale or mustard leaves and mix it together with the creamy mixture of corn flour, immediately taking it out of the heat. Just before serving she would grill some sardines directly over the coal fire, the sardines just like they come, with scales and all. This way it won't break or stick in the grill. Then she would serve the creamy cabbage mixture, and we would make a little hole in the middle and fill it with olive oil. We would take the sardines with our fingers, dip them in the oil and then the 'esparregadas' and eat it.

This is a typical example of the adaptation of a recipe. Alzira's mother certainly invented these 'esparregadas' on arrival to this new country where spinach and cream were not easily found, and her children have perpetuated her recipe in spite of the fact that something quite different is presented today in Portuguese restaurants and recipe books.

Ultimately, then, culinary traditions and food memories define us, offering solidarity with and a sense of distance from our familial, social and ethnic groups. But, in keeping and adapting familiar recipes, we are able to create practices that, even as they recall the past, initiate new traditions, new identities, new selves.

Notes

1   The work described in this essay is part of a larger Food and Memory project. The sociological survey was conducted by the writer and Rosa Beluzzo in 1997–1998 as part of a research work at the Department of Law and Social Sciences of Getulio Vargas Business School in São Paulo, together with the Brazilian Centre for Latin American Studies of the Memorial of Latin America. The survey was edited and published as Heck and Belluzzo, *Cozinha dos Imigrantes: Memorias e Receitas*, 1998. A second part of this research (the analysis of the interviews in relation to immigration) has been undertaken by the writer during a Visiting Fellowship at the Institute of

Advanced Studies of the University of London aided by a post-doctoral grant of
FAPESP, Research Funding Institution of São Paulo.

2   The comments quoted in the following pages derive both from the published research,
Heck and Belluzzo, 1998, and from further interviews conducted for the purposes of
the present essay.

Bibliography

Acton, Eliza (1845), *Modern Cookery in All its Branches*, London: Longman, Brown, Green and Longmans.

Adams, Elsie and Briscoe, Mary Louise (eds) (1971), *Up Against the Wall Mother*, Canada: Glencoe.

'The Adulteration of Food' (1887), *Westminster Review* **128**, 1090-1099.

Akhtar, Miriam and Humphries, Steve with Ros Belford (2000), *Some Liked It Hot: The British on Holiday at Home and Abroad*, London: Virgin Books.

Alencastro, Luis Felipe and Renaux, M. L. (1997), 'Caras e Modos dos Migrantes e Imigrantes' in Novaes, Fernando (org.), *Historia de Vida Privada no Brasil Volume 2*, São Paulo: Cia das Letras.

Allen, Ida Bailey (1927), *The Modern Method of Preparing Delightful Foods*, New York: Corn Products Refining Company.

Alvim, Zuleica (1998), 'Imigrantes: A Vida Privada des Pobres do *Campo*', in Noaes, Fernando (ed.), *Historia de Vida Privada no Brasil*, Volume 2, São Paulo: Cia das Letras.

Ames, Kenneth L. (1992), *Death in the Dining Room and Other Tales of Victorian Culture*, Philadelphia: Temple University Press.

Andrews, Maggie (1997), *The Acceptable Face of Feminism*, London: Lawrence and Wishart.

Andrews, Maggie and Talbot, M. (2000), *All the World and Her Husband*, London: Cassell.

Anonymous [1857] (1886), 'Curry', in Parton, James (ed.), *The Humorous Poetry of the English Language*, Boston: Houghton Mifflin, pp. 474-475.

Anonymous (1870), *The Manuscript Receipt Book and Household Treasury*, third edition, Philadelphia: Claxton.

Anonymous (c. 1830), Unpublished cookbook, University of Delaware Special Collections, Newark, DE.

Appadurai, Arjun (1988), 'How to Make a National Cuisine', *Comparative Studies* **30**, 3-24.

Arata, Stephen (1990), 'The Occidental Tourist: *Dracula* and the Anxiety of Reverse Colonization', *Victorian Studies* **33**, 621-645.

Attar, Dena (1987), *Bibliography of Household Books Published in Britain, 1800-1914*, London: Prospect Books.

Atwood, Margaret (1969), *The Edible Woman*, London: Virago.

Atwood, Margaret (1985), *The Handmaid's Tale*, London: Virago.

Azim, Firdous (1993), *The Colonial Rise of the Novel*, New York and London: Routledge.

Bakhtin, Mikhail [1965] (1984), *Rabelais and His World*, trans. Hélène Iswolsky, Bloomington: Indiana University Press.

Ballaster, Ros, Beetham, Margaret, Frazer, Elizabeth and Hebron, Sandra (1991), *Women's Worlds: Ideology, Femininity and the Women's Magazine*, Basingstoke: Macmillan.

Bardwick, J. M. (1980), *Women in Transition: How Feminism, Sexual Liberation and the Search for Self-Fulfilment have Altered Our Lives*, Brighton: Harvester.

Barnes, Julian (2002), *Something to Declare*, London: Picador.

Barr, Pat (1976), *The Memsahibs: In Praise of the Women of Victorian India*, London: Secker and Warburg.

Barthes, Roland (1972), *Mythologies*, trans. Annette Levers, New York and London: Vintage.

Bateman, Michael (1999), 'An American Revolution', *Independent on Sunday*, 24 January.

Beardsmore, Alan and Keil, Teresa (1997), *Sociology on the Menu: An Invitation to the Study of Food and Society*, London: Routledge.

Beck, Leonard B. (1984), *Two 'Loaf-Givers'*, Washington: Library of Congress.

Bedell, Geraldine (2001), 'Sex and Food', *The Observer*, 11 November.

Beecher, Catherine and Beecher Stowe, Harriet [1869](1985), *American Woman's Home*, Hartford, CT: Stowe-Day Center.

Beeton, Isabella (1861), *Beeton's Book of Household Management*, London: S. O. Beeton.

Beetham, Margaret (1996), *A Magazine of Her Own? Domesticity and Desire in the Woman's Magazine 1800-1914*, London: Routledge.

Beetham, Margaret (2001), 'Women and the Consumption of Print', in Shattock, J. (ed.), *Women and Literature 1800-1900*, Cambridge: Cambridge University Press, pp. 55-77.

Best War Time Recipes (1918), New York: Royal Baking Powder Company.

Bevan, David (ed.) (1988), *Literary Gastronomy*, Amsterdam: Rodopi.

Bhabha, Homi K. (1994), *The Location of Culture*, New York and London: Routledge.

Bocock, R. (1993), *Consumption*, London and New York: Routledge.

Boone, Joseph (1987), *Tradition Counter Tradition: Love and the Form of Fiction*, Chicago: Chicago University Press.

Borden, E. S. (c. 1873), Doc. 191, Unpublished Cookbook, Henry Francis du Pont Winterthur Museum Library, Wilmington, DE.

Bourdieu, Pierre [1979] (1984), *Distinction: A Social Critique of the Judgement of Taste*, trans. Richard Nice, London: Routledge Kegan Paul.

Bower, Anne (ed.) (1992), *Recipes for Reading: Community Cookbooks, Stories, Histories*, Amherst, MA: University of Massachusetts Press.

Braithwaite, Brian (1995), *Women's Magazines: The First 300 Years*, London: Peter Owen.

Brand, G. and Scannell, P. (1991), 'Talk, Identity and Performance: The Tony Blackburn Show', in Scannell, P., *Broadcast Talk*, London: Sage, pp. 201-226.

Brantlinger, Patrick (1988), *Rule of Darkness: British Literature and Imperialism, 1830-1914*, Ithaca: Cornell University Press.

Brears, Peter (1994), 'A La Française: The Waning of a Long Dining Tradition', in Wilson, C. Anne (ed.), *Luncheon, Nuncheon and Other Meals: Eating with the Victorians*, Stroud: Alan Sutton, pp. 91-116.

Brillat-Savarin, Jean-Anthèlme (1926), *Physiology of Taste, or Meditation on Transcendental Cookery*, New York: Boni and Liveright.

British Broadcasting Corporation (2002), *The Food Programme*, 12 May.

British Broadcasting Corporation (1999), *The Naked Chef*.

British Broadcasting Corporation (1996), *Two Fat Ladies*.

Bruch, Hilda (1973), 'How Vital Are Your Statistics?', *Spare Rib* **11**, May, 31-33, 38.

Bulwer Lytton, Edward (1833), *England and the English*, London: Richard Bentley.

Burchill, Julie (2000), 'The New Domesticity', *The Guardian*, 4 November.

Burton, Antoinette B. (1994), *Burdens of History: British Feminists, Indian Women and Imperial Culture, 1865-1915*, Chapel Hill: University of North Carolina Press.

Buzard, James (1997), 'Home Ec With Mrs. Beeton', *Raritan* **17**, Fall, 121-135.

Camporesi, Piero (1998), *The Magic Harvest*, London: Polity Press.

Cardoso, Ruth (1988), 'Aventuras de antropólogos em campo ou como escapar das armadilhas do método', in *A Aventura Antropológica*, São Paulo: Paz e Terra.

Carter, Angela (1991), *Wise Children*, London: Chatto and Windus.

Chaney, Lisa (1998), *Elizabeth David: A Mediterranean Passion*, London: Macmillan.

Channel 4 (1998), *In the Footsteps of Elizabeth David*.

Channel 4 (1999), *Nigella Bites*.

Chase, Hattie (c. 1880-1890), Doc. 358, Recipe Book, Henry Francis du Pont Winterthur Museum Library, Wilmington, DE.

Chaudhuri, Nupur (1992), 'Shawls, Jewelry, Curry and Rice in Victorian Britain', in Chaudhuri, N. and Strobel, M. (eds), *Western Women and Imperialism*, Bloomington: Indiana University Press, pp. 231-246.

Chaudhuri, Nupur and Strobel, Margaret (eds), *Western Women and Imperialism*, Bloomington: Indiana University Press.

Coates, Jenefer (1974), 'Shared Housework', *Spare Rib* **25**, 28-29.

Cogan, Frances (1989), *The All-American Girl: The Ideal of Real Womanhood in Mid-Nineteenth-Century America*, Athens, GA: University of Georgia Press.

Colley, Linda (1992), 'Britishness and Otherness: An Argument', *Journal of British Studies* **31**, 309-329.

Connolly, Cyril (1947), 'Comment', *Horizon* **15** (87), 151-154.

Conrad, Jessie [1923] (1933), *A Handbook of Cookery for a Small House*, London: Heinemann.

Cooper, Artemis (1999), *Writing at the Kitchen Table: The Authorized Biography of Elizabeth David*, London: Michael Joseph.

Corner, J. (1995), *Television Form and Public Address*, London: Edward Arnold.

Cotter, Colleen (1997), 'Claiming a Piece of the Pie: How the Language of Recipes Defines Community', in Bower, Anne L. (ed.), *Recipes for Reading:*

Community Cookbooks, Stories, Histories, Amherst: University of Massachusetts Press, pp. 51-71.

Coultrap-McQuin, Susan (1990), *Doing Literary Business: American Women Writers in the Nineteenth Century*, Chapel Hill: University of North Carolina Press.

Counihan, Carole M. (1998), 'Food and Gender: Identity and Power', in Counihan, C. M. and Kaplan, S. L. (eds) (1998), *Food and Gender: Identity and Power*, Netherlands: Harwood, pp. 1-10.

Counihan, Carole M. (1999), *The Anthropology of Food and Body: Gender, Meanings and Power*, London and New York: Routledge.

Courtney, William Leonard (1904), *The Feminine Note in Fiction*, London: Chapman and Hall.

Coward, Ros (1984), *Female Desire: Women's Sexuality Today*, London: Paladin.

Curtin, Deane W. and Heldke, Lisa (eds) (1992), *Cooking, Eating, Thinking: Transformative Philosophies of Food*, Bloomington and Indianapolis: Indiana University Press.

D'Avigdor, Elim Henry [pseud. 'Wanderer'] (1885), *Dinners & Dishes*, London: Simpkin, Marshall and Co.

David, Elizabeth (1950), *A Book of Mediterranean Food*, London: John Lehmann.

David, Elizabeth (1951), *French Country Cooking*, London: John Lehmann.

David, Elizabeth (1954), *Italian Food*, London: MacDonald.

David, Elizabeth (1955), *Summer Cooking*, London: Museum Press.

David, Elizabeth (1960), *French Provincial Cooking*, London: Michael Joseph.

David, Elizabeth (1986), *An Omelette and a Glass of Wine*, Harmondsworth: Penguin.

David, Elizabeth (1994), *Harvest of the Cold Months: The Social History of Ice and Ices*, London: Michael Joseph.

David, Elizabeth (2000), *Is There a Nutmeg in the House?* London: Michael Joseph.

Davidoff, Leonore and Hall, Catherine (1987), *Family Fortunes: Men and Women of the English Middle Classes: 1780-1850*, London: Hutchinson.

Davidson, Cathy (1998), Preface, 'No More Separate Spheres!', *American Literature* **70** (3), September, 443-465.

De Certeau, Michel, Giard, Luce and Mayol, Pierre (1998), *The Practice of Everyday Life II: Doing and Cooking*, trans. Timothy J. Tomasik, Minneapolis: University of Minnesota Press.

Devitt, Mrs Charles W. (1871), Doc. 324, Recipe Book, Henry Francis du Pont Winterthur Museum Library, Wilmington, DE.

Dickens, Charles (1836), *Pickwick Papers*, London: Chapman and Hall.

Dickens, Charles (1850), *The Personal History of David Copperfield*, London: Bradbury and Evans.

Douglas, Ann (1977), *The Feminization of American Culture*, New York: Alfred A. Knopf.

Douglas, Mary (1975), 'Deciphering a Meal', *Implicit Meanings: Essays in Anthropology*, London: Routledge.

Driver, Christopher (1985), *The British at Table*, London: Chatto and Windus.

Driver, Elizabeth (1989), *A Bibliography of Cookery Books Published in Britain, 1875-1914*, London: Prospect Books.

Du Pont, Louisa Gephard (c. 1850), Recipe Book, Hagley Museum and Library, Wilmington, DE.

Dunbar, Paul Laurence (1896), *Howdy Honey Howdy*, New York: Dodd and Mead.

Edmunds, J. (1903), *Curries and How to Prepare Them*, London: Food and Cookery Publishing Agency.

Elias, Norbert (1994), *The Civilizing Process: Sociogenetic and Psychogenetic Investigations*, trans. Edmund Jephcott, revised edition, Oxford: Blackwell.

Ellis, J. (1982), *Visible Fictions*, London: Routledge.

Ellis, Sarah Stickney (1844), *The Family Monitor and Domestic Guide*, New York.

Ellman, Lucy (1988), *Sweet Desserts*, London: Virago.

Ephron, Nora (1983), *Heartburn*, New York: Alfred A. Knopf.

Esquivel, Laura (1993), *Like Water for Chocolate: A Novel in Monthly Instalments with Recipes, Romances and Home Remedies*, trans. Carol and Thomas Christiensen, London: Black Swan.

Extension Circular No. 21 (1917), *Food Emergency Demonstrations*, New Hampshire College Extension Service, September.

'*The Feasts of Autolycus*', Review (1923), *The Nation* **62**, 30 April, 349-350.

Ferguson, Marjorie (1985), *Forever Feminine: Women's Magazines and the Cult of Femininity*, Aldershot: Gower.

Ferguson, Sheila (1989), *Soul Food*, New York: Grove.

Fischler, Claude (1988), 'Food and Self Identity', *Social Science Information* **27**, 275-291.

Fisher, Abby [1881] (1995), *What Mrs Fisher Knows about Old Southern Cooking: Soups, Pickles, Preserves etc.*, Bedford, MA: Applewood Press.

Fisher, M. F. K. (1983), 'The Anatomy of the Recipe', in *With Bold Knife and Fork*, London: Chatto and Windus.

Fiske family (c. 1810-1890), Doc. 723. Cookbook, Henry Francis du Pont Winterthur Museum Library, Wilmington, DE.

Flint, Kate (1993), *The Woman Reader, 1837-1914*, Oxford: Clarendon Press.

Floyd, Janet (2002), *Writing the Pioneer Woman*, Columbia, MO.: Missouri University Press.

Fogarrty, Fran (1972), 'Munchy Business', *Spare Rib* **3**, September, 31-33.

Fordyce, Eileen (1987), 'Cookbooks of the 1800s', in Grover, Kathryn (ed.), *Dining in America*, Amherst: University of Massachusetts Press, pp. 85-113.

Foucault, Michel (1980a), *History of Sexuality*, Volume 1, trans. R. Hurley, New York: Vintage.

Foucault, Michel (1980b), *Power/Knowledge: Selected Interviews and Other Writings*, New York: Pantheon Books.

Francatelli, Charles E. (1861), *A Plain Cookery Book for the Working Classes*, London: Bosworth and Harrison.

Franks, Thetta Quay (1917), *The Margin of Happiness: The Reward of Thrift*, New York: Knickerbocker.

Freeman, Caroline (1973), 'When is a Wage not a Wage?', *Red Rag* **5**, August, 16-18.

Freeman, Sarah (1989), *Mutton and Oysters: The Victorians and their Food*, London: Victor Gollancz.

Freud, Sigmund [1905] (1991), *On Sexuality*, The Penguin Freud Library 7, Harmondsworth: Penguin Books.

Fussell, Paul (1975), *The Great War and Modern Memory*, New York: Oxford University Press.

Fussell, Paul (1980), *Abroad: British Literary Traveling Between the Wars*, New York and Oxford: Oxford University Press.

Gates, Henry Louis Jr (1987), 'Talking Books', in Henry Louis Gates Jr and McKay, Nellie (eds), *The Norton Anthology of African American Literature*, New York and London: Norton, pp. xxvii-xli.

Gates, Henry Louis Jr (1988), *The Signifying Monkey: A Theory of African-American Literary Criticism*, New York and Oxford: Oxford University Press.

Gates, Henry Louis Jr (1987), *Figures in Black: Words, Signs and the 'Racial' Self*, New York and Oxford: Oxford University Press.

Giard, Luce (1998), 'Doing Cooking', in De Certeau, Michel, Giard, Luce and Mayol Pierre, *The Practice of Everyday Life*, Minneapolis: University of Minnesota Press, pp. 149-223.

Gilman, Sander (1985), *Difference and Pathology: Stereotypes of Sexuality, Race and Madness*, Ithaca: Cornell University Press.

Goldman, Anne (1992), '"I Yam What I Yam": Cooking, Culture and Colonialism', in Smith, S and Watson, J. (eds), *De/Colonizing the Subject: The Politics of Gender in Women's Autobiography*, Minneapolis: University of Minnesota Press, pp. 169-195.

Goody, Jack (1977), *The Domestication of the Savage Mind*, Cambridge and New York: Cambridge University Press.

Goody, Jack (1998), *Food and Love: A Cultural History of East and West*, London and New York: Verso.

Goodyear, Rachel (1975), 'Tradition, Innovation and Borrowing in Nineteenth-Century Household Books: *An Encyclopaedia of Domestic Economy* and *Beeton's Book of Household Management*', MA Diss., Leeds University.

Gray, Rose and Rogers, Ruth (1995), *The River Café Book*, London: Ebury Press.

Grimley, Gordon (ed.) (1973), *The Victorian Cookery Book*, London: Abelard-Schuman.

Gronniosaw, James A. U. [1770] (1813), *A Narrative of the Most Remarkable Particulars in the Life of James Albert Ukawsaw, an African Prince as Related by Himself*, Leeds: G. Wilson.

Habegger, Alfred (1982), *Gender, Fantasy, and Realism in American Literature*, New York: Columbia University Press.

Hall, Stuart (1991), 'The Local and the Global', in King, Anthony (ed.), *Culture, Globalization and the World System*, Basingstoke: Macmillan, pp. 19-39.

Hamilton, Roberta (1978), *The Liberation of Women: A Study of Patriarchy and Capitalism*, London: Allen and Unwin.

Harding, J. (1998), *Sex Acts*, London: Sage.

Hardyment, Christine (1995), *A Slice of Life: The British Way of Eating since 1945*, London: BBC.

Harris, Jessica B. (1989), *Iron Pots and Wooden Spoons: Africa's Gifts to New World Cooking*, New York: Fireside.

Harris, Jessica B. (1995), *A Kwanzaa Keepsake: Celebrating the Holiday with New Traditions and Feasts*, New York: Fireside.

Heck, Marina and Belluzzo, Rosa (1998), *Cozinha dos Imigrantes: Memorias e Receitas*, São Paulo: DBA/ Melhoramentos.

Heldke, Lisa M. (1992), 'Foodmaking as a Thoughtful Practice', in Curtin, Deane W. and Heldke, Lisa (eds), *Cooking, Eating, Thinking: Transformative Philosophies of Food*, Bloomington and Indianapolis: Indiana University Press, pp. 203-229.

Heldke, Lisa M. (1992), 'Recipes for Theory-Making', in Curtin, Deane W. and Heldke, Lisa (eds), *Cooking, Eating, Thinking: Transformative Philosophies of Food*, Bloomington and Indianapolis: Indiana University Press, pp. 251-265.

Hermes, Joke (1995), *Reading Women's Magazines: An Analysis of Everyday Media Use*, Cambridge: Polity Press.

Hess, John L. and Karen (1972), *The Taste of America*, Columbia: University of South Carolina Press.

Hess, Karen (1992), *The Carolina Rice Kitchen: The African Connection*, Columbia: University of South Carolina Press.

Hess, Karen (1995), Historical Notes, *What Mrs Fisher Knows about Old Southern Cooking: Soups, Pickles, Preserves etc.*, Bedford, MA: Applewood Press.

Hibbert, C. (ed.) (1985), *Queen Victoria in Her Letters and Journals: A Selection*, New York: Penguin Books.

Hill, Janet M. (1918), 'Food Suggestions for August–September', *American Cookery* 23 (2), August/September, 124-125.

Hill, Janet M. (1918), 'Queries and Answers', *American Cookery* 23 (2), August/September, 135-140.

Hill, Janet M. (1918), 'Seasonable and Tested Recipes', *American Cookery* 22 (7), February, 500-505.

Hill, Janet M. (1918), *War Time Recipes*, Cincinnati: Proctor and Gamble Company.

Hoffman, Alice [1990] (1992), *Seventh Heaven*, London: Virago.

Hoover, Herbert (1917), 'What I Would Like Women to Do', *Ladies' Home Journal*, August, 24.

Hoover, Herbert (1941), Introduction. *History of the United States Food Administration: 1917-1919*, Stanford: Stanford University Press.

'How to Mend a Toilet' (1977), *Spare Rib*, July, 20.

Humble, Nicola (2000), Introduction, *Mrs Beeton's Book of Household Management*, Oxford: Oxford University Press.

'Humble Pie' (1971), *Shrew* 3 (7), August.

Hunter, Lynette (1994), 'Proliferating Publications: The Progress of Victorian Cookery Literature', in Wilson, C. Anne (ed.), *Luncheon, Nuncheon and Other Meals: Eating with the Victorians*, Stroud: Alan Sutton, pp. 51-70.

Hurston, Zora Neale (1934), 'Characteristics of Negro Expression', in Cunard, N. (ed.), *Negro: An Anthology*, London: Wishart.

Jaivin, Linda (1996), *Eat Me*, London: Chatto and Windus.

James, Allison (1996), 'Cooking the Books: Global or Local Identities in Contemporary British Food Cultures?' in Howes, D. (ed.), *Cross-Cultural Consumption: Global Markets, Local Realities*, London: Routledge, pp. 77-92.

James, Selma and Dalla Costa, Mariarosa (1972), *The Power of Women and the Subversion of the Community*, London: Falling Wall Press.

'Jane's Journal' (1977), *Femme*, June, 4.

Jeffries, Stuart (2001), *Mrs Slocombe's Pussy*, London: HarperCollins.

Jones, Steve and Taylor, Ben (2001), 'Food Writing and Food Cultures: The Case of Elizabeth David and Jane Grigson', *Cultural Studies* **4** (2), 171-188.

Kelley, Mary (1984), *Private Woman, Public Stage: Literary Domesticity in Nineteenth-Century America*, New York: Oxford University Press.

Kennedy, David M. (1980), *Over Here: The First World War and American Society*, Oxford: Oxford University Press.

Kenney Herbert, Colonel [1878] (1885), *Culinary Jottings for Madras*, Madras: Higginbotham and Co.

Kilgour, Maggie (1990), *From Communion to Cannibalism: An Anatomy of Metaphors of Incorporation*, Princeton: Princeton University Press.

Lacan, Jacques (1982), *Feminine Sexuality*, trans. J. Mitchell and J. Rose, London: Pantheon Books.

Lanchester, John (1996), *The Debt to Pleasure*, London: Picador.

Langland, Elizabeth (1995), *Nobody's Angels: Middle-Class Women and Domestic Ideology in Victorian Culture*, Ithaca: Cornell University Press.

Lawson, Nigella (1998a), 'Can't Cook, Don't Want To', *The Guardian*, 13 October.

Lawson, Nigella (1998b), *How to Eat*, London: Chatto and Windus.

Lawson, Nigella (2000), *How to Be a Domestic Goddess*, London: Chatto and Windus.

Lawson, Nigella (2001), *Nigella Bites*, London: Chatto and Windus.

LeCroy, Anne (1989), 'Cookery Literature or Literary Cookery', in Schofield, Mary Anne (ed.), *Cooking By the Book: Food in Literature and Culture*, Bowling Green, Ohio: Bowling Green State University Popular Press, pp. 7-24.

Left Overs: War Edition (c. 1918), Lowell, MA: C. I. Hood Company.

Lehmann, John (1955), *The Whispering Gallery*, London and New York: Longmans, Green and Co.

Leonardi, Susan J. (1989), 'Recipes for Reading: Summer Pasta, Lobster à la Riseholme, and Key Lime Pie', *PMLA* **104**, May, 340-347.

Levenstein, Harvey A. (1988), *Revolution at the Table: The Transformation of the American Diet*, New York: Oxford University Press.

Leverson, Ada (1893), 'An Afternoon Party', *Punch* **15**, July, 13.

Lévi-Strauss, Claude (1966), 'The Culinary Triangle', *Partisan Review* **33**, 586-595.

Lévi-Strauss, Claude (1987), *Anthropology and Myth*, Oxford: Basil Blackwell.

Macaulay, Thomas Babington [1835] (1972), 'Minute on Indian Education', in Clive, J. and Pinney, T. (eds), *Selected Writings*, Chicago: University of Chicago Press, pp. 235-251.

Mackay, Jane and Thane, Pat (1986), 'The Englishwoman', in Colls, R. and Dodd, P. (eds), *Englishness: Politics and Culture: 1880-1920*, London: Croom Helm, pp. 191-229.

Mackenzie, John (1984), *Propaganda and Imperialism: The Manipulation of British Public Opinion 1880-1960*, Manchester: Manchester University Press.

Mars, Valerie (1993), 'Parsimony and Plenty, Views from Victorian Didactic Works on Food For Nursery Children', in Mars, Gerald and Valerie (eds), *Food, Culture and History* 1, London: The London Food Seminar, pp. 152-162.

Mars, Valerie (1994), 'A La Russe: The New Way of Dining', in Wilson, C. Anne (ed.), *Luncheon, Nuncheon and Other Meals: Eating with the Victorians*, Stroud: Alan Sutton, pp. 117-144.

Marshall, Agnes B. (1890), *Mrs A. B. Marshall's Cookery Book*, London: Simpkin, Marshall, Hamilton, Kent and Co.

Marshall, Kate (1982), *Real Freedom: Women's Liberation and Socialism*, New York: Junius Publications.

Mayle, Peter (1989), *A Year in Provence*, London: Pan Books.

Mayle, Peter (1991), *Toujours Provence*, London: Pan Books.

Mayle, Peter (1993), *Hotel Pastis: A Novel of Provence*, New York: Alfred A. Knopf.

McCracken, Ellen (1993), *Decoding Women's Magazines: From Mademoiselle to Ms*, Basingstoke: Macmillan.

McCullough, Kate (1996), 'Slavery, Sexuality, and Genre: Pauline Hopkins and the Representations of Female Desire', in Gruesser, John (ed.), *The Unruly Voice: Rediscovering Pauline Elizabeth Hopkins*, Urbana: University of Illinois Press, pp. 21-49.

McIntosh, William Alex and Zey, Mary (1998), 'Women as Gatekeepers of Food Consumption: A Sociological Critique', in Carole M. Counihan and Steve Kaplan (eds), *Food and Gender: Identity and Power*, Netherlands: Harwood, pp. 21-49.

Mennell, Stephen (1985), *All Manners of Food: Eating and Taste in England and France from the Middle Ages to the Present*, Oxford: Basil Blackwell.

Merritt, Albert N. (1920), *War Time Control of Distribution of Foods: A Short History of the Distribution Division of the United States Food Administration, its Personnel and Achievements*, New York: Macmillan.

Metcalf, Thomas R. (1964), *The Aftermath of Revolt: 1857-1870*, Princeton: Princeton University Press.

Michie, Helena (1987), *The Flesh Made Word: Female Figures and Women's Bodies*, New York: Oxford University Press.

Mink, Louis (1980), 'Everyman His or Her Own Annalist', in Mitchell, W. J. T. (ed.), *On Narrative*, Chicago: University of Chicago Press, pp. 233-239.

Moores, S. (2000), *Media and Everyday Life in Modern Society*, Edinburgh: Edinburgh University Press.

Moseley, R. (2000), 'Makeover Takeover on British Television', *Screen* **41** (3), 299-314.

Mulkerrins, J. (2001), 'Focus', *The Sunday Times*, 16 December, 19.

Mullendore, William Clinton (1941), *History of the United States Food Administration: 1917-1919*, Stanford: Stanford University Press.

Muxel, Anne (1996), *Individu et Memoire Familiare*, Paris: Nathan.

Narayan, Uma (1997), *Dislocating Culture*, New York and London: Routledge.

Nash Smith, Henry (1974), 'The Scribbling Women and the Cosmic Success Story', *Critical Inquiry* **1** (1), September, 47-71.

'Natural Earth Drinks' (1972), *Spare Rib*, August, 25.

Nelson, Elizabeth (1989), *The British Counter-Culture 1966-1973: A Study of the Underground Press*, Basingstoke: Macmillan.

Norman, Jill (1993), 'South Wind in the Kitchen', in Castell, H. and Griffin K. (eds), *Out of the Frying Pan: Seven Women who Changed the Course of Postwar Cookery*, London: BBC Books, pp. 31-50.

Northend, Mary Harrod (1918), *American Cookery* **23** (2), August/September, 91-94.

Observer Food Magazine 14, May 2002.

Oakley, Ann (1974), *The Sociology of Housework*, Oxford: Martin Robinson.

Oliver, Jamie (2000), *The Return of the Naked Chef*, Harmondsworth: Penguin.

Oliver, Jamie (2001), *Happy Days with the Naked Chef*, London: Michael Joseph.

Orbach, Susie (1976), 'Fat is a Feminist Issue', *Spare Rib*, November and December, 6-9 and 42-45.

Orbach, Susie (1979), *Fat is a Feminist Issue*, London: Hamlyn.

Ortins, A. (2000), *Portuguese Home Style Cooking*, New York: Interlink Books.

Parker, Rozsika (1977), 'Portrait of the Artist as a Housewife' *Spare Rib*, July, 5-8.

Patten, Marguerite (1970), *500 Recipes for Working Wives*, London: Hamlyn.

Patten, Marguerite (1973), *Busy Cook's Book*, London: Hamlyn.

Patterson, Mrs Fred (1870), Doc. 391, Recipe Book, Henry Francis du Pont Winterthur Museum Library, Wilmington, DE.

Pennell, Elizabeth Robins (1903), *My Cookery Books*, Boston: Little, Brown and Co.

Pennell, Elizabeth Robins (1910), *Our House and the People in it*, Boston and New York: Houghton Mifflin.

Pennell, Elizabeth Robins (1916), *Nights: Rome and Venice in the Aesthetic Eighties, London and Paris in the Fighting Nineties*, Philadelphia: J. B. Lippincott.

Pennell, Elizabeth Robins [1896] (1923), *A Guide for the Greedy, by a Greedy Woman*, repr of *The Feasts of Autolycus*, Philadelphia: J. B. Lippincott.

Pennell, Elizabeth Robins [1901] (2000), *The Delights of Delicate Eating*, repr of *The Feasts of Autolycus*, Urbana and Chicago: University of Illinois Press.

Pennell, Elizabeth Robins and Joseph (1891), *The Stream of Pleasure*, London: Unwin.

Perera, Suvendrini (1991), *Reaches of Empire: The English Novel from Edgeworth to Dickens*, New York: Columbia University Press.

Phelps, Mrs E. A. (1873), Doc. 191, Cookbook, Henry Francis du Pont Winterthur Museum Library, Wilmington, DE.

Pierce, Charles (1857), *The Household Manager*, London: George Routledge.

Pilsbury, H.N. (1847), Doc. 275, Recipe Book, Henry Francis du Pont Winterthur Museum Library, Wilmington, DE.

Plumley, Ladd (1918), 'The Basis of Victory', *American Cookery* 22 (7), February, 484.

Ponsonby, Arthur (1918), *Falsehood in War-time*, New York: Dutton.

Poole, Gaye (1999), *Reel Meals, Set Meals: Food in Film and Theatre*, Sydney: Currency Press.

Porter, Dilwyn (1997), '"Never Never Land": Britain Under the Conservatives 1951-1964', in Tiratsoo, N. (ed.), *From Blitz to Blair: A New History of Britain since 1930*, London: Weidenfeld and Nicholson, pp. 102-131.

Postgate, Raymond (1951), *The Good Food Guide*, London: Cassell.

Prince, Rose (1997), 'Elizabeth the First', *Independent on Sunday*, 5 October, 7-12.

Probyn, Elspeth (2000), *Carnal Appetites: FoodSexIdentities*, London and New York: Routledge.

Pullar, Phillippa (1970), *Consuming Passions*, Harmondsworth: Penguin Books.

Ramusak, Barbara N. (1990), 'Cultural Missionaries, Maternal Imperialists, Feminist Allies: British Women Activists in India, 1865-1945', *Women's Studies International Forum*, 13, 309-321.

'Recipe for Brown Bread' (1975), *Bread and Roses*, Autumn, 9.

'Recipe for a Delicious Macaroni Cheese' (1975), *Bread and Roses*, Spring, 10.

Recipes for War Breads (1918), Philadelphia: Dr D. Jayne & Son.

Reed, Evelyn (1971), *Problems of Women's Liberation: A Marxist Approach*, New York: Pathfinder Press.

Richards, Thomas (1990), *The Commodity Culture of Victorian England: Advertising and Spectacle, 1851-1914*, Stanford: Stanford University Press.

Roberts, Michèle (1990), *In the Red Kitchen*, London: Methuen.

Roberts, Michèle (1992), *Daughters of the House*, London: Virago.

Roberts, Michèle (1993), 'The Bishop's Lunch', in *During Mother's Absence*, London: Virago.

Robinson, John A. (1978), 'Autobiographical Memory', in Gruneberg, M. and Morris, P. (eds), *Aspects of Memory I: The Practical Aspects*, London: Routledge, pp. 223-251.

Rogers, Ruth and Gray, Rose (1997), *The River Café Book*, London: Ebury Press.

Rombauer, Irma S. (1931), *The Joy of Cooking*, New York: Bobbs.

Romines, Ann (1992), *The Home Plot: Women, Writing, and Domestic Ritual*, Amherst, MA: University of Massachusetts Press.

Romines, Ann (1997), 'Growing Up with Methodist Cookbooks', in Bower, Anne L. (ed.), *Recipes for Reading: Communities, Cookbooks, Stories, Histories*, Amherst, MA: University of Massachusetts Press, pp. 75-88.

Rowbotham, Sheila (1999), *A Century of Women: The History of Women in Britain and the United States*, London: Penguin.

Rowbotham, Sheila (2000), *Promise of a Dream: Remembering the 60s*, London: Penguin.

Rowbotham, Sheila, Segal, Lynne and Wainwright, Hilary (1979), *Beyond the Fragments: Feminism and the Making of Socialism*, London: Merlin Press.

Rowe, Marsha (ed.) (1982), *Spare Rib Reader*, London: Penguin.

Rule, Vera (2000), 'First Leach Your Brawn', *The Guardian*, 1 April.

Rundell, Maria (1851), *Modern Domestic Cookery*, London: John Murray.

Ruskin, John (1865), 'Of Queen's Gardens', *Sesame and Lilies*, London: Smith and Elder.

Russett, Cynthia Eagle (1989), *Sexual Science: The Victorian Construction of Womanhood*, Cambridge: Harvard University Press.

Said, Edward (1993), *Culture and Imperialism*, New York: Vintage.

Scales, Mrs Melrose (1918), 'Hoover Hooverize', Dallas: Scales Publishing Company.

Sceats, Sarah (2000), *Food, Consumption and the Body in Contemporary Women's Fiction*, Cambridge: Cambridge University Press.

Schaffer, Talia (2000), *The Forgotten Female Aesthetes: Literary Culture in Late-Victorian England*, Charlottesville: University Press of Virginia.

Schaffer, Talia and Psomiades, Kathy A. (1999), *Women and British Aestheticism*, Charlottesville: University Press of Virginia.

Schofield, Mary Anne (ed.), *Cooking By the Book: Food in Literature and Culture*, Bowling Green, Ohio: Bowling Green State University Popular Press.

Scholes, Robert (1980), 'Language, Narrative, and Anti-Narrative', in Mitchell, W. J. T. (ed.), *On Narrative,* Chicago: Chicago University Press, pp. 200-208.

Scott, Mrs Anna B. (1918), 'How to Save Half the Wheat', *The North American* (Philadelphia), 14 April, Supplement.

Seale, Bobby (1988), *Barbeque'n with Bobby*, Berkeley, CA: Ten Speed Press.

Selected Recipes for Wartimes (1918), Calumet Baking Powder Company.

Shange, Ntozake (1998), *If I Can Cook / You Know God Can*, Boston: Beacon Press.

Shapiro, Laura (1986), *Perfection Salad: Women and Cooking at the Turn of the Century*, New York: Farrar, Straus and Giroux.

Sharpe, Jenny (1993), *Allegories of Empire: The Figure of the Woman in the Colonial Text*, Minneapolis: University of Minnesota Press.

Shute, Jenefer (1993), *Life-Size*, London: Mandarin.

Silverstone, Roger (1990), 'Television and Everyday Life: Towards an Anthropology of the Television Audience', in Ferguson, M. (ed.), *Public Communication: The New Imperatives. Future Directions for Media Research*, London: Sage, pp. 173-189.

Silverstone, Roger (2000), *Why Study Media?* London and New York: Routledge.

Simmons, Amelia [1796] (1984), *The First American Cookbook: A Facsimile of American Cookery*, New York: Dover Publications.

Simpson, Helen (1992), 'Sugar and Spice', in Smith, Joan (ed.), *Femmes de Siècle: Stories from the '90s: Women Writing at the End of Two Centuries*, London: Chatto and Windus, pp. 26-32.

Slater, Nigel (2000), *Appetite: So What Do We Want to Eat Today?* London: Fourth Estate.

Smith, Delia (2000), *How to Cook*, London: BBC.

Smith, Mary (1874), Unpublished cookbook, University of Delaware Special Collections, Newark, DE.

Smith, Stephanie (1994), *Conceived by Liberty: Maternal Figures and 19th-Century American Literature*, Ithaca: Cornell University Press.

Smith-Rosenberg, Caroll (1975), 'The Female World of Love and Ritual: Relations between Women', *Signs* **1** (1), 1-29.

Sokolow, R. (1991), *Why We Eat What We Eat: How the Encounter Between the New World and the Old Changed the Way Everyone on the Planet Eats*, New York: Summit Books.

Southgate, Henry (1876), *Things a Lady Would Like to Know*, London: William P. Nimmo.

Spain, Nancy (1948), *Mrs. Beeton and her Husband*, London: Collins.

Steel. Flora A. (1888), *The Complete Indian Housekeeper and Cook*, London: W. Heinemann.

Stokes, Eric (1959), *The English Utilitarians and India*, Oxford: Clarendon Press.

Storey, John (2001), *Cultural Theory and Popular Culture: An Introduction*, Third Edition, Harlow: Prentice-Hall.

Strange, N. (1998), ' Perform, Educate and Entertain: Ingredients of the Cookery Genre', in Lusted, D. and Geraghty, C. (eds), *The Television Studies Book*, London: Edward Arnold.

Strasser, Susan (1982), *Never Done: A History of Housework*, New York: Pantheon Books.

Suleri, Sara (1992), *The Rhetoric of British India*, Chicago: University of Chicago Press.

Sumner, Caroline Louise (1918), 'A Hoovercessional!' *American Cookery* **22** (7), March, 590.

Suppes, Patrick (1992), 'Model of Justified Procedures', in Curtin, Deane W. and Heldke, Lisa M. (eds), *Cooking, Eating, Thinking: Transformative Philosophies of Food*, Bloomington and Indianapolis: Indiana University Press, pp. 235-243.

Taylor, Mary (1991), 'America's First Cookbook', *Early American Life* **21** (1), 40-43.

Tebbutt, Val (1976), 'Use Rice Instead of the Expensive Spud', *Brass Tacks* **2**, June.

Thackeray, William [1848] (1993), *Vanity Fair*, Oxford: Oxford University Press.

Theophano, Janet (2002), *Eat My Words*, New York and Basingstoke: Palgrave.

Thompson, Eleanor (1947), *Education for Ladies, 1830-1860: Ideas on Education in Magazines for Women*, New York: King's Crown Press.

Thorne, John (1992), *Outlaw Cook*, New York: Farrar, Straus and Giroux.

Tichi, Cecilia (1991), *The Electronic Hearth*, New York and Oxford: Oxford University Press.

'To Teach Cooking to College Girls' (1918), *American Cookery* **22** (7), March, 575-576.

Todorov, Tzvetan (1977), *The Poetics of Prose,* trans. Richard Howard, Ithaca: Cornell University Press.

Tomlinson, Graham (1986), 'Thought for Food: A Study of Written Instructions', *Symbolic Interaction* **9**, 201-216.

Trusler, John (1788), *Honours of the Table*, Dublin: W. Sleater.

United States Food Administration (1917), *War Cook Book for American Women*, comp. Frederic J. Haskin, Washington: National Capitol Press.

United States Food Administration (1918), *War Economy in Food*, Hammond, IN: W. B. Conkey.

United States National War Garden Commission (1919), *Home Canning and Drying of Vegetables and Fruits*, Washington: National War Garden Commission.

United States, Food Administration (1918), *Food Saving and Sharing*, New York: Doubleday, Page and Co.

United States, *Food and the War: A Textbook for College Classes* (1918), Boston: Houghton Mifflin.

Urry, John (1995), *Consuming Places*, London and New York: Routledge.

Veblen, Thorstein (1899), *The Theory of the Leisure Class: An Economic Study in the Evolution of Institutions*, New York: Macmillan.

Visser, Margaret (1991), *The Rituals of Dinner*, Toronto: HarperCollins.

Viswanathan, Gauri (1989), *Masks of Conquest: Literary Study and British Rule in India*, New York: Columbia University Press.

Waldman, Marilyn Robinson (1980), '"The Otherwise Unnoteworthy Year 711": A Reply to Hayden White', in Mitchell, W. J. T. (ed.), *On Narrative*, Chicago: University of Chicago Press, pp. 240-248.

Waltman, John Lawrence (1976), *The Early London Diaries of Elizabeth Robins Pennell*. Diss: University of Texas at Austin.

Wandor, Michelene (1972), *The Body Politic: Women's Liberation in England 1969-1972*, London: Stage 1.

Ware, Vron (1992), *Beyond the Pale: White Women, Racism and History*, London: Verso.

Warner, Susan [1850] (1992), *The Wide, Wide World*, New York: Oxford University Press.

Warren, Eliza (1864), *How I Managed on Two Hundred Ponds a Year*, London: Houlston & Wright.

Watson, Shane (2001), 'Living with KPA', *The Observer*, 21 December.

Weekes, J. (1989), *Sex, Politics and Society since 1800*, London: Longman.

Weldon, Fay (1977), 'Pearly Oats', *Spare Rib*, July, 54-57.

Welter, Barbara (1966), 'The Cult of True Womanhood: 1820-1860', *American Quarterly* **18**, 151-174.

White, Anna Hadley Louise (c. 1880-1890), Doc. 134, Cookbook, Collection, Henry Francis du Pont Winterthur Museum Library, Wilmington, DE.

White, Cynthia L. (1970), *Women's Magazines 1693-1968*, London: Michael Joseph.

White, Florence [1932] (1962), *Good Things in England*, London: Jonathan Cape.

White, Hayden (1987), *The Content of the Form: Narrative Discourse and Historical Representation*, Baltimore: Johns Hopkins Press.

White, Patricia (1972), 'The Edible Present', *Spare Rib*, December, 32-33.

Wilde, Oscar [1885] (1991), 'Dinners and Dishes', in Jackson, John Wyse (ed.), *Aristotle at Afternoon Tea: The Rare Oscar Wilde*, repr. from *The Pall Mall Gazette*, 7 March 1885, London: Fourth Estate, p. 194.

Williams, Jacqueline Bock (2000), Introduction, *The Delights of Delicate Eating*, Urbana and Chicago: University of Illinois Press.

Williamson, Judith (1978), *Decoding Advertisements*, London: Marion Boyars.

Williamson, Judith (1986), *Consuming Passions*, London: Marion Boyars.

Wilson, C. Anne (1994), 'Meal Patterns and Food Supply in Victorian Britain', in *Luncheon, Nuncheon and Other Meals: Eating With the Victorians*, Stroud: Alan Sutton, pp. xi-xvi.

Wilson, Elizabeth (1980), *Only Halfway to Paradise: Women in Postwar Britain: 1948-1968,* London: Tavistock.

Winship, Janice (1987), *Inside Women's Magazines*, London: Pandora.

Winfrey, Oprah (1994), Introduction, *In the Kitchen with Rosie: Oprah's Favorite Recipes*, New York: Alfred A. Knopf.

'The Wiser Person' (1918), 'On "Having a Case"', *American Cookery* **22** (7), March, 588-590.

Witt, Doris (1999), *Black Hunger: Food and the Politics of US Identity*, New York and Oxford: Oxford University Press.

Young, Robert (1995), *Colonial Desire: Hybridity in Theory, Culture and Race*, New York and London: Routledge.

Zeldin, Theodore (1994), *An Intimate History of Humanity*, London: Sinclair-Stevenson.

Name Index

Subject Index

IN THE AT TABLE SERIES

To order or obtain more information
on these or other University of
Nebraska Press titles, visit
www.nebraskapress.unl.edu.